CHRISTIANS
GOING TO
HELL

CHRISTIANS GOING TO HELL

SEUNG WOO BYUN

CREATION HOUSE
A STRANG COMPANY

CHRISTIANS GOING TO HELL by Seung Woo Byun
Published by Creation House
A Strang Company
600 Rinehart Road
Lake Mary, Florida 32746
www.creationhouse.com

Cover design by Terry Clifton

Translated by Jennifer Seo

Library of Congress Control Number: 2005932812
International Standard Book Number: 1-59185-871-2

First Edition

06 07 08 09 10 — 9 8 7 6 5 4 3 2 1
Printed in the United States of America

If you read *Heaven Is So Real!* you must read this book.

Christians Going to Hell is related to *Heaven Is So Real!* I had the book written so that people would repent before My Second Coming. This is a book that I am pleased with, a book that is very important to Me.

—THE VOICE
HEARD BY CHOO THOMAS WHILE PRAYING

CONTENTS

PREFACE

MY HEART SINCERELY wishes that all would believe in Jesus, receive the assurance of salvation, and not go to hell.

> Not everyone who says to me, "Lord, Lord," will enter the kingdom of heaven, but only he who does the will of my Father who is in heaven.
>
> —MATTHEW 7:21

These words are truth and will be fulfilled. Jonathan Edwards, John Wesley, George Whitfield, Charles Finney, Richard Baxter, Thomas Watson, and Joseph Alleine very clearly proclaimed this truth. Charles Hodge, Dwight Moody, Aiden W. Tozer, Martyn Lloyd-Jones, and John Stott followed the same truth. However, most of the modern church has lost this truth. As a result, many souls are being deceived and face the danger of destruction.

At such a time, I think it is very fortunate that *Heaven Is So Real!*, written by Mrs. Choo Thomas and translated by Pastor Yonggi Cho, has come out. This book was long overdue, testifying and re-emphasizing the fact that those whose hearts are impure and who are disobedient will definitely not enter heaven.

Heaven Is So Real! is a testimony of Mrs. Thomas's experience of going to heaven seventeen times. In the book, the Lord sighed over the fact that "only about 20 percent of churches are putting Me first; the rest of them are worrying about what people say and how much money they will have."[1] Also He said, "Only about 20 percent of Christians are actually pleasing Him."[2] In the book, the following shocking information is recorded:

The Lord touched my head, and took my hand, leading me down a dark tunnel, and we emerged on another rough road that ran very far and to the edge of the pit. This mountain road led through tall trees and huge rocks. When we got to the top, I looked out over a brown and lifeless valley. Everywhere there was brown. The whole region seemed to be filled with dead grass.

I noticed multitudes of people who were wearing sand-colored robes roaming aimlessly in the vicinity of the pit's yawning mouth. Their heads were hanging low, and they looked very dejected and hopeless.

"Who are these people, Lord?" I asked.

"They are disobedient 'Christians.'"

"How long will they have to stay in this barren, lifeless place?"

"Forever, My daughter. The only ones who will enter My kingdom are the pure of heart—My obedient children."

He went on to explain: "Many who call themselves 'Christians' do not live by My Word, and some of them think that going to church once a week is enough. They never read My words, and they pursue worldly things. Some who even know My words never have their hearts with Me."

The whole plan and purpose of God was beginning to clarify in my thinking. I remembered how Jesus had warned that it is hard to enter His kingdom, and now I had an inkling of what that meant.

"My daughter, My Word says that it is hard to enter the kingdom of heaven, but so few really believe this and understand its importance. I am revealing this to you so you can warn them," He explained.[3]

In another part of the book, Jesus solemnly warned that those who barely come to Sunday worship, those who are stingy and do not tithe, those with lukewarm faith, and those who love the world more than the Lord cannot enter heaven even though they are Christians. Further, the Lord warned "that many pastors will go into the valley... [of the shadow of death], then their congregations will follow."[4]

I must ask you a question: Do you truly understand the words that Jesus said to Choo Thomas? In other words, are you convinced that these words are the truth from Scripture?

By the mercy and grace of God, I had known this truth for twenty years and had proclaimed it solitarily. Now, I believe that it is time for me to share the biblical doctrine of salvation, which the Holy Spirit taught me. That is why I wrote this book.

While Mrs. Choo Thomas's book is an experiential book on the doctrine of salvation, my book is one that supports biblical, revelatory messages about the doctrine of salvation. So I urge you, do not hesitate to buy and read this book. I hope you will believe in Jesus and avoid hell. Furthermore, I hope you will believe in Jesus in a proper way and go to heaven.

—Pastor Seung woo Byun
March 4, 2004
From Great Faith Church in Ulsan, Korea

FOREWORD

ITHANK AND PRAISE God for allowing me to be part of Pastor Seung Woo Byun's book.

The Lord told me that He had caused Pastor Byun to write the book *Christians Going to Hell* for people who are confused about hell and for Christians who do not know what they must do to go to heaven. Every Christian must read *Christians Going to Hell*, a book filled with God's truth.

Because the Lord showed me only partially about hell, He used Pastor Byun to shed more light and teach more in depth about hell. Sister Mary Baxter experienced hell many times as recounted in her book *A Divine Revelation of Hell*, and it is too terrifying to describe it. The Lord told me that there are few places in hell more dreadful than the one Sister Baxter described, and He is not pleased at all that some pastors never mention hell. The Lord spoke of hell so many times while He was on the earth because He does not want anyone to go there.

I thank God that He chose Pastor Byun to write this book, because some Christians never hear about hell from sermons or from Bible studies. They truly do not realize what a terrifying place hell is. Furthermore, some Christians have no idea what will happen after they die. They blindly believe that they will not remember anything after life on Earth. I know this because I have received too many letters about it. How sad it is! Our bodies will die, but our souls and spirits never die. We will feel pain, joy, sadness, and all the emotions we felt while we were living on Earth. Whether we go to hell or heaven, we will live eternally.

Christians Going to Hell is filled with the knowledge of God's Word that we should learn and the things we need to do in order to fulfill God's will and please Him. I was led by the Holy Spirit as I wrote this introduction. The Lord told me to write this. He also told me that this book is the voice that wakens the souls before His second coming.

Through this introduction, I believe that the righteous God gave me the opportunity to show my gratitude to Pastor Yonggi Cho for translating my book *Heaven Is So Real!* Pastor Cho had to obey the Lord. When I was an unknown person, almighty God used Pastor Cho's fame for *Heaven Is So Real!* While Pastor Cho was reading and rejoicing in this book, God specially anointed him for this task.

Before translating the book into Korean, Pastor Cho read it three times. Pastor Cho's life and thoughts are completely in the Spirit. He had no choice but to translate this book as God's power came upon him mightily for this book. Usually it takes six months to translate a book, but it took him only two months. This fact surprised the American publisher Creation House. They told me that such a thing has not happened before. The Lord told me that Pastor Cho would translate my book. *Heaven Is So Real!* is Jesus' book for all Christians. Praise the Lord!

I am absolutely convinced that *Christians Going to Hell* is related to *Heaven Is So Real!* Otherwise, the Lord would not have allowed me to write this recommendation. I realize how important this book is for all Christians everywhere. Before the coming of Jesus Christ, I want to recommend this book to everyone. This book is very important to the Lord. He wants all of His people to go to heaven. Heavenly Father, thank You so much for loving us! I give all the glory to God. Praise the Lord!

—CHOO-NAM THOMAS

– Chapter 1 –

DO NOT GO TO HELL!

There was a rich man who was dressed in purple and fine linen and lived in luxury every day. At his gate was laid a beggar named Lazarus, covered with sores and longing to eat what fell from the rich man's table. Even the dogs came and licked his sores.

The time came when the beggar died and the angels carried him to Abraham's side. The rich man also died and was buried. In hell, where he was in torment, he looked up and saw Abraham far away, with Lazarus by his side. So he called to him, "Father Abraham, have pity on me and send Lazarus to dip the tip of his finger in water and cool my tongue, because I am in agony in this fire."

But Abraham replied, "Son, remember that in your lifetime you received your good things, while Lazarus received bad things, but now he is comforted here and you are in agony. And besides all this, between us and you a great chasm has been fixed, so that those who want to go from here to you cannot, nor can anyone cross over from there to us."

He answered, "Then I beg you, father, send Lazarus to my father's house, for I have five brothers. Let him warn them, so that they will not also come to this place of torment."

Abraham replied, "They have Moses and the Prophets; let them listen to them."

"No, father Abraham," he said, "but if someone from the dead goes to them, they will repent."

He said to him, "If they do not listen to Moses and the Prophets, they will not be convinced even if someone rises from the dead."

– LUKE 16:19-31

CHRISTIANS GOING TO HELL

W<small>E CALL THIS</small> passage the parable of the rich man and Lazarus. Many insist that this is a true story, not just a parable.

For instance, John Wesley wrote about this passage:

> But is the…account merely a parable, or a real history? It has been believed by many, and roundly asserted, to be a mere parable, because of one or two circumstances therein, which are not easy to be accounted for. In particular, it is hard to conceive, how a person in hell could hold conversation with one in paradise. But, admitting we cannot account for this, will it overbalance an express assertion of our Lord: "There was," says our Lord, "a certain rich man."—Was there not? Did such a man never exist? "And there was a certain beggar named Lazarus."—Was there, or was there not? Is it not bold enough, positively to deny what our blessed Lord positively affirms? Therefore, we cannot reasonably doubt, but the whole narration, with all its circumstances, is exactly true. And Theophylact (one of the ancient commentators on the Scriptures) observes upon the text, that, "according to the tradition of the Jews, Lazarus lived at Jerusalem."[1]

The legend also says that the rich man's name was either Nineve or Phinees.[2] Therefore, it is probable that the story was an actual event.

Even if it is only a figurative story, this does not present a problem for us, because Jesus was the One who told the story, and He knows about afterlife more than anyone else. Moreover, it can be an advantage for us if it turns out that the story did not actually occur, because a factual story only shows a partial aspect of afterlife, while a parable reveals a general truth.

1. Death is not the end, but the beginning of eternity.

Many people believe that death is the end, so they live irresponsible lives, even committing suicide. However, death is not the end of existence. After we die, there will be judgment (see Hebrews 9:27), and we will be assigned eternally to heaven or hell. That is the basic truth revealed in this passage.

The Seventh-day Adventist church does not believe in the immortality of souls. They insist on the mortality of souls. Since they believe that upon death one's soul will be destroyed, they deny hell as the Jehovah's Witnesses do. They deny that the story of a rich man and Lazarus is an actual event, and they believe that it is one of the "Egyptian folk tales," which Jesus quoted.

Whether or not the passage is a real event or a parable, it is a fact. Besides this passage, all the scriptural passages about heaven and hell are real truth. This truth is found not only in Scripture, but it also has been proven in modern medical science.

Many years ago, Dr. Maurice Rawlings wrote several books on the topic of death. He had been a personal physician to General Dwight D. Eisenhower, and he is currently a specialist in cardiovascular disease and an international expert on CPR. He became the author of the best-seller *Beyond Death's Door* and is a wealthy owner of a personal jet and a lakefront house.

Maurice Rawlings has been a lifelong doctor who witnessed death almost every day. He never seriously thought about death, though. He believed that afterlife was either a dream or a fantasy.

One day, a forty-eight-year-old postman named Charles McKaine was admitted to the hospital. While Dr. Pam Charlesward was conducting an ECG test on Charles, he suddenly experienced heart failure. To the two doctors' surprise, he did not realize that his heart had stopped, and he kept on talking. After four or five seconds, he looked confused—as though he wanted to ask a question—when his eyes rolled backward and he fell into unconsciousness. A nurse ran to conduct mouth-to-mouth CPR, called "a kiss of life," while another nurse prepared an intravenous injection. Dr. Rawlings used a heart controller to make Charles's heart beat regularly again.

Suddenly Charles screamed, "Don't stop! I'm in hell! I'm in hell!"

Dr. Rawlings thought Charles was seeing an illusion, so he replied, "You wrestle with hell. I am busy trying to save your life!"

This was a very rare case. Most patients would complain to the doctor, "Stop jabbing my ribs! You are going to break my ribs!" The chest compressions cause very severe pain, even breaking the ribs of some patients, but the man wanted to come back desperately.

Thinking that his response was unusual, Dr. Rawlings knocked on Charles's chest and asked, "Why don't you want me to stop?"

Charles cried out, "I am in hell!"

Dr. Rawlings replied, "You mean, you are afraid to go to hell."

Upon hearing the doctor's words, Charles yelled, "No, I am in hell. Don't let me go. Please, don't let me go. Don't you understand? I'm in hell. Whenever you stop the CPR, I am in hell again. Please, don't let me go to hell again!"

Until then, Dr. Rawlings had disregarded the complaints of patients, but this patient was very serious. First of all, he was surprised at the look on his patient's face. He had not seen such a terrified look on anyone's face in the past twenty-five years. Charles's face was livid with fear, and it was clear that he was in the most frightening time of his life. Dr. Rawlings continued to try to save his patient's life. Suddenly, Charles yelled with a panicked voice, "How can I escape from hell?"

Dr. Rawlings replied, "How about praying to God?" Charles asked him to pray for him.

Startled, Dr. Rawlings grumbled, "I am not a pastor," but the sharp looks from the nurses prompted him to reluctantly come up with a prayer: "Follow after me, Jesus Son of God! Save me from hell. If I live again, I will live for you."

The patient repeated his prayer desperately, then a miracle took place. He became peaceful and soon returned to a normal state.

The next day, when Dr. Rawlings went to Charles's room, he was reading the Bible.[3]

This is a true story. It shocked Maurice Rawlings, and he became interested in death not as a doctor, but as a human being. It also caused him to study death with a whole-hearted devotion, using two methods.

First, he talked with people who had had near-death experiences, then he analyzed and compared their stories.

As a result, he discovered that these experiences had strong commonalities. He had generally believed that only a few people could have similar illusions. However, he came to conclude that it was impossible for so many patients to have essentially the same and continual illusions. Furthermore, these patients were normal, discerning people who could judge reality correctly and believed their experiences to be real and not fantasies.

Second, he began a comparative study of world religions. He compared and analyzed the religious theories from holy books including the laws and Talmud of Judaism, the Quran of Islam, Vedas of the Indian Upanishad, Brahman of Hinduism, the Zoroastrian holy book, the sayings and analects of Confucius, the Agama of Jainism, Buddhist holy books, the Japanese Shinto Kojiki, and Lao Tzu's Taoism. Subsequently, he realized that only one book most accurately described the near-death experiences of his patients: the Christian Bible.

Through his study, he became convinced that Christianity was the only true religion. He was not a believer before his study, but he became a faithful Christian afterward. Heaven and hell are not fiction, but reality.

I once read about a man who was an atheist and a gambler. After he died, the inscription on his gravestone was written as follows: "Here lies a dicer; long in doubt if death could kill the soul, or not: Here ends his doubtfulness; at last convinced;— but, ah! the die is cast!"[4]

Tryon Edwards said, "Hell is a reality seen too late—duty neglected in its season."[5] It is a place where one regrets that one had disregarded what one ought to have done.

The rich man in the passage realized too late that heaven and hell really do exist and therefore could not avoid going to hell. Be careful that you also do not realize this truth too late. As you read this, believe in the existence of afterlife, of heaven and hell. I wish that you would avoid hell and receive heaven as your inheritance.

2. Please be anywhere but in hell!

The Bible speaks about hell much more than heaven. It is probably because more people will end up in hell than in heaven. In the Bible, the person who mentions the most about hell is Jesus. Obviously, Jesus knew about hell more than any other person.

In 1747, John Wesley wrote the following words: "I desire to have both heaven and hell ever in my eye, while I stand on this isthmus of life, between these two boundless oceans; and I verily think the daily consideration of both highly becomes all men of reason and religion."[6]

Nowadays many preachers commit the sin of being silent about hell. They do not preach about hell because people do not like to hear those sermons. Jonathan Edwards wrote of the necessity of preaching about hell.

> Another thing that some ministers have been greatly blamed for, and I think unjustly, is speaking terror to them who are already under great terrors, instead of comforting them. Indeed if ministers in such a case go about to terrify persons with that which is not true, or to affright them by representing their case worse than it is, or in any respect otherwise than it is, they are to be condemned; but if they terrify them only by still holding forth more light to them, and giving them to understand more of the truth of their case, they are altogether to be justified. When consciences are greatly awakened by the Spirit of God, it is but light imparted, enabling men to see their case, in some measure, as it is; and, if more light be let in, it will terrify them still more. But ministers are not therefore to be blamed that they endeavor to hold forth more light to the conscience, and do not rather alleviate the pain they are under, by intercepting and obstructing the light that shines already. To say any thing to those who have never believed in the Lord Jesus Christ, to represent their case any otherwise than exceeding terrible, is not to preach the word of God to them; for

the word of God reveals nothing but truth; but this is to delude them.[7]

I agree with this statement wholeheartedly. I also believe that preachers must not concern themselves with what people think; they should preach about hell more often. The first topic they must preach about is hell's real existence. The next topic should be "What kind of place is hell?" Well, what kind of place is hell?

Thomas á Kempis says this about hell: "One hour in this hellhole will produce more pain than a hundred years of penitential practice."[8] The following two points help us to realize how painful the suffering of hell is.

First, hell is the lake that burns with fire and brimstone.

> Father Abraham, have pity on me and send Lazarus to dip the tip of his finger in water and cool my tongue, because I am in agony in this fire.
>
> —LUKE 16:24

> ...where "their worm does not die, and the fire is not quenched." Everyone will be salted with fire.
>
> —MARK 9:48–49

What do you think will bring the most severe suffering in the world to a person? I believe it is fire. The most fearful injury is a burn. Its cure is most painful. Hell is a place full of fire. In Revelation, fire is described as "the lake of fire" (Rev. 20:15) or "the lake which burns with fire and brimstone" (Rev. 21:8, NKJV).

The following shocking testimony shows how frightening the fire of hell is. In 1948, George Godkin of Alberta, Canada, died after a prolonged illness. At that time, he experienced hell for a moment. He introduced his experience as follows:

> I was guided to the place in the spirit world called hell. This was a place of punishment for all those who rejected Jesus Christ. I not only witnessed hell, but felt the torment of those who will go there. The darkness of hell was so intense that it seemed to have a pressure per square inch. Truly it was extremely black, dismal, desolate, heavy, and thick. It gave individuals a crushing, despondent feeling of loneliness.
>
> There was heat of the most drying, dehydrating type. The eyeballs felt so dry that it seemed red, hot coals were in their sockets. The tongue and lips were parched and cracked with intense heat. The breath from the nostrils felt like the blast from a furnace. The exterior of the body felt as though it were encased within a white-hot stove. The interior of the body felt the tormenting sensation of scorching, hot air being forced through it. The agony and loneliness of hell which the human souls feel cannot be clearly expressed; it has to be experienced!"[9]

The fire of hell, described above, is a place of torturous suffering. The worst place in the universe is hell. We must avoid going to hell at all cost.

Hell is an eternal place. The fire of hell never dies, and there is no death in hell. Therefore, hell's torment is eternal.

One time, I heard through a radio about a man who, after separating from his wife and feeling despair, prayed that he might die by fire. Imagine a person who jumps into the fire wishing to die and yet does not die, but suffers agonizing torment in the unquenchable fire. How terrible that would be! Hell is such a place! The fire of hell never dies. Because of the deep pit, it is impossible to escape. A suicide is impossible, too. That is why the Bible records people who fell into hell as follows:

> He will be tormented with burning sulfur in the presence of the holy angels and of the Lamb. And the smoke of their torment rises for ever and ever. There is no rest day or night....
>
> —REVELATION 14:10–11

Richard Baxter, the famous Puritan preacher, wrote about the suffering of hell.

> But the greatest aggravation of these torments will be their *eternity*. When a thousand millions of ages are past, they are as fresh to begin as the first day. If there were any hope of an end, it would ease the damned to foresee it; but *For ever* is an intolerable thought! They were never weary of sinning, nor will God be weary of punishing. They never heartily repented of sin, nor will God repent of their suffering. They broke the laws of the eternal God, and therefore shall suffer eternal punishment.... As the joys of heaven are beyond our conception, so are the pains of hell. Everlasting torment is inconceivable torment. [10]

I have never read such a vivid testimony as that of a woman named Susan, about the unending suffering of hell. One night, Susan was sitting on the sofa in her living room. Suddenly, she felt the presence of God and was filled with the Holy Spirit. She heard the Lord's voice: "Look! Keep your eyes on hell!"

As soon as she heard the words, a burning wall appeared in front of her. A blue-hot flame like a column of fire rose fiercely from the bottom of a brown floor. A jelly-like figure stood in the middle of the fire. While she was gazing at it, it began to tremble with fear.

A loud cry broke out with a sob, "Oh, God, please help me. Please help me!" It kept weeping.

Then the Lord spoke, "My beloved daughter, the soul that you see in the fire is a man who has been in hell for the last one thousand eight hundred years. He still keeps crying out to me like this."

Why are you surprised? Do you think one thousand eight hundred years is long? No, it is not long. One thousand years is not even close to one second in hell. That is because hell is an eternal place. Samuel Davies once described eternity vividly as follows:

> Eternity! It is a duration that excludes all number and computation; days, and months, and years, yea, and ages, are lost in it, like drops in the ocean. Millions of millions of years, as many years as there are sands on the seashore, or particles of dust in the globe of the earth, and these multiplied to the highest reach of number, all these are nothing to eternity. They do not bear the least imaginable proportion to it, for these will come to an end, as certain as day: But eternity will never, never come to an end. It is a line without end; it is an ocean without a shore...It is an infinite, unknown something, that neither human thought can grasp, nor human language describe....Suppose a bird were to pick up and carry away a grain of sand or dust from the globe of this earth once in a thousand years, till it should be at length wholly carried away; the duration which this would take up appears a kind of eternity to us.[11]

Several years ago, I saw a bonfire on the grounds of my grandfather's house. I threw a big log into the fire. The log burned all day, but only the surface of it was burned. Watching it reminded me of hell. The log looked like someone's thigh. I shuddered with fear as I thought about the souls being eternally tormented in hell.

We mistakenly believe that the world in which we live today will be eternal. There is an end to this world, but heaven and hell, which seemed not real to us, truly exist and are everlasting. Therefore, we must be careful not to go to hell.

3. Do not be assured because you are baptized and go to church. You must repent of your sins.

Why did the rich man fall into Hades? Why did he go to hell? "No, father Abraham...but if someone from the dead goes to them, they will repent" (Luke 16:30). As implied in the verse, the rich man went to hell because he did not repent. The reason he went to hell is the same reason his five brothers will go to hell. They would not repent.

Many Christians are convinced that they will go to heaven because they have faith in Jesus, but I want to ask them, "Have you repented of your sins?" Faith without repentance is false faith, which will not rescue us from hell.

Do you want to go to heaven? Then you must repent. (See 2 Peter 3:8–9.) What sins should you repent of? There is no one particular sin of which you must repent. You must repent of *all* your sins. If you ask, "God, what sin must I turn away from?" then God will definitely say, "From all sins!" In Ezekiel 18:30–32, God commanded:

> Therefore, O house of Israel, I will judge you, each one according to his ways, declares the Sovereign Lord. Repent! Turn away from all your offenses; then sin will

not be your downfall. Rid yourselves of all the offenses you have committed, and get a new heart and a new spirit. Why will you die, O house of Israel? For I take no pleasure in the death of anyone, declares the Sovereign Lord. Repent and live!

Repentance is not merely regretting and confessing your sins, but cutting off your sins. At the same time, repentance is cutting off "all your offenses" (Ezek. 18:30). Thomas Watson said, "They are but half-turned who turn from many sins but are unturned from some special sin."[12] However, many are ignorant of this crucially important point about repentance. I want to introduce to you some of the most well-known sayings regarding repentance.

> Yet be it evermore remembered, no sinner can find a welcome before the face of God unless he returns most deeply penitent. Ah! You do not know God at all if you suppose He can receive you without the most thorough penitence and the most ample restitution.[13]
>
> —Charles Finney

> O sirs, In God's name let me tell you, it is not the giving up of one sin, nor fifty sins, which is true repentance; it is the solemn renunciation of every sin. If thou dost harbour one of those accursed vipers in thy heart, thy repentance is but a sham. If thou dost indulge in but one lust, and dost give up every other, that one lust, like one leak in a ship, will sink thy soul. Think it not sufficient to give up thy outward vices; fancy it not enough to cut off the more corrupt sins of thy life; it is all or none which God demands.[14]
>
> —Charles Spurgeon

More importantly, this is what our Lord Jesus Christ said:

> If your hand causes you to sin, cut it off. It is better for you to enter life maimed than with two hands to go into hell, where the fire never goes out. And if your foot causes you to sin, cut it off. It is better for you to enter life crippled than to have two feet and be thrown into hell...where "their worm does not die, and the fire is not quenched." Everyone will be salted with fire.
>
> —MARK 9:43–49

Some people might question how this passage is relevant to what I was talking about. It is relevant because Jesus is saying that it does not take hand, foot, and eye—in other words, many different sins—to go to hell; if there is even one sin that we have not gotten rid of, we will be thrown into hell along with that sin. In a parable that teaches about repentance, Jesus also said:

> I tell you that in the same way there will be more rejoicing in heaven over one sinner who repents than over ninety-nine righteous persons who do not need to repent.
>
> —LUKE 15:7

Previously I used to think that because of the words "in heaven," the "ninety-nine righteous persons" referred to saints in heaven. I must have thought so because they were described as "persons who do not need to repent," but the "ninety-nine righteous persons who do not need to repent" refer to those on earth who have truly repented. This fact is clear, because it is written in Luke 15:4:

Suppose one of you has a hundred sheep and loses one of them. Does he not leave the ninety-nine in the open country and go after the lost sheep until he finds it?

Now please pay attention to what I am about to say! There are two kinds of people. One kind consists of those in Christ who have repented; while the second kind consists of those outside His fold who have not repented. In other words, one group of people will go to heaven; the other group will go to hell.

What does the Bible say about people who have repented? It says they are "righteous persons who do not need to repent." Therefore, those who want to go to heaven must have no need to repent. They must not have even one sin remaining in them. All sins must be repented. Only truly repentant persons deserve to go to heaven.

Some people may have great difficulty digesting this truth, because they may confuse repentance with confession. Repentance and confession are different. The object of repentance is habitual sin, and the object of confession is accidental sin. In principle, non-believers repent, and believers confess. Therefore, it does not mean that a person who has sins to confess is not repentant and will go to hell. It means that a person who has habitual sin—in other words, sin that needs to be thrown away—is not repentant and will go to hell.

In order to facilitate your decision, I will tell an important story. One day, Rev. T. L. Osborne, an international evangelist, was waiting for his ship to leave the harbor. He had enough time to walk around the streets. Then an interesting scene took place right in front of him. A herd of pigs was following its herder in a row without going astray.

As many of you know, pigs are very hard to control. When you beat them with a stick to the left, they will go to the right. When you beat them with a stick to the right, they will go left. No matter how much you try, they will go wherever they please.

Rev. Osborne had often seen herders using both hands to grab pigs' tails in order to control them, and the pigs would kick their legs to run away from them, but he had never seen a row of pigs following their herder so obediently. Puzzled, he followed them, and to his surprise, they arrived at a slaughterhouse. The pigs entered the large iron barred gate without hesitation! Rev. Osborne, watching such a humorous and pitiful sight of pigs, waited for the herder to come out. Upon meeting him, the reverend asked the secret of the herder's amazing ability.

"It is simple. Pigs like beans. When I walk, I drop a handful of beans on the road, and they follow the beans, not me. They are so intent on eating the beans that they do not realize they are walking toward their death."[15] He was shocked by these words! He realized that the people who are busy indulging themselves with pleasure and self-interest are just like these pigs.

My beloved friend, pigs like beans the most. What sin do you like the most? That sin is Satan's bean, the bait that he uses to drag you to hell. When you sin, do not say that "I cannot stop this sin because I like it too much." Just as pigs that follow the beans were actually following the herder who led them to the slaughterhouse, we who follow our favorite sin are in reality following Satan who steals, kills, and destroys. Our destination is hell, which Jesus described as "everlasting fire prepared for the devil and his angels" (Matt. 25:41, NKJV). Therefore, I wish that you would open your eyes to this reality and cut off your sin right now.

4. We must boldly spread the gospel with compassion for the lost souls.

The rich man in hell requested two things from Abraham. First, he begged for a drop of water for himself, and then he asked for Lazarus to be sent to his brothers on Earth. The best-written book on hell is by Pastor Mary Baxter, titled *A Divine Revelation of Hell*. Recording a thirty-day eyewitness testimony of hell, the content of the book is very similar to the following passage.

> Next we came to the fire pot. The size of this fire pot was the same as the first, and skeletal figures were in it. The voice spoke, "Lord, have mercy on me!" Only when he spoke did I realize whether it was a man or a woman.
>
> He spoke with a sob. "Lord...I have been wrong. Please forgive me...Please take me out of here. I have been in this misery...for so many years. Please let me out!" While he was begging, his skeletal figure trembled violently.
>
> I looked at Jesus and saw Him crying, too. He looked above and said, "My Father, My Father, have mercy!"
>
> "Lord Jesus, haven't I suffered long enough for the sins I committed?" the voice cried out from the fire. "I have been here for forty years."
>
> Jesus spoke, "It is written, the righteous will live by faith. It is not by paying the penalty for your sins that you are saved, but it is by having faith in Me, Jesus Christ, while you were on earth that you are saved. You did not believe in the truth. Even when My people were sent to you to show you the way, you did not listen to them. You scorned them and rejected the gospel. Even though I died for you, you mocked Me and did not repent from

your sins. My Father gave you many opportunities to receive salvation. If only you had listened then..." Jesus shed His tears.

"I know, Lord. I know!" the man wailed. "But I am repenting now."

"It is too late," said Jesus. "The judgment is ended."

The man continued to weep. "Lord, even now the unrepentant people still come here. Please allow me to tell them that they must repent from their sins while on earth. I do not want them to come here."[16]

Like this man, people in hell are ready to share the gospel if only they are given the opportunity.

Those who have seen hell are fired up for evangelism. Pastor Jung Pyeo Lee, the director of Hansin Ministry Development, shared his testimony one day.[17] While he was in middle school, his close friend gave him a book, *A Calendar of Wisdom* by Tolstoy. The book contained many famous sayings of Buddha, Confucius, Lao Tzu, Jung-tzu, Socrates, and others, but what touched his heart were the words of Jesus. He asked his friend if there was a book with only the sayings of Jesus, and his friend handed him the New Testament. While he was reading it, he felt shocked at the story of the rich man and Lazarus in Luke 16. He determined that he must believe in Jesus just so he would avoid going to hell!

One morning, during his second year of high school, he coughed up blood. From the X-ray taken at the hospital, it was discovered that his right lung had a hole that caused the bleeding. The medication prescribed for him did not work at all. With great despair, he went to the pharmacy and bought a large dose of sleeping pills. Before taking the pills to cause his death, he closed his eyes for a moment, and suddenly hell appeared. He saw tormented skeletons screaming with pain. The vision caused his eyes to open wide in shock, but the memory of it did not immediately disappear. When he closed his eyes again, the scene reappeared. Out of fear, he gave up his plan to commit suicide. Instead, he desperately held on to God, was healed, and became a pastor. He described the effect the vision of hell had on him.

> I could not help but spread the gospel because I have seen the vision of hell. In whatever church or community that I went to, I earnestly evangelized with a cry, "Believe in Jesus!"
>
> While in An-yang, I served as an army chaplain. While sharing the gospel there, I habitually told the soldiers, "If it weren't for hell, I would not be preaching the gospel like this. But hell is real."

We must spread the gospel. That is because hell really exists. If we do not share the gospel, people around us will go to hell.

Now this is my conclusion.

> The time came when the beggar died and the angels carried him to Abraham's side. The rich man also died and was buried.
>
> —LUKE 16:22

In later Judaic thought, it is believed that when a righteous man dies, his soul is carried away by good angels, but when an evil man dies, his soul is carried by dark angels. In old Korean myths, there are dark spirits in black garb, but no angels. That is because without Jesus, there is no salvation. This means that before the gospel reached Korea, the nation's main religions of Buddhism and Confucianism were not able to save one soul, but sent all people to hell.

Charles Finney, the great evangelist, said:

> In all ages it has been common for some dying saints to hear music which they supposed to be of heaven and to see angels near and around them. With eyes that see what others cannot see, they recognize their attending angels as already come, "Don't you hear that music?" say they. "Don't you see those shining ones? They come, they come!" But attending friends are yet too carnal to see such objects and to hear such sounds; for it is the mind and not the body that has eyes. It is the mind that sees, and not the body. No doubt in such cases, they do really see angelic forms and hear angelic voices. The Bible says, "Precious in the sight of the Lord is the death of his saints." How gloriously do these closing scenes illustrate this truth.
>
> If this be true of saints, then doubtless wicked spirits are allowed to drag the wicked down from their dying beds to hell. Nor is it unreasonable to suppose that they too really see awful shapes and hear dreadful sounds. "Who is that weeping and wailing? Did I not hear a groan? Is there not some one weeping as if in awful agony? O, that awful thing; take him away, take him away! He will seize me and drag me down; take him away, away!"[18]

This is true, and there are too many real-life cases like this. Due to time limitations, I will introduce only two short cases.

In the book *People Who Met Angels* written by Joan Wester Anderson, the following story appears. An 11-year-old Christian boy was dying of peritonitis. He suddenly told those around him, "Look, Mom! There are angels around us. One angel is prettier than the other angels."

Mom replied, "I cannot see anything." Thinking that he was seeing an illusion, she tried to console him.

Nevertheless, the son kept saying, "Look. The angels are here. They are so close I can touch them." At last, the parents realized that their boy was seeing a reality and felt greatly comforted.[19]

In another case, Rev. Dr. David Nelson recorded the near-death experiences of people. He observed the incidents as a doctor while he was still an unbeliever. He wrote that the unbelievers scream, "Ah, the frightful figure! Please take him out of this room. Why don't you take him out?"[20]

When the repentant die, angels come to escort them, but when the unrepentant die, evil spirits come to take them away. If you were to die, who do you think will come to escort you? Who would you like to escort you? Of course, you would like the angels to come. Then I wish that you would at once rely upon the blood of Jesus, confess all your sins, and cut off all your sins.

— Chapter 2 —

The Repentance That Leads to Salvation

Godly sorrow brings repentance that leads to salvation and leaves no regret, but worldly sorrow brings death.

—2 Corinthians 7:10

WHAT MUST WE do to be saved? In answer to this question, most people reply, "Only by faith!" However, this is not a complete answer. That is because the Bible tells us that for salvation, we need faith and repentance.

"The time has come," he said. "The kingdom of God is near. Repent and believe the good news!"

—Mark 1:15

I have declared to both Jews and Greeks that they must turn to God in repentance and have faith in our Lord Jesus.

—Acts 20:21

Therefore let us leave the elementary teachings about Christ and go on to maturity, not laying again the foundation of repentance from acts that lead to death, and of faith in God.

—Hebrews 6:1

Thomas Watson, one of the exemplary leaders of the Puritan movement in England, wrote a book concerning questions and answers of Christian doctrines in Westminster Conference. In the preface of his book titled *The Doctrine of Repentance* he wrote:

> "If there are two kinds of grace which are absolutely necessary for believers in their lives, one is repentance, and the other, faith. These are two necessary wings that are essential for believers to fly to heaven."
>
> A bird cannot fly with only one wing. Likewise, we cannot go to heaven with only repentance or with faith. We must repent from our sins and have faith in Jesus to go to heaven.[1]

Joseph Alleine said, "The devil has many people repenting falsely and he deceives them with one thing or another."[2]

Charles Finney said, "Every time you tell sinners to repent, you should explain what true repentance is. Since there are false doctrines and principles and too many mysterious factors concerning this word, you should also inform what repentance is not. The meaning of certain words that used to be very clear before has been so distorted that additional explanation is needed. Without clarification, these words frequently convey wrong meanings to sinners. The word *repentance* is one of them."[3] Therefore, we must understand the meaning of true repentance and repent genuinely. Then what is genuine repentance?

In his book *The Doctrine of Repentance*, Thomas Watson introduced six characteristics of true repentance as:

1. Discovery of sin
2. Remorse toward sin
3. Confession of sin

4. Shame for sin
5. Hatred of sin
6. Turning away from sin

He said that if one of them is missing, repentance would not be effective. False repentance has some of these characteristics, while genuine repentance has all of them.[4] Thus I want to introduce these elements of true repentance next.

The Recognition of Sin

> Jesus answered them, "It is not the healthy who need a doctor, but the sick. I have not come to call the righteous, but sinners to repentance."
>
> —LUKE 5:31–32

Here "sinners" refers to those who recognize their sin. Therefore, repentance is possible to those who realize that they are sinners. Then how do we recognize that we are just hopeless sinners? The famous evangelist D. L. Moody said that there are three things that make people recognize their sin, and they are: conscience, the Word of God, and the Holy Spirit.[5]

1. People recognize their sin through their conscience.

Conscience is God's voice from within us. Conscience always insists that we do the right things. Conscience acknowledges the difference between the right and the wrong and judges our conduct as good or bad. To be more specific, we can recognize our sin through the pang of our conscience.

2. People recognize their sin through the law.

Certainly our conscience helps us to recognize our sin, but it alone is not enough. Since our conscience has been affected by our corrupt nature, it needs to be illumined by God.

The famous Baptist preacher Charles H. Spurgeon realized that he was a sinner at age fourteen. At the time, thoughts of "God's majesty and my wretchedness" surged upon him like a wave and filled him with fear and regret. He recalls the experience during that time as follows:

> I could confidently say that anyone who examines my life would find no specific sin. However, when I examined myself, I saw that I had sinned tremendously before God. I was not like the boys who were unfaithful, dishonest, and foul. But at certain point, I met the law and Moses who had the Ten Commandments. While I was reading them, I saw that they were condemning me before the Most Holy God.[6]

Through the law, we become conscious of sin. (See Romans 3:20.) Through the law, sin is taken into account (see Romans 5:13), and sin is recognized as sin, and sin becomes utterly sinful. (See Romans 7:13.)

3. People recognize their sin through the Holy Spirit.

The Holy Spirit descended upon the earth for largely two purposes: one is to convict people of sin, and the other is to testify Christ so that people might believe in Him. Regarding the former, Jesus says:

> When he comes, he will convict the world of guilt in regard to sin...because men do not believe in me.
> —JOHN 16:8–9

When someone does something wrong, he is rebuked so that he may learn to recognize his fault. Likewise, the Holy

Spirit rebukes us so that we will correct our sin. In particular, He focuses on the sin of not believing in Jesus.

Dr. A. J. Gordon said, "The verse, 'in regard to sin, because men do not believe in me' means that [the] Holy Spirit awakens men to recognize their sin—the sin of not believing in Jesus. The Bible does not say that [the] Holy Spirit awakens men to recognize the sin of stealing, lying, and committing adultery. [The] Holy Spirit convicts men to recognize their sin of not believing in Jesus Christ." [7]

You may have heard about the book *I Will Keep My Eyes on It* by Elder Young Moon Park. This book is a testimony about how he became a new creation when he visited heaven and hell right before his plot to murder the eight family members of his wife. While he was standing before the judgment throne of God, he was surprised to discover two sins that are not considered sin in a free nation such as South Korea. Those two were not believing in Jesus and persecuting those who believe in Jesus.[8]

The sin of not believing in Jesus is the greatest among all sins, but people do not realize how great this sin is. That is why the Holy Spirit is working to convict people of this sin.

As you have seen above, we can recognize sin through our conscience, the law of God, and the Holy Spirit. It is our first step of faith to recognize our sin through these three means, and this is extremely important.

We must know precisely what it means to recognize sin. Today, there are many people who recognize their sin superficially. Recognizing sin is not merely acknowledging sin at an intellectual level.

Charles Hodge wrote:

> The essential element in repentance is humbly realizing one's worthlessness, thereby becoming humble and

remorseful. Most people are willing to acknowledge that they are sinners, and yet think lightly of their sin and basically believe that they are good. They also tend to think that God's law is too severe upon frail human beings, and that it is unfair to punish them harshly when the demands of the law are not met by them. Repentance, however, completely breaks the mentality of those who consider themselves righteous. Repentance is the soul's total surrender before God, realizing that his sin is inexcusable. It is not condemning oneself and seeing God as a harsh master, but acknowledging that God's demands and judgment are righteous.[9]

One who has truly recognized his sinfulness as described above sees his sin as utterly sinful. It is important to recognize our sin deeply, not superficially. This importance is well indicated by D. L. Moody:

When someone does not recognize his sin deeply, that is a clear indication that he did not genuinely repent. Those who think lightly of their sin will fall into that same sin sooner or later. If one becomes a Christian and confesses his faith without realizing the severity of his sin, he will likely become a Christian with a stony heart that cannot produce fruit. Upon being persecuted, rejected, or ridiculed, he will be drawn back to the world.[10]

My ministry experience has revealed that this is definitely true. Therefore, we must recognize our sin deeply.

Godly Sorrow

After I have preached about biblical repentance, one of the most frequent questions I receive from people is, "Pastor, I want to repent, but I can't. How can I do it?" The answer to this question is found in Paul's writing.

> Godly sorrow brings repentance that leads to salvation and leaves no regret, but worldly sorrow brings death. See what this godly sorrow has produced in you: what earnestness, what eagerness to clear yourselves, what indignation, what alarm, what longing, what concern, what readiness to see justice done. At every point you have proved yourselves to be innocent in this matter.
>
> —2 CORINTHIANS 7:10–11

In this passage, we can find significant cause-and-effect links regarding repentance.

- First is "Godly sorrow."
- Second is "Repentance that leads to salvation."
- Third is "Salvation [that] leaves no regret."

Always, the salvation of souls occurs in this order: godly sorrow, which leads to repentance, which leads to salvation that leaves no regret.

Joseph Alleine, author of *Alarm to the Unconverted,* and who had great influence on George Whitfield and Charles Spurgeon, said in regard to repentance:

> What is it that you count necessary? Is your bread necessary? Is your breath necessary? Then your conversion [and repentance] is much more necessary. Indeed, this is the one thing necessary. Your possessions are not neces-

sary; you may sell all for the pearl of great price, and yet be a gainer by the purchase. Your life is not necessary; you may part with it for Christ to infinite advantage. Your reputation is not necessary; you may be reproached for the name of Christ, and yet be happy; yes, you may be much more happy in reproach than in repute. But your conversion [and repentance] is necessary; your salvation depends on it; and is it not needful in so important a matter to take care? On this one point depends your making or marring to all eternity.[11]

Truly salvation depends upon repentance. Therefore, what we need the most is repentance. However, it is godly sorrow that produces repentance. Without godly sorrow, one cannot repent. If godly sorrow is the root of repentance, repentance is its fruit. Godly sorrow quickens a person's heart and allows him to repent. On the other hand, worldly sorrow interferes with repentance and makes it impossible for a person to repent. That is why Paul said:

> Godly sorrow brings repentance that leads to salvation and leaves no regret, but worldly sorrow brings death.
> —2 CORINTHIANS 7:10

However, the majority of people who come to church to listen to sermons are not concerned with godly sorrow, but their hearts are filled with worldly sorrow. They are neither ashamed of their sin (see Ezra 9:6 and Ezekiel 43:10–11), sorrowful (see Psalm 6:6; 38:18; Matthew 5:4; Luke 7:38; and James 4:9), nor fearful of God for their sin. (See Psalm 4:4 and Proverbs 3:7; 14:6.) They are not interested in salvation of souls; they are entirely focused on the world. Of course, they are not without any concern for the salvation of souls, but show only momentary interest when listening to sermons. On the way home, or even right after the preaching is over, their seriousness or their interest in lost souls vanishes quickly. With the conclusion of the sermon comes the end of concern. They never bring godly sorrow into their homes. That is why they are not able to repent.

Do you really want to repent genuinely? When the Word of God pricks your conscience and gives you conviction of sin, bring godly sorrow to your home. Bring it to your workplace and into your daily life, then repentance will become possible for you.

The Change of Heart Toward Sin

Let those who love the LORD hate evil.

—PSALM 97:10

Hate evil.

—AMOS 5:15

Hate what is evil; cling to what is good.

—ROMANS 12:9

It is absolutely necessary for us to loathe sin (see Proverbs 8:13), which God so hates. (See Proverbs 6:16–19.) Charles Finney said, "Repentance in its meaning always contains hatred for sin."[12] Thomas Watson assumed that "a genuine convert is the one who loathes sin," and asserted emphatically the importance of hatred for sin in repentance as follows:

It is more important to loathe sin than to avoid it. Like the person throwing away gold vessels and treasures out into the sea in the midst of a storm, a person can leave sin purely out of fear…but without loathing sin, one cannot truly love Christ and long for heaven.…Loving sin is more evil than committing sin. A good man may fall into sin out of ignorance, but there is no hope for a person who takes pleasure in sinning. What makes a pig enjoy wallowing in the mud? When a person loves sin, it shows that the person's will is with sin; thus the more will resides with sin, the greater the sin is. If a person sins deliberately, there is no sacrifice that can cleanse it away [see Hebrews 10:26].[13]

One time, while attending the Family Mission School sponsored by YWAM (Youth With a Mission), I heard a preacher say, "Only those who loathe sin have the power to overcome sin…The moment I loathe sin do I have the power to overcome it. That is when I finally prevail over sin." Hating sin is one of the core elements of repentance. Therefore, we must loathe sin.

The problem is that people love to sin. Except for a minority of faithful Christians, the whole world loves to sin. People suffer from more than one particular sin.

> You adulterous people, don't you know that friendship with the world is hatred toward God? Anyone who chooses to be a friend of the world becomes an enemy of God.
>
> —JAMES 4:4

Scripture says that before repentance, everyone is in an adulterous friendship with the world. (See Romans 3:23.) Sin is people's close friend and their alluring mistress. Since they are in love with sin, whenever they are away from sin, they long for it and cannot stand to be without it. Eventually, they meet sin again.

However, there is one hope. Second Samuel 13:15 states, "Then Amnon hated her with intense hatred. In fact, he hated her more than he had loved her." In the same way, we can end up hating sin seven times more than we had loved it. This is possible through the grace of God. Therefore, ask the Holy Spirit to help you through prayer.

The Confession of Sin

Many people confuse repentance with confession. Confession is not the same as repentance. It is only one part of repentance.

> He who conceals his sins does not prosper.
> —PROVERBS 28:13

> Only acknowledge your guilt...
> —JEREMIAH 3:13

> If we confess our sins, he is faithful and just and will forgive us our sins.
> —1 JOHN 1:9

Likewise, the Bible commands us to confess our sins. However, not all confessions of sin bring forth forgiveness. In Scripture, the wicked people like Pharaoh, Balaam, King Saul, and Judas Iscariot all confessed their sins, but they did not receive forgiveness. Therefore, we must confess genuinely, which means we must pay attention to three factors:

1. Individual sins must be confessed separately.

Many people acknowledge themselves to be sinners, but their confession of sin is general. That is, they confess, "Lord, I have sinned," but they do not confess each individual sin. On the other hand, like the patient who tells his doctor all the individual symptoms of his illness, a true confessor must confess his sin in detail to the doctor of his soul, the Christ. If a person has ten wounds, all of these wounds must be treated. Even if the wounds are the same type but in different places, they must be treated individually. In the same manner, each type of sin must be confessed separately, and each number of sins must be confessed separately. This is what Charles Finney wrote regarding confession:

> Look back at your past. Be sure to recall each individual sin you have committed. I am not saying that you must glance at your past, agree that your life has been filled with sin, and make a holistic confession of your sins all summed up. That is not the right way. You must deal with your individual sins one at a time. As you deal with specific sins, it is a good idea to write down each of them with a paper and pencil as it comes to your mind. Be sure to examine your sins like a merchant examining his inventory. As you remember additional sins, include them on your paper. You must never confess your sins all together because you have committed your sins one by one.[14]

Before the throne of God are the book of life and the book of conducts. In the book of conducts, all the sins we have committed with our mouths and our actions in our lifetimes are recorded without missing even one. God gives according to our deeds.

But I will rebuke you and accuse you to your face.
—PSALM 50:21

Likewise, God deals with our sin individually. Therefore, our confession must be made individually.

2. Confession must be made with a pure heart.

Confessing my sins with a sin cherished in my heart (see Psalm 66:18)—in other words, with sinful desire conceived in my heart (see James 1:15)—is offensive to God. Therefore, prior to confessing my sin, I must abort the sin in my heart. I must confess with a strong determination never to sin again.

Many people confess with their mouths, but their words do not agree with what they have confessed in their hearts. Like a thief who is forced to confess his crime upon being caught but still loves to steal, false repenters may confess their sins but still cherish their sins in their hearts. As an example, St. Augustine said that before he repented, he would confess his sin and ask God for the power to overcome his sin. However, his heart deep inside would whisper, "No, not yet, Lord."[15] This is not the right attitude. In order to repent, one must not have any remaining regrets toward sin. Ezra 10:10–12 shows a great model of confession:

> Then Ezra the priest stood up and said to them, "You have been unfaithful; you have married foreign women, adding to Israel's guilt. Now make confession to the LORD, the God of your fathers, and do his will. Separate yourselves from the peoples around you and from your foreign wives." The whole assembly responded with a loud voice: "You are right! We must do as you say."

Likewise, true confession is made with a strong, decisive will to cut off sin.

3. Confession must be made to God and people.

Sins committed against God can be confessed to God alone, but if a sin has been committed against other people, the confession must be made to God and to those people, because you have wronged both God and people. Surprisingly, many people wrongly believe that they need only to confess to God.

> Therefore, if you are offering your gift at the altar and there remember that your brother has something against you, leave your gift there in front of the altar. First go and be reconciled to your brother; then come and offer your gift.
>
> —MATTHEW 5:23–24

Listen to what the scripture is saying. How can such reconciliation occur without confessing one's sin to the other person?

> So watch yourselves. If your brother sins, rebuke him, and if he repents, forgive him. If he sins against you seven times in a day, and seven times comes back to you and says, 'I repent,' forgive him.
>
> —LUKE 17:3–4

This scripture also says the same thing. If we do not need to confess our sins to those we have wronged, Jesus would not have said these words.

Charles Finney said:

If you have sinned against someone and that person lives close to you, you must go and confess your sin to him. If the person lives too far away for you to go, write a letter to him at once without deferring. Be sure to resolve it right away. Do not postpone it. The more you defer, the more difficult it will be for you. If you sinned against God, confess to God; if you sinned against a person, confess to the person.[16]

Do not take confession lightly. Whether you have sinned against God or a person, if you have not confessed your sin, you are living in that sin even if you do not repeat it. It means that you are still in that sin. Therefore, you must confess your sins.

On the other hand, after we have confessed our sin, we must receive the forgiveness of God by faith. Many people confess their sins to God, but not many believe that their sins have been forgiven. It is the work of the Holy Spirit that convicts us of sin (see John 16:8), but it is the work of Satan that accuses and evokes feelings of condemnation. (See Revelation 12:10.) Some people have been convicted of their sins, but they live with continuous feelings of guilt and despair, believing that they cannot escape from them. Such thoughts and feelings are not from God. They are from Satan. People who, after having confessed their sins, cannot find assurance of forgiveness have a misunderstanding about the "basis of forgiveness."

Let me ask you a question. When God forgives our sins, does He forgive us based on His mercy or His righteousness? Many people will probably answer "mercy," but that is wrong.

If we confess our sins, he is faithful and just and will forgive us our sins and purify us from all unrighteousness.

—1 JOHN 1:9

Of course, God is a God of mercy and love, but if God could have forgiven our sins simply with His mercy, Jesus would not have hung on the cross. Jesus, as the Righteous One, died on the cross for the unrighteous. (See 1 Peter 3:18.) As a result of His work on the cross, the forgiveness is not a matter of mercy, but a matter of justice. Jesus paid the penalty of our sins on the cross. Therefore, by simply appealing to God's justice, not to His mercy, we can be forgiven.

Since Jesus Christ took up the cross for us, God has no choice but to forgive us morally and legally. Based on this fact, we can request God's forgiveness and receive it by faith. Therefore, having the assurance of God's forgiveness of our sins is not a presumption.

The Compensation for Sin

Whoever damages other people's property must compensate for it conscientiously.

> If a man steals an ox or a sheep and slaughters it or sells it, he must pay back five head of cattle for the ox and four sheep for the sheep. If a thief is caught breaking in and is struck so that he dies, the defender is not guilty of bloodshed; but if it happens after sunrise, he is guilty of bloodshed. A thief must certainly make restitution, but if he has nothing, he must be sold to pay for his theft. If the stolen animal is found alive in his possession—whether ox or donkey or sheep—he must pay back double.
>
> —Exodus 22:1–4

As the scripture declares, if a thief slaughters or sells the stolen animal, he must pay back five head of cattle for the ox and four sheep for the sheep. That is because such a thief's action reveals his premeditated evil intention. If the thief is not capable of paying back, he must become a slave to make restitution. However, if the thief had kept the animal undamaged, he must compensate for it double. When David became enraged after hearing Nathan's story and said the man must pay for the lamb four times over (2 Samuel 12:6), he was basing his judgment on the scripture.

> The LORD said to Moses: "If anyone sins and is unfaithful to the LORD by deceiving his neighbor about something entrusted to him or left in his care or stolen, or if he cheats him, or if he finds lost property and lies about it, or if he swears falsely, or if he commits any such sin that people may do—when he thus sins and becomes guilty, he must return what he has stolen or taken by extortion, or what was entrusted to him, or the lost property he found, or whatever it was he swore falsely about. He must make restitution in full, add a fifth of the value to it and give it all to the owner on the day he presents his guilt offering. And as a penalty he must bring to the priest, that is, to the LORD, his guilt offering, a ram from the flock, one without defect and of the proper value. In this way the priest will make atonement for him before the LORD, and he will be forgiven for any of these things he did that made him guilty."
>
> —LEVITICUS 6:1–7

The important words are "give it all" (v. 5), signifying that a restitution or penalty was made before the guilt offering. Only when the restitution was made to the person, the guilt offering was presented to God. This is a truth that must be applied automatically to all Christians. The sin offering of Himself, which

Jesus Christ presented to God on behalf of people, is never a substitute for restitutions that we must make when we sin.

> That person...must confess the sin he has committed. He must make full restitution for his wrong, add one fifth to it and give it all to the person he has wronged.
>
> —Numbers 5:7

Therefore, confession of sin is not everything. There must always be restitution. Do not believe that this only applies to people in the Old Testament. In Luke 19:8–9, Zacchaeus told Jesus, "Look, Lord! Here and now I give half of my possessions to the poor, and if I have cheated anybody out of anything, I will pay back four times the amount." At that point, Jesus did not explain to him that he did not have to follow the convention of the Old Testament times, but instead, He said to him, "Today salvation has come to this house, because this man, too, is a son of Abraham." Therefore, compensation for damage must be made. Now, let me answer some questions that you might have regarding the issue of compensation.

First, what happens when the victim to whom you want to make restitution has died? In that case, you must compensate to the victim's family.

What if the victim does not have any family or relatives, or if the victim is alive but you do not know his whereabouts? In that case, you must give a guilt offering to God.

> The LORD said to Moses, "Say to the Israelites: 'When a man or woman wrongs another in any way and so is unfaithful to the LORD, that person is guilty and must confess the sin he has committed. He must make full restitution for his wrong, add one fifth to it and give it all to the person he has wronged. But if that person has

no close relative to whom restitution can be made for the wrong, the restitution belongs to the LORD and must be given to the priest, along with the ram with which atonement is made for him.'"

—NUMBERS 5:5–8

Lastly, what happens if you want to make restitution but you cannot afford it? In that case, you must compensate as much as you can, and then faithfully promise to pay the rest as soon as you are able. Then God will forgive your sin.

Turning From All Sin

One Sunday, while John Bunyan, author of *The Pilgrim's Progress,* was exercising on the grass, a question suddenly crossed his mind. *Will you go to hell with your sin? Or will you go to heaven with your sin thrown away*? This question troubled him to death, but eventually, he determined to throw away his sin.[17] As you see in John Bunyan's case, repentance is the determination to throw away your sins. Ezekiel 18:30–32 is a good example that shows the characteristics of repentance.

> Therefore, O house of Israel, I will judge you, each one according to his ways, declares the Sovereign LORD. Repent! Turn away from all your offenses; then sin will not be your downfall. Rid yourselves of all the offenses you have committed, and get a new heart and a new spirit. Why will you die, O house of Israel? For I take no pleasure in the death of anyone, declares the Sovereign LORD. Repent and live!
>
> —EZEKIEL 18:30–32

In this passage, we learn two important lessons on repentance.

1. First, repentance is turning away from sin.

> He who conceals his sins does not prosper, but whoever confesses and renounces them finds mercy.
>
> —PROVERBS 28:13

> Let the wicked forsake his way and evil man his thoughts. Let him turn to the LORD, and he will have mercy on him, and to our God, for he will freely pardon.
>
> —ISAIAH 55:7

> Produce fruit in keeping with repentance. And do not think you can say to yourselves, "We have Abraham as our father." I tell you that out of these stones God can raise up children for Abraham. The ax is already at the root of the trees, and every tree that does not produce good fruit will be cut down and thrown into the fire.
>
> —MATTHEW 3:8–10

> First to those in Damascus, then to those in Jerusalem and in all Judea, and to the Gentiles also, I preached that they should repent and turn to God and prove their repentance by their deeds.
>
> —ACTS 26:20

Many people wrongly believe that they will be forgiven when they only confess their sins, but that is a misconception. Anyone who does not turn away from sin will not be forgiven.

Charles Spurgeon said:

One should not expect his king to forgive him as long as he is acting in a treasonous way. In the same way, we should not imagine that the Judge of this world will wipe away our sin when we refuse to turn away from it.[18]

Also, Joseph Alleine said:

As their foundation of hope, many people rely on the fact that Christ has died for sinners. But the fact needs to be emphasized that Christ did not die for the stubborn ones who do not repent and continue to live in sin…To believe that Christ will save you when you are holding on to sin is to make Christ a sinner. It is to lower God's dignity more than what all the wicked people and demons in hell have done and can do. Still, do you hold on to that presumptuous hope?[19]

Finally, this is what Charles Finney said:

The individual who truly repents, not only sees sin to be detestable and vile and worthy of abhorrence, but he really abhors it, and hates it in his heart…when he truly repents, he most heartily abhors and renounces it. [20]

Therefore, we must turn away from sin.

2. Next, repentance is turning away from *all* sins.

Thomas Watson said, "There is no postponing or compromising with sin when it comes to true repentance."[21] If we ask, "God, what sin must I turn away from?" Then God will definitely reply, "From all sins!"

The true convert abhors sin on account of its hateful nature, because it dishonors God, and therefore he desires to repent of it.[22]

—CHARLES FINNEY

If you reserve in one sin, God will not accept you. All your sins must die. Otherwise, you must die.[23]

—JOSEPH ALLEINE

If one sin has dominion of us we are not the Lord's free men. A man who is held by only one chain is still a captive. There is no going to heaven with one sin ruling within us, for of the saints it is said, "Sin shall not have dominion over you."[24]

—CHARLES SPURGEON

Therefore, do not think, *I will be okay since I have given up all sins except this little one.* That is not wisdom. Instead, think, *I cannot risk destruction now after having given up all sins because of this little sin,* and throw away your last sin.

On the other hand, some people feel despair after hearing sermons on repentance. They ask, how can such repentance be possible? For these people, let me make one comment. The repentance that the Bible requires consists of turning away from all sins. That does not mean we will never sin again. As an example, this is what Charles Finney said:

These (1 John 5:1, 4, 18) and similar passages expressly teach the persevering nature of true religion, through the indwelling of the Holy Spirit: in other words, they teach that the truly regenerate cannot sin, in the sense at least of living in anything like habitual sin. They teach, that with all truly regenerate souls, holiness is at least the rule, and sin only the exception; that instead of its being true, that the regenerate souls live a great majority of their days subsequent to regeneration in sin, it is true that they so seldom sin, that in strong language it may be said in truth, they do not sin. This language so strongly and expressly teaches that perseverance is an unfailing attribute of Christian character, that but for the fact that other passages constrain us to understand these passages as strong language used in a qualified sense, we should naturally understand them as affirming that no truly regenerate soul does at any time sin. But since it is a sound rule of interpreting the language of an author, that he is, if possible, to be made consistent with himself; and since John, in other passages in this same epistle and elsewhere, represents that Christians, or truly regenerate persons, do sometimes sin; and since this is frequently taught in the Bible, we must understand these passages just quoted as only affirming a general and not a universal truth; that is, that truly regenerate persons do not sin anything like habitually, but that holiness is the rule with them, and sin only the exception.[25]

Repentance is not the completion of faith but the starting point of it. To explain it theologically, repentance is not sanctification. Therefore, I believe the words of Joseph Alleine most appropriately explain what the repentant person is like.

God will not smile on that soul that smiles on sin, nor have any peace with him that is at peace with his enemy. Other enemies you must forgive, and love, and pray for; but for these spiritual enemies, all your affections, and all your prayers must be engaged against them; yea, you must admit no parley.[26]

Now let me lead you to the conclusion. There is a pastor named Yong-Kyu Park in South Korea. He is a pastor of First Sung Nam Church, a Presbyterian mega-church that he planted, which now has forty-five thousand members. He also established Song Lim Middle and High School and became the youngest headmaster and member of the board of trustees in the nation. Additionally, he wrote fifty-seven books besides the one made into a movie titled *Guide Me, O My Great Redeemer.*

However, when Pastor Park became hospitalized due to God's punishment, God showed him the vision of heaven and hell. The size of hell was so huge that he was quite surprised and asked an angel, "Dear angel, what is the population of hell?" It is hard to believe, but the angel told him, "The ratio of people entering hell and heaven is one thousand to one." Upon hearing that, he asked, "Dear angel, what kinds of people are in hell?" What the angel said is very important.

> There are two kinds of people in hell. One kind is those who did not believe in Jesus. Those who did not believe in Jesus come to hell 100 percent. The other kind is the people who went to church but died without repenting.[27]

In the story of the rich man and Lazarus, the rich man said:

> "No, father Abraham," he said, "but if someone from the dead goes to them, they will repent." He said to him, "If they do not listen to Moses and the Prophets,

they will not be convinced even if someone rises from the dead."

—LUKE 16:30–31

In addition, the apostle Peter testified in 2 Peter 3:8–9:

But do not forget this one thing, dear friends: With the Lord a day is like a thousand years, and a thousand years are like a day. The Lord is not slow in keeping his promise, as some understand slowness. He is patient with you, not wanting anyone to perish, but everyone to come to repentance.

Therefore, to go to heaven we must definitely repent from all sins.

Finally, remember this one thing. Thomas Aquinas, the famous theologian in the thirteenth century, said, "God who forgives the penitents never made a promise that he would give them a tomorrow to repent."[28]

There is an illustration that dramatically shows this truth. The famous evangelist D. L. Moody was preaching on the topic of repentance during the evening service at a church in Chicago. He ended the sermon with the words, "Well the time has gone up, so I cannot preach anymore this evening. Please come back to the meeting next Sunday." A few days later, a great fire broke out over the entire Chicago area, killing many people, including those who had attended Moody's meeting. It caused Moody to regret greatly as he sighed, "Why didn't I tell the people to repent that day, instead of telling them to return the next Sunday evening!"[29] As this illustration shows, nobody knows when a person will die.

Do not boast about tomorrow, for you do not know
what a day may bring forth.

—PROVERBS 27:1

Why, you do not even know what will happen tomorrow.
What is your life? You are a mist that appears for a
little while and then vanishes.

—JAMES 4:14

Thomas Watson said, "Is there a guarantee that we will
live one more day? We are marching quickly out of the world,
disappearing from the stage. Our lives are but a little frag-
ment of a candle that will soon burn out, or a wildflower that
withers more quickly than grass. [See Psalm 103:15.] The life
of human beings is not more than a flying shadow."[30] Nobody
knows when a person will die. Therefore, please repent before
it is too late.

– Chapter 3 –

FAITH MORE PRECIOUS THAN GOLD

Simon Peter, a servant and apostle of Jesus Christ, To those who through the righteousness of our God and Savior Jesus Christ have received a faith as precious as ours: Grace and peace be yours in abundance through the knowledge of God and of Jesus our Lord.

–2 PETER 1:1-2

SOME TIME AGO I read a book titled *Real Christians* by Charles Price. It is an outstanding book worth recommending to others. In the book he said, "If someone asks me to list some of the most misunderstood words used by Christians, the first on my list would be 'faith.'" [1]

When I read the sentence, my heart felt so refreshed because even though this is a definite fact, only a very few recognize this truth.

Charles Finney said:

> We must warn the sinners to believe the gospel. Also, we must explain to them what belief is and what belief is not. If sinners are told to believe, eight out of ten say, 'Yes, I believe the gospel.' The truth is, they were merely taught to agree that the gospel is true, but they do not believe the gospel and do not know the evidence of their belief. In the end, their belief is nothing more than an acknowledgment without

evidence...Strangely, they do not see that they have deceived themselves, and are convinced that they believe. It is most difficult to let them realize that they do not believe the gospel.[2]

Now, do you understand what Finney is saying? Perhaps you do not yet comprehend it. However, after you have read this chapter, you will clearly understand it.

Nowadays, many people believe that since salvation is by faith, all they have to do is to believe to go to heaven. Some people even think that salvation is by faith and reward in heaven is by works; therefore, even if they do not obey God and live in sin, they can still be saved. This is a very dangerous mentality caused by their lack of true biblical understanding regarding belief. The Bible records those who believed and yet were not saved.

> To the Jews who had believed him, Jesus said, "If you hold to my teaching, you are really my disciples. Then you will know the truth, and the truth will set you free....I tell you the truth, everyone who sins is a slave to sin. Now a slave has no permanent place in the family, but a son belongs to it forever. So if the Son sets you free, you will be free indeed...Why is my language not clear to you? Because you are unable to hear what I say. You belong to your father, the devil, and you want to carry out your father's desire."
>
> —JOHN 8:31–32, 34–36, 43–44

Here it is written, "the Jews who had believed him," but Jesus reveals that their father was not God, but Satan.

But when they believed Philip as he preached the good news of the kingdom of God and the name of Jesus Christ, they were baptized, both men and women. Simon himself believed and was baptized. And he followed Philip everywhere, astonished by the great signs and miracles he saw... When Simon saw that the Spirit was given at the laying on of the apostles' hands, he offered them money and said, "Give me also this ability so that everyone on whom I lay my hands may receive the Holy Spirit." Peter answered: "May your money perish with you, because you thought you could buy the gift of God with money! You have no part or share in this ministry, because your heart is not right before God."

—ACTS 8:12–13, 18–21

Simon also clearly believed and was baptized, but he did not know the way of the cross nor shared in this ministry.

What good is it, my brothers, if a man claims to have faith but has no deeds? Can such faith save him?... You believe that there is one God. Good! Even the demons believe that—and shudder. You foolish man, do you want evidence that faith without deeds is useless?... As the body without the spirit is dead, so faith without deeds is dead.

—JAMES 2:14, 19–20, 26

Some people believed in Jesus, but James tells them that their faith not accompanied by action could not lead them to salvation.

Look! All these scriptural passages show people who believed, but astonishingly, none of them received salvation.

In these passages, none of the believers were saved. Then why were they not saved? It is because their belief was not a genuine belief. Even today, there are too many people who say they are believers but have false belief. Out of my love for you, I want to share with you what is biblical belief.

What Is Faith?

In the Bible, what is faith? Let us investigate together.

1. Faith is accepting the testimony of Jesus (John 3:11–12).

Charles Hodge said, "Most generally, faith is agreeing to the truth of the evidence when the evidence is shown."[3] This is true. Faith is agreeing with the evidence and testimony of Jesus.

Jesus testified that He is the Son of God and the promised Messiah in the Scripture. He also testified about His redemptive death, our salvation through faith, and the necessity of our rebirth, as well as the true existence of heaven and hell, His second coming, and His final judgment. Therefore, we must believe that Jesus is the Son of God and the Messiah. We must also believe that His death was not a failure but redemption. We must also believe that we are saved not by works but by faith. We must believe all of these as facts. That is faith. However, we must take caution! This is just *part* of faith, not *all* of it. Therefore, just believing in these facts alone does not lead us to salvation.

Earlier, John Wesley said that Satan has given a substitution of faith which resembles faith and which only a few can discern as false. This substitution is called the intellectual understanding of the truth of the gospel.

Charles Finney confessed in his book *Power From On High,*

"I learned from one seminary professor that faith means 'the intellectual activity or state of assurance.' And I always heard people describing faith in such a term...They said 'faith is being firmly convinced of the doctrines regarding Christ.'"[4]

In the latter part of this book Finney reveals that such a faith is not saving faith. That is correct. Such faith can never lead to salvation. Therefore, we must never remain in this state. However, today many people show their ignorance regarding this matter.

2. Faith is accepting Jesus (John 1:12).

Gary Collins pointed out an important factor in one of his books.

> Evangelists have succeeded in planting faith in Jesus Christ to new believers, but they have failed to teach them that real faith is to submit to Christ's sovereignty and renounce their sin.[5]

In reality, many preachers succeed in planting faith in Christians, but fail repeatedly to explain what true faith is and to plant that faith in them. Then what is faith? Simply put, faith is accepting Jesus.

> Yet to all who received him, to those who believed in his name, he gave the right to become children of God.
>
> —JOHN 1:12

Faith is receiving Jesus into our heart, but as *what* do we receive Him? That is the important question. Many people wrongly believe that they will be saved when they receive Jesus as their Savior. That is not true. We must receive Jesus as our King and our Savior, and then we will have salvation. This truth is so clearly revealed in the Bible that it is strange that so many people miss it.

> He came to that which was his own [this means Jesus is King over his people], but his own did not receive him. Yet to all who received him [not simply as a Savior, but as a King], to those who believed in his name, he gave the right to become children of God.
>
> —JOHN 1:11–12

> Therefore let all Israel be assured of this: God has made this Jesus, whom you crucified, both Lord and Christ.
>
> —ACTS 2:36

> God exalted him to his own right hand as Prince and Savior that he might give repentance and forgiveness of sins to Israel.
>
> —ACTS 5:31

> Believe in the Lord Jesus, and you will be saved—you and your household.
>
> —ACTS 16:31

> That if you confess with your mouth, "Jesus is Lord," and believe in your heart that God raised him from the dead, you will be saved. For it is with your heart that you believe and are justified, and it is with your mouth that you confess and are saved.
>
> —ROMANS 10:9–10

Therefore, we must not simply receive Jesus as our Savior, but as our King. This truth is not a doubtful truth that only a few of us proclaim. Very many fathers of faith recognized this truth clearly and testified to it powerfully.

First, Jonathan Edwards said that the one who receives Christ by living faith enters into an intimate relationship with the Savior and King who rules over him. He does not simply receive the Lord as a priest who removes his sin.

Next, Richard Baxter said:

> Faith receives Christ as Savior and Lord. The one who cannot receive Christ as Savior and Lord cannot receive him at all. Faith accepts Christ's suffering, forgiveness, and glory, as well as submitting to His sovereignty, rule, and way of salvation.[6]

Charles Spurgeon said the following:

> Who do you belong to? Answer this question. If you are convinced that you belong to Christ, his title to [you] is 'Emperor' or else he must be nothing at all. If Christ is not your emperor or king or monarch, he has nothing to do with you.[7]

A. W. Tozer said:

> There is no Savior without Lord. Christ is Savior and Lord. It is a modern-day heresy to say that a sinner can receive him as the Savior, but not as the Lord... Christ's status as the Savior is connected to his sovereignty forever.[8]

John Stott, the great evangelical theologian said:

The appropriate response to the gospel is faith, truly faith alone. But true living faith in Christ includes in essence the element of obedience. [See Romans 10:3.] Also, since the object of faith is "Jesus Christ our Lord" (Rom. 1:4) or "Lord Jesus Christ" (Rom. 1:7), faith inevitably leads to lifetime obedience... This is our answer to those who insist that they can accept Jesus Christ as Savior without submitting to him as Lord. We cannot accept Jesus Christ as our Savior if we have not acknowledged him as our Lord.[9]

I will share one more thing. There is a book written by Juan Carlos Ortiz, the famous Bible teacher, titled *The Kingdom of God*. The book points out an important factor: salvation is not simply going to heaven once you die, but is turning away from being your own master. In other words, salvation is putting your life under the sovereignty of God.

Therefore, why do you not open the door of your heart and receive Jesus as your King and Savior?

3. Faith is depending on Jesus (Matthew 18:2–3).

Since a young child is helpless, he is completely dependent on his parents. In the same way, we must depend on Jesus. That is faith.

Dr. Oswald Smith wrote a sermon titled "What Does It Mean to Believe?" In the sermon he asserts:

People who translated the *King James Version* three hundred fifty years ago had difficulty translating one Hebrew word into English. Finally, they decided on the word *trust*. As a result, the Old Testament contains this word one hundred sixty-two times.

When these people were translating the New Testament, they labored over the same word. This time the word had to be translated from Greek, and they tried hard to come up with the correct English translation. The reason is not known, but they decided on the word *believe*. The Old Testament word *trust* was not used in the New Testament, but instead, the word *believe* was chosen. This word appears many times, especially in the gospel of John and Paul's epistles. As a result, there are many confusions and misunderstandings... Today, too many people believe without trusting in God.

The Old Testament tells of the way of salvation: "Trust Jehovah." But the New Testament speaks of "believing the Lord." The Old Testament translation is the correct translation. Salvation comes when you trust in the Lord.[10]

In addition, I found an outstanding explanation that shows that faith is trusting. Charles Price, in his excellent book *Real Christians*, defined the word *faith* and pointed out that it could be used in two ways. The difference between these two ways was illustrated in these two questions: "Do you believe in the monster of Loch Ness in Scotland?" and "Do you believe in aspirin?"[11]

The question about the monster of Loch Ness asks whether you believe in the fact that there is a monster with a long neck and two camel-like humps that hides whenever the people of Loch Ness go on the monster hunt. The answer to this question can be yes or no. You may believe in the monster's existence or you may deny it. It is not important how you answer this question because the answer one way or the other will not affect you. In this case, faith is an intellectual matter.

But the question about aspirin is assuming that you already

know the existence of aspirin and its painkilling capability, and is asking whether you would take aspirin to get rid of your headache. In this case, faith is not simply acknowledging its existence, but trusting its power.

It is the second type of faith that is the New Testament faith that illustrates our relationship with Jesus Christ. This faith does not merely believe in the existence of Jesus Christ, but it enables Jesus Christ to work. Of course, because "anyone who comes to him must believe that he exists" (Heb. 11:6), we must possess the first type of faith, too. However, the first kind of faith does not benefit us. James said, "You believe that there is one God. Good! Even the demons believe that—and shudder" (James 2:19).

Therefore, we must not stay on the first kind of faith. Based on the first type of faith, we must go on to the second type of faith, so that we can experience the work of Christ who sets us free from the power of sin. Such faith is the only faith that saves us from sin and hell. The essence of this kind of faith is well illustrated in the metaphor of the vine and the branches:

> Remain in me, and I will remain in you. No branch can bear fruit by itself; it must remain in the vine. Neither can you bear fruit unless you remain in me. I am the vine; you are the branches. If a man remains in me and I in him, he will bear much fruit; apart from me you can do nothing. If anyone does not remain in me, he is like a branch that is thrown away and withers; such branches are picked up, thrown into the fire and burned.
>
> —JOHN 15:4–6

The fact that we are the branches of Jesus is a precious, heartwarming truth. If the branch is disconnected from the vine, it cannot survive and maintain its life. The sap supplied from the vine is the life source for all the plant's leaves, sprouts, flowers, and fruits. If the branches are cut from the vine, they will wither and die. In the same way, we, the branches of Jesus, do not possess life, strength, and spiritual power on our own. By faith, all that we possess comes from Jesus. Today, we are who we are, what we feel, and what we do by the grace, help, and power that come from Jesus. Therefore, we do not need to feel despair about our salvation, thinking that we can never go to heaven. Saints are not those who accomplish something by their own strength and power. Christ is our root, and everything in Christ is for our benefit. Therefore, we must do all we can to remain in the Lord.

> Now those who had been scattered by the persecution in connection with Stephen traveled as far as Phoenicia, Cyprus and Antioch, telling the message only to Jews. Some of them, however, men from Cyprus and Cyrene, went to Antioch and began to speak to Greeks also, telling them the good news about the Lord Jesus. The Lord's hand was with them, and a great number of people believed and turned to the Lord. News of this reached the ears of the church at Jerusalem, and they sent Barnabas to Antioch. When he arrived and saw the evidence of the grace of God, he was glad and encouraged them all to remain true to the Lord with all their hearts.
>
> —ACTS 11:19–23

Likewise, the most important thing about faith is for believers to remain in the Lord, in other words, to depend on Jesus.

There are three elements of faith: intellect, volition, and

dependence. The intellectual aspect of faith involves understanding and agreeing with the truth of the gospel; the volitional aspect of faith involves receiving Jesus as King and Savior and determining in our heart to live according to His will; and the dependent aspect of faith involves wholly trusting the power of the Lord to overcome inner corruption and to be free from sin for the life of daily obedience. Out of these, the third element of faith can be further analyzed into three parts.

1. Humility

> See, he is puffed up; his desires are not upright—but the righteous will live by his faith.
>
> —Habakkuk 2:4

Jonathan Edwards confessed that he drew near to Christ to receive His salvation and be poor in spirit, to exalt Him humbly, and to grow and learn from Him. This means putting God, who is in Christ, above everything, and living a life of total and humble reliance upon Him by faith that He is the Son of God.

Likewise, the core of Christian faith is emptying oneself to exalt Christ humbly and relying on Him. Therefore, the first element of dependence is humility.

> But he gives us more grace. That is why Scripture says: "God opposes the proud but gives grace to the humble."
>
> —James 4:6

God opposes the proud and gives grace to the humble. This grace is the sap of the true vine, the Holy Spirit. As Paul said, "I have become who I am by the grace of God" (see 1

Corinthians 15:10), all of us can overcome sin through this grace, and live obediently before the Lord. Grace is given to the humble person, and that grace transforms him.

2. Trust

The first element of dependence is humility. Humility has to do with us rather than God; humility is not relying on ourselves. Further, humility is not abasing ourselves but seeing ourselves with spiritual eyes, as God sees us. All human beings are corrupt, deceitful above all things, and desperately wicked. Therefore, anyone who becomes aware of his true inner state will overcome pride and be humble.

Does our humility solve all problems? No, it cannot. We must go on to the next level, which is trusting the Lord.

> The disciples were even more amazed, and said to each other, "Who then can be saved?" Jesus looked at them and said, "With man this is impossible, but not with God; all things are possible with God."
>
> —MARK 10:26–27

Whenever I think about faith, I think of this passage. Salvation from sin—in other words, cutting away of all sins—cannot be done by humans. That must be our starting point. If someone believes that this is possible, he believes in himself, not the Lord. We must come to the point where we fully realize our own inner corruption, moral incapability, and spiritual bankruptcy, and desperately cry out, "I cannot do it on my own. My determination, effort, labor, and self-development are all insufficient. Lord, have mercy on me, a sinner!" Then there is hope.

In *The Final Quest,* the Lord told Rick Joyner:

It is good to lose your self-confidence...[But] that is not enough. You must fill the empty place with trust in Me, otherwise, it will only lead to anxiety.[12]

Again, Flora Slosson Wuellner said:

It is the most sorrowful and vain thing to try to live a Christian life without relying on the power of Christ...Try loving and continually praying without the daily dependence on the life-giving well of Christ. We will eventually see our own dry well.[13]

Therefore, we must not remain in our own self-dejection, but go on to the next level of reliance on God. In other words, we must go on to the level of "I can do nothing on my own. I can do all things in God." This is the level of believing and trusting in the power of the Lord to rescue us from sin.

3. Prayer

The third aspect of faith, dependence, begins with humility. From the starting point of humility, it goes on to trust, and then to prayer—or to express more accurately, to desperate cry. At this time, the chain of sin will be broken and the soul will gain freedom. In other words, the soul receives salvation.

Salvation is not achieved by simply understanding the doctrine of salvation with the mind and being convinced of its truth theoretically. That is the belief of demons. The true faith that saves us has the three elements, which are intellect, volition, and dependence. Furthermore, the dependence aspect of faith includes having humility, trust, and "hosanna" prayer. Hosanna prayer is a prayer that thirsts after salvation.

"For I will take you out of the nations; I will gather you from all the countries and bring you back into your own land. I will sprinkle clean water on you, and you will be clean; I will cleanse you from all your impurities and from all your idols. I will give you a new heart and put a new spirit in you; I will remove from you your heart of stone and give you a heart of flesh. And I will put my Spirit in you and move you to follow my decrees and be careful to keep my laws. You will live in the land I gave your forefathers; you will be my people, and I will be your God..." This is what the Sovereign LORD says: Once again I will yield to the plea of the house of Israel and do this for them.

—EZEKIEL 36:24–28, 37

Jesus answered her, "If you knew the gift of God and who it is that asks you for a drink, you would have asked him and he would have given you living water."

—JOHN 4:10

And everyone who calls on the name of the Lord will be saved.

—ACTS 2:21

Just as the blind beggar Bartimaeus desperately cried out to Jesus, "Jesus, Son of David, have mercy on me!" despite the rebukes from people (see Mark 10:47), we must pray, "Lord, forgive my sins and deliver me from the bondage of sin. Please save me!" when we realize our own moral bankruptcy and Christ's power of salvation.

How long must we pray like this? Just as Bartimaeus cried out until he received the Lord's answer, we must pray with faith and perseverance until the Lord answers us. When we do that, Jesus, the perfect Lord, will bring us true salvation: forgiveness of sin and freedom from the bondage of sin.

The Role of Faith

What do you think is the role of faith? Many people consider it merely as providing forgiveness for sin or giving privilege of being the child of God. They do not think more than that, because they have imperfect understanding of faith.

However, faith is not just consenting to the basic Christian doctrine but receiving Jesus as King and Savior and trusting the Lord to live a new, obedient life to God. Therefore, the role of faith goes beyond the incomplete view of faith. Then what are the specific roles of faith?

1. Faith purifies our heart (Acts 15:9).

In Mrs. Choo Thomas's book *Heaven Is So Real!* (translated by Pastor Yonggi Cho), the Lord says, "Only the pure-hearted and obedient people will go to heaven."[14] Some people might wonder, "Why does he say that since we are saved by faith?" However, the Lord is right. This is what the Bible says:

> He made no distinction between us and them, for he purified their hearts by faith.
>
> —ACTS 15:9

True faith causes hearts to be pure. That is why Paul says in the Bible:

> To the pure, all things are pure, but to those who are corrupted and do not believe, nothing is pure. In fact, both their minds and consciences are corrupted. They claim to know God, but by their actions they deny him.

They are detestable, disobedient and unfit for doing anything good.

—TITUS 1:15–16

John Wesley said that the fruit of faith that comes from God is the power to overcome sin. First, it is the power to overcome external sin, such as evil speech and actions. Next, it is the power to overcome interior sin because faith purifies our hearts from unholy lust and fleshly nature.

Therefore, no matter how much one claims to have faith, he is not a true believer if his heart is impure.

2. Faith makes us holy.

...to open their eyes and turn them from darkness to light, and from the power of Satan to God, so that they may receive forgiveness of sins and a place among those who are sanctified by faith in me.

—ACTS 26:18

Faith not only makes us righteous, but makes us holy as well. Jesus has become for us not only our righteousness, but also our holiness. (See 1 Corinthians 1:30.) Therefore, when we believe in Jesus with a true heart, we will become righteous and holy. That is why Charles Finney said in his book *The Secret of Holiness* that if a Christian wants to be holy, the only answer is by faith. All other answers are legalistic. Without understanding the most important and fundamental secret of faith, it is impossible to become holy no matter how hard one tries. Not only righteousness, but also holiness, must be gained by faith.

3. Faith enables us to obey God.

> Through him and for his name's sake, we received grace and apostleship to call people from among all the Gentiles to the obedience that comes from faith.
>
> —ROMANS 1:5

Paul wrote his purpose for spreading the gospel.

- First, it is for the name of the Lord. In other words, it is to give glory to the Lord.

- Second, it is not only so that the Gentiles might believe, but that they may obey the Lord.

Note that Paul did not say, "have faith and obey"; rather, he said, "to the obedience [result] that comes from faith [cause]." Faith and obedience cannot be separated. They are connected through the rule of cause and effect. Do not separate what God has connected into one. Otherwise, deception will arise.

When we are speaking about living faith that includes deeds, we are not asserting that we must add obedience to faith in order to have true faith and be saved. In other words, when obedience does not result from faith, it does not mean that a person did not simply obey, but that his faith was not real to begin with. Real faith grants him salvation.

True faith always leads to obedience. Therefore, one of the roles of faith is to cause obedience.

4. Faith firmly establishes the law.

During my Christian walk, I have heard many preachers and saints say, "How fortunate that we need only to believe in Jesus to be saved, while in the Old Testament, the Israelites had to obey every single law to be saved!" As this statement illustrates, many people believe that faith has replaced the law. However, this is a misunderstanding. Faith is not given to replace the law, but to enable us to fulfill the law. That is why Paul says:

> Do we, then, nullify the law by this faith? Not at all! Rather, we uphold the law.
>
> —ROMANS 3:31

In this verse, the phrase "uphold the law" appears. In the New Living Translation, it is written:

> Well then, if we emphasize faith, does this mean that we can forget about the law? Of course not! In fact, only when we have faith do we truly fulfill the law.
>
> —ROMANS 3:31, NLT

Firmly upholding the law means obeying it firmly. (Out of ethical, ritual, and civil laws, *law* here refers to ethical law.) What upholds the law? It is faith that upholds the law. Faith is not an indulgence that pardons lack of obedience; it is the secret to obeying the law. Faith plays the role of enabling us to keep the law.

5. Faith brings us what we hope for.

> Now faith is being sure of what we hope for and certain of what we do not see.
>
> —HEBREWS 11:1

What should we hope for? Jesus! In Jesus we find righteousness, peace, joy, holiness, love, and heavenly kingdom. All of these are found in Him.

Do you just hope for Jesus and all these things, or have you received all of them? Faith is the substance of things we hope for. Therefore, real faith gives us the substance of our hope. By human effort, we cannot possess the things that we hope for, but when we truly have faith in Jesus and rely on Him, we can possess all these things. Possessing what we hope for is the role and function of faith.

6. Faith allows us to live a life pleasing to God.

> And without faith it is impossible to please God, because anyone who comes to him must believe that he exists and that he rewards those who earnestly seek him.
> —Hebrews 11:6

No one can please God without faith. What is it that pleases God? Many people do not understand the true meaning of this verse. The words *please God* do not mean that the Lord is displeased with lack of faith and pleased with faith. The meaning of this verse is that without faith, one simply cannot live a life that is pleasing to God. John 15:4–5 restates this:

> Remain in me, and I will remain in you. No branch can bear fruit by itself; it must remain in the vine. Neither can you bear fruit unless you remain in me. I am the vine; you are the branches. If a man remains in me and I in him, he will bear much fruit; apart from me you can do nothing.

The truth of what I am saying becomes clear when we see Hebrews 11:6 in context with the previous verse.

> By faith Enoch was taken from this life, so that he did not experience death; he could not be found, because God had taken him away. For before he was taken, he was commended as one who pleased God.
>
> —HEBREWS 11:5

Here, "he was commended as one who pleased God" means that people who had observed Enoch's life acknowledged and testified that he had lived a life that was pleasing to God. The next verse, "and without faith, it is impossible to please God," means that faith is the secret to living a life pleasing to God. This is the role and function of faith. Faith allows us to live a life like Enoch's, one that is pleasing to God. As a result, like Enoch, we will be lifted up to heaven (rapture).

7. Faith overcomes the world.

> ...for everyone born of God overcomes the world. This is the victory that has overcome the world, even our faith. Who is it that overcomes the world? Only he who believes that Jesus is the Son of God.
>
> —1 JOHN 5:4–5

Faith enables us to overcome the world. Anyone who does not have faith cannot overcome the world. What is the word *world* referencing in this verse?

> Do not love the world or anything in the world. If anyone loves the world, the love of the Father is not in him. For everything in the world—the cravings of sinful man, the lust of his eyes and the boasting of what he has and does—comes not from the Father but from

the world. The world and its desires pass away, but the man who does the will of God lives forever.

—1 JOHN 2:15–17

The first part of this passage says, "Do not love the world or anything in the world" (v. 15). Therefore, the world is the object that we must not love. In 2 Timothy, Paul points out the three objects that we must not love: self, money, and pleasure. (See 2 Timothy 3:2–4.) To say that the world represents selfishness, greed, and lust are not incorrect. In verse 16, the meaning of "the world" is specified as "the cravings of sinful man, the lust of his eyes and the boasting of what he has and does."

"The cravings of sinful man, the lust of his eyes and the boasting of what he has and does"—these are the things of the world. Therefore, it is very clear what it means to overcome the world. It means to overcome the cravings of our flesh, the lust of our eyes, and the boasting of what we have and do. When these three things tempt and attack us, we must not succumb to them but attack them and strike them down. That is overcoming the world. It is the role of faith to overcome them. Those who have faith overcome the world. Only he who overcomes will inherit the kingdom of God. (See Revelation 21:7.)

The Touchstone of Faith

Examine yourselves to see whether you are in the faith; test yourselves. Do you not realize that Christ Jesus is in you—unless, of course, you fail the test?

—2 CORINTHIANS 13:5

We must examine and check our faith to discern whether it is true or false. So we must make sure that even after believing in Jesus, we do not fall into hell. How can we know whether our faith is true or false? There are four touchstones of faith. Through these four touchstones, test your faith step-by-step, and then you will surely know whether your faith is true or false.

1. Assurance

Some churchgoers maintain that no matter how hard they try they simply cannot believe. They are unbelievers. They are not Christians.

2. Deeds

> What good is it, my brothers, if a man claims to have faith but has no deeds? Can such faith save him?
> —JAMES 2:14

Jesus warned His disciples to be aware of false prophets, and He said that by their fruit we would know them. What was the reason that these false prophets were cast away? They were evildoers. (See Matthew 7:23.) In others words, they did not live according to the Word of God. This is only one reason God would reject someone. Therefore, we must examine our faith through our biblical obedience—our deeds.

3. Love

> For in Christ Jesus neither circumcision nor uncircumcision has any value. The only thing that counts is faith expressing itself through love.
> —GALATIANS 5:6

Thomas Manton said, "Faith is our response to God's love toward us and giving that love back to God."[15]

Jonathan Edwards said:

> Saving faith has both light and heat. Speculative faith has light, but not the heat. It is the faith of demons, different from faith of love...Love is the life and spirit of faith. Faith without life is the same as dead bodies without spirit. Love discerns between true faith and false ones.[16]

Wherever a person goes, his shadow follows. Shadow always follows the substance. In the same way, deeds always follow true faith.

Where do deeds come from? They come from love. As Paul said, love is the perfection of law. Therefore, we must check whether or not our faith is derived from love. If our deeds do not arise from love but from fear, expectation, or hope, we are not being biblically obedient, and that kind of faith cannot be true faith.

4. Humility

> See, he is puffed up; his desires are not upright—but the righteous will live by his faith.
>
> —HABAKKUK 2:4

What do you see? Do you see the contrast between pride and faith? Pride and faith cannot coexist. We must realize that pride exists under lack of faith, while humility exists under faith. One of the key reasons people do not believe in Jesus is pride. Prideful people cannot believe in Jesus.

> How can you believe if you accept praise from one
> another, yet make no effort to obtain the praise that
> comes from the only God?
>
> —JOHN 5:44

Only the humble can believe in Jesus. That is why Jesus said the following:

> I tell you the truth, unless you change and become
> like little children, you will never enter the kingdom of
> heaven. Therefore, whoever humbles himself like this
> child is the greatest in the kingdom of heaven.
>
> —MATTHEW 18:3–4

While I was preaching a few days ago, the Holy Spirit said to me regarding verse 3: "Do you know exactly what it means when it says that unless you change and become like little children, you will never enter the kingdom of heaven? It means that you can only be saved when you are humble enough to receive the Word, not as knowledge but as revelation."

Let me help you understand this in an easy way.

- First, anyone who wishes to enter heaven must change and become like a little child.

- Second, becoming like little children means being humble. As verse 4 shows, little children are symbols of humility.

- Third, only to the humble the Word comes, not as knowledge but as revelation.

At that time Jesus said, "I praise you, Father, Lord of heaven and earth, because you have hidden these things from the wise and learned, and revealed them to little children."

—MATTHEW 11:25

Here, the word *revealed* signifies revelation. "Now this is eternal life: that they may know you, the only true God, and Jesus Christ, whom you have sent" (John 17:3). However, Jesus said, "No one knows the Son except the Father, and no one knows the Father except the Son and those to whom the Son chooses to reveal him" (Matt. 11:27). Only the humble can receive this revelation. In other words, the Word of God that touches the spirit with revelation, not knowledge, comes only to those who listen to it with a humble heart. As a result, one is able to have faith and receive salvation.

After hearing Peter's confession of faith, Jesus said, "This was not revealed to you by man, but by my Father in heaven" (Matt. 16:17). Paul also said, "Faith comes from hearing the message, and the message is heard through the word of Christ" (Rom. 10:17). Here "the word" is *rhema*—the revelatory word. In the parable of the sower, understanding the Word with our mind is different from realizing the Word with our heart. Understanding is the function of the brain, while realization is the function of the spirit (heart). Only through revelation do we have realization. Without revelation, there is no realization of sin or the truth of the gospel. Without revelation, there is no repentance or faith. Revelation is given only to the childlike, the humble in heart. Therefore, please remember that only the humble possess the true faith and receive salvation.

Humility is the touchstone of faith. Genuine Christians, even though there are differences in degree, are all humble. Kathryn Kuhlman said that faith goes beyond conviction, confidence, and reliance, and is not self-conceit. Charles Hodge said, "Without humility, no one can be a Christian…Without humility, there cannot exist true faith, communion with God, internal peace and external power."[17]

Through my observations and past experiences as a preacher, I found some people to be good and humble. They have "good soil" in their heart, and when they hear the message of the gospel, they immediately receive salvation. Certain people are evil, yet humble. They are like the tax collectors and prostitutes in the Bible. They have no big problem receiving salvation, although not as easily as the first group of people. People who are good and yet prideful have difficulty receiving salvation. Their pride must be broken in order for them to receive salvation. The most difficult are the people who are evil and prideful. To be honest, I have rarely seen such people receive salvation. There is not much hope for them. It is a miracle among miracles for them to be saved. In most cases, these people fall into hell. If they realize they are evil and prideful and repent by turning away from their sins, they can receive salvation.

One day, the Holy Spirit said these words to me: "Humility lies within true faith. Some people have faith but do not possess humility. They are nominal Christians, Christians by name only. Such people cannot be saved. Furthermore, there are people who have faith but lack humility, possessing pride instead. Such people are hypocrites who are twice as much the sons of hell. Therefore, they will not only be thrown into hell, but they will also be punished twice as much in hell."

How fearful these words are! Just as blood flows in blood vessels, humility flows in faith. Just as blood is life, the humility that flows within faith is the life of faith. All blood vessels are not the same, but there is the main artery into which much blood flows. In the same way, there are believers who have more humility and therefore, bigger faith. The name of our church is Great Faith Church. "Great faith" does not just signify strong assurance. Think about the Canaanite woman to whom Jesus said, "Woman, you have great faith! Your request is granted" (Matt. 15:28). This woman was so humble; she did not even refute when she was called a dog. Likewise, the centurion had humility that was rare to find in a conquering general, and he received a complement from Jesus: "I tell you the truth, I have not found anyone in Israel with such great faith" (Matt. 8:10). Therefore, the size of one's faith is not measured by the size of one's assurance, but the size of one's humility. To measure faith, we must always measure humility.

In conclusion, I will now lead you to the summary of faith. In order to understand faith at once, let us draw a picture to illustrate it. Use paper and pencil to draw it yourself so that you will clearly remember it.

- First, draw a small circle.

- Next, draw six progressively larger circles around it so it looks like a target. You will have seven circles altogether. Within each circle, you will write a simple explanation and a scriptural verse. On the smallest circle in the center, write "The Word (revelation, Romans 10:17)."

- On the second circle, write "Humility (Habakkuk 2:4)."

- On the third circle, write "Relying on Jesus (John 15:4–5)."

- On the fourth circle, write "Prayer (calling on the

name of the Lord, Acts 2:21)."

- On the fifth circle, write "Love (grace, Galatians 5:6)."

- On the sixth circle, write "Deeds (James 2:14)."

- On the seventh and last circle, write "Knowledge and assurance in the gospel."

- The seventh element is the part that forms the "shell" of faith. The other six inner circles are actual contents of faith, which is the "kernel" of faith. Therefore, those who have the first through sixth are the grain, and those who only have the seventh are chaff.

Now, I will briefly explain each circle that makes up true faith.

1. Faith begins by hearing the *rhema*—the revelatory words, not *logos*.

> Consequently, faith comes from hearing the message, and the message is heard through the word of Christ.
> —ROMANS 10:17

Rhema indicates the word of revelation. Therefore, in order to be saved, we need revelatory word.

2. When the Word comes to a person as knowledge, he becomes proud, but when it comes as a revelation, he becomes humble.

In other words, through the revelatory light of God's Word, the person faces himself honestly and becomes lowly in heart, because he sees not only his external sinfulness, but also his inward corruption.

> See, he is puffed up; his desires are not upright—but the righteous will live by his faith.
>
> —HABAKKUK 2:4

3. Humility denies ourselves and depends on Jesus to become the source of our righteousness and holiness.

> Remain in me, and I will remain in you. No branch can bear fruit by itself; it must remain in the vine. Neither can you bear fruit unless you remain in me. I am the vine; you are the branches. If a man remains in me and I in him, he will bear much fruit; apart from me you can do nothing.
>
> —JOHN 15:4–5

4. Humility and the heart of reliance on Jesus are revealed through prayer.

> Jesus answered her, "If you knew the gift of God and who it is that asks you for a drink, you would have asked him and he would have given you living water."
>
> —JOHN 4:10

> And everyone who calls on the name of the Lord will be saved.
>
> —ACTS 2:21

5. When we call on the name of the Lord, He pours His love into our hearts.

> For in Christ Jesus neither circumcision nor uncircumcision has any value. The only thing that counts is faith expressing itself through love.
>
> —GALATIANS 5:6

Here, the word *grace* or *the Holy Spirit* can replace the word *love*.

6. After these steps, we can finally live according to the Word of God by grace.

> What good is it, my brothers, if a man claims to have faith but has no deeds? Can such faith save him?
>
> —JAMES 2:14

This is true faith. This is the secret of faith and the process by which faith is formed. Therefore, use this picture to examine your own faith and to teach and share with others what true faith is.

Finally, I want to share this word with you. We must possess true faith, but having true faith is not the end. The Bible speaks about those who at one time possessed faith, but were destroyed at the end.

> But my righteous one will live by faith. And if he shrinks back, I will not be pleased with him.
>
> —HEBREWS 10:38

Some people used to have faith, but gave it up and no longer live in faith. Therefore, even those who live in true faith are still in danger of destruction. We must follow the example of Paul.

> I have fought the good fight, I have finished the race, I have kept the faith.
>
> —2 TIMOTHY 4:7

Paul kept the faith until the end. Revelation 14 is similar.

> This calls for patient endurance on the part of the saints who obey God's commandments and remain faithful to Jesus.
>
> —REVELATION 14:12

Therefore, taking Paul and the saints mentioned in Revelation as examples, we must keep our faith until the end. Perhaps the words I say are very unfamiliar to some people. Furthermore, some people may even feel deep resistance against my words, but please believe what I am saying. It is not enough to just believe. We must continue to believe and not retreat. In other words, we must live in faith.

> [Paul and Barnabas returned,] strengthening the disciples and encouraging them to remain true to the faith. "We must go through many hardships to enter the kingdom of God," they said.
>
> —ACTS 14:22

As the verse says, Paul exhorted people to remain true to the faith.

> Once you were alienated from God and were enemies in your minds because of your evil behavior. But

now he has reconciled you by Christ's physical body through death to present you holy in his sight, without blemish and free from accusation—if you continue in your faith, established and firm, not moved from the hope held out in the gospel.

—COLOSSIANS 1:21–23

Only those who remain in faith will stand before God without blemish and free from accusation.

But women will be saved through childbearing—if they continue in faith, love and holiness with propriety.

—1 TIMOTHY 2:15

Only by remaining in faith can we be saved. These words were written for women, but they apply to men as well.

Examine yourselves to see whether you are in the faith; test yourselves. Do you not realize that Christ Jesus is in you—unless, of course, you fail the test?

—2 CORINTHIANS 13:5

Paul did not ask, "Do you have faith?" He asked, "Are you in the faith?" In other words, Paul's question is, "Are you remaining in faith? Are you continually living in faith?" Even though I had faith in the past, if I do not have it now, I will fail the test and will be cast away. Therefore, always remember this fact, and like Paul, let us not draw back. I wish every one of you success in keeping your faith.

– Chapter 4 –

FAITH AND OBEDIENCE

What good is it, my brothers, if a man claims to have faith but has no deeds? Can such faith save him? Suppose a brother or sister is without clothes and daily food. If one of you says to him, "Go, I wish you well; keep warm and well fed," but does nothing about his physical needs, what good is it? In the same way, faith by itself, if it is not accompanied by action, is dead.

But someone will say, "You have faith; I have deeds."

Show me your faith without deeds, and I will show you my faith by what I do. You believe that there is one God. Good! Even the demons believe that—and shudder.

You foolish man, do you want evidence that faith without deeds is useless? Was not our ancestor Abraham considered righteous for what he did when he offered his son Isaac on the altar? You see that his faith and his actions were working together, and his faith was made complete by what he did. And the scripture was fulfilled that says, "Abraham believed God, and it was credited to him as righteousness," and he was called God's friend. You see that a person is justified by what he does and not by faith alone.

In the same way, was not even Rahab the prostitute considered righteous for what she did when she gave lodging to the spies and sent them off in a different direction? As the body without the spirit is dead, so faith without deeds is dead.

–JAMES 2:14-26

IN THE BEGINNING when Adam was created he was neither good nor evil, but was in a state of neutrality. Even though he was made in the image of a good God he was neutral, because without the involvement of human free will, there could not be the formation of good or evil. That was why his future rested upon his own choice. In other words, his future depended on his good or evil decision.

After Adam ate of the forbidden fruit and sinned against God, all human beings, like a fetus that catches a virus from his infected mother, are born evil through the original sin of Adam. As proof, billions of people have been born and have died since Adam, but not one of them was righteous, nor did what was right, and never sinned. (See Ecclesiastes 7:20.) Because this has become the norm, no one expects anyone to be perfect and sinless.

All human beings are sinners. Therefore, the belief that if one lives righteously he will go to heaven, but if one lives wickedly, he will go to hell is very incorrect. The statement "if you believe in Jesus, you will go to heaven, but if you don't believe in Him, you will go to hell" sounds wrong and unfair at first, but it is true. That is because all human beings are sinners, and sin must be forgiven. Sin cannot be compensated by good deeds, and only Jesus is able to forgive the sin of humankind.

In other words, heaven is not for good people, but for those who believe. We are not saved by our good deeds or by the works of the law, but only by faith. That is why the Bible records the following words:

> We...know that a man is not justified by observing the law, but by faith in Jesus Christ. So we, too, have put our faith in Christ Jesus that we may be justified by

faith in Christ and not by observing the law, because by observing the law no one will be justified.

—GALATIANS 2:16

For it is by grace you have been saved, through faith—and this not from yourselves, it is the gift of God—not by works, so that no one can boast.

—EPHESIANS 2:8–9

These verses do not mean that as long as we believe, and are not necessarily living by God's Word, we can go to heaven. No one who does not live by the Word of God can go to heaven. There is no exception, even for believers. That is why the Bible records the following:

Not everyone who says to me, "Lord, Lord," will enter the kingdom of heaven, but only he who does the will of my Father who is in heaven.

—MATTHEW 7:21

What good is it, my brothers, if a man claims to have faith but has no deeds? Can such faith save him?

—JAMES 2:14

It is certain that we are saved by faith, but it is just as certain that those who do not live by the Word of God will not enter heaven. These two truths are revealed clearly in the Bible and cannot be denied. However, many people wonder how these two truths can coexist at the same time. They do not have the whole understanding of these truths.

Many people believe one truth one day, and the other truth another day. Even preachers preach one sermon one day and a different sermon the next, without having a clear, coherent understanding. Unintentionally, they bring confusion and deception upon people. However, such confusion and deception will disappear like a morning mist once we understand the true meaning of faith and obedience and the relationship between the two. By introducing the difficulties that brought me to my present understanding about faith and obedience (deeds), I hope to give you help that will bring you instant understanding.

1. Questions about the doctrine of salvation and the beginning of realization.

I was unusually interested in the doctrine of salvation ever since I was young, because I believed in the existence of heaven and hell and did not want to go to hell. My Sunday school teachers taught me that, even within the church, some people would go to heaven and some would go to hell. I wanted to know exactly why this was the case. I did not want to be surprised on Judgment Day; I wanted to be well prepared so that I would go to heaven. I was not a rebellious child, but because of these reasons, I did not listen to different explanations that my pastor and my teachers gave regarding salvation. Rather, I held on to the following two verses in the Bible:

> Not everyone who says to me, "Lord, Lord," will enter the kingdom of heaven, but only he who does the will of my Father who is in heaven.
> —MATTHEW 7:21

> What good is it, my brothers, if a man claims to have faith but has no deeds? Can such faith save him?
> —JAMES 2:14

When I heard sermons that were contrary to these verses, I knew clearly in my spirit that they were not the truth, even though I was young. I continued to hold on to those verses.

However, in today's Christianity, the situation is different. Many pastors and saints may say they agree, but they do not believe these verses at face value. They believe that since we are saved by faith, these verses are merely emphatic expressions that must not be taken too literally. They believe that they will go to heaven, even though they do not live by the Word of God. How did people end up having such a risky and dangerous faith? The cause is not immediately seen, but it is closely related to how Protestantism was birthed. Sundar Singh said that churchianity and Christianity are not the same. Just as Roman Catholicism became distorted in its beliefs, Protestantism also became skewed in its beliefs. It is not enough to become a member of a church, but one must become a disciple of Christ.

As you are well aware, Protestantism was derived from Roman Catholicism. Just as Moses delivered Israel from Egypt, the reformer Martin Luther "delivered" Protestantism from Roman Catholicism. Martin Luther is said to be the father of Protestantism.

While I was in seminary, I was skimming the pages of William Barclay's commentary, and found a shocking fact: Martin Luther did not acknowledge the Book of James as scriptural.[1]

Before Luther, there were people who questioned its canonicity. In the writings of Jerome and Eusebius, there are passages that doubt the scriptural authority of the book. They were referring to someone else's words, but the contents threatened the authority of the Book of James. Jerome wrote that even though with time, James's authority in the church was acknowledged, it may be likely that someone else wrote the letter using James' name.[2]

Eusebius wrote:

> Such is the story of James, to whom is attributed the first of the "general" epistles.[3]

This means that since it is a general epistle, it cannot be acknowledged as canonical. These were the first words that doubted the canonicity of James.

Later, the Book of James received harsher treatments from Cajetan, Erasmus, and Luther. Cajetan and Erasmus did not show any interest in the Book of James, while Luther did not treat James as scriptural. Luther commented rudely on the Book of James as "an epistle of straw."[4] Luther's ignorance and prejudice did not end here; he even tried to exclude the Books of Hebrews, Jude, and Revelation as not being canonical. As proof, his German translation of the New Testament has only twenty-three books, not the full twenty-seven. He left out these four books in his New Testament, but recorded them at the end of the text as appendices. This was not a simple problem. Revelation 22:18–19 warns:

> I warn everyone who hears the words of the prophecy of this book: If anyone adds anything to them, God will add to him the plagues described in this book. And if anyone takes words away from this book of prophecy, God will take away from him his share in the tree of life and in the holy city, which are described in this book.

Luther was blatantly prejudiced regarding the Bible. Because the four scriptural books spoke about salvation that has deeds, he did not acknowledge them as part of the Bible. The reformative works of this man formed Protestantism. Therefore, it may be natural that today's church also suffers from such serious prejudice and ignorance regarding faith and works.

The biggest issue on the topic of faith and works arises from the writings of Paul and James when they both refer to the righteousness credited to Abraham. We can read two different statements regarding one character.

> What then shall we say that Abraham, our forefather, discovered in this matter? If, in fact, Abraham was justified by works, he had something to boast about—but not before God. What does the Scripture say? "Abraham believed God, and it was credited to him as righteousness."
>
> —ROMANS 4:1–3

> Was not our ancestor Abraham considered righteous for what he did when he offered his son Isaac on the altar? You see that his faith and his actions were working together, and his faith was made complete by what he did. And the scripture was fulfilled that says, "Abraham believed God, and it was credited to him as righteousness," and he was called God's friend. You see that a person is justified by what he does and not by faith alone.
>
> —JAMES 2:21–24

When we look at these two passages, they seem to contradict each other. In reality however, they form a perfect harmony. In order to understand these passages, we must realize that the word *faith* that Paul and James use, and the words *works* and *deeds* used by them respectively are different in meaning from each other. I do not know the exact time period, but, by God's grace, I had learned that there was such difference. At the time, I explained the differences by analyzing and breaking them down into smaller categories, but I do not think that is necessary here.

Simply put, Paul's *faith* is the cause that produces works, and therefore it is the faith that is accompanied by works. Paul used the word *faith* with this meaning in mind. On the other hand, James understood the gospel truth of Christianity and used the word *faith* to express the truthfulness of it. Of course, that is faith, too, but it is not describing the same kind of faith that saves us.

John Wesley said that Satan has given a substitution of faith which resembles faith and which only a few can discern as false. This substitution is called "the intellectual understanding of the truth of the gospel."

Charles Finney confessed in his book *Power From On High:*

> I learned from one seminary professor that faith means "the intellectual activity or state of assurance." And I always heard people describing faith in such a term…They said "faith is being firmly convinced of the doctrines regarding Christ."[5]

In the latter part of this book Finney reveals that such a faith is not saving faith. That is correct. Such faith can never lead to salvation. Therefore, we must never remain in this state.

Now, we will find out the difference between the words *works* and *deeds.*

Jonathan Edwards wrote in his book, *The Heart of Christianity,* that the statement that we are justified by faith is not contradictory to apostle Paul's frequent assertions that we cannot be justified by the works of the law. Likewise, the statement that biblical obedience is related to righteousness is not contradictory to apostle Paul's frequent assertions that we cannot be justified by the works of the law.

It is certain that Jonathan Edwards knew the difference between works and deeds. Works and deeds are different from each other, but how? The word *works*, which Paul used negatively, signifies the self-effort to receive salvation, as in "the works of the law" (Rom. 9:32, NKJV). This is a foolish attempt. The word *deeds* used by James is fundamentally different in meaning from the works of the law mentioned in the Book of Romans, and it signifies deeds of faith.

The former is the action that appears before salvation, while the latter is the action that appears to those who have already been saved. The former is impossible to accomplish, while the latter is possible; the former can lead to self-righteousness, while the latter is achieved by the grace of God, and thus brings glory to Him.

Even though the words *works* and *deeds* seem like synonyms, they are actually different in meaning. Therefore, once we understand this and read the two passages about Abraham being credited as righteous, there is no contradiction; the two passages are totally harmonious and complementary to each other. As a result, we do not have to accept one passage and reject the other; both passages by Paul and James are complete and literal truths. This means that if we "have faith but no deeds," we are not in danger of losing heavenly rewards, but our own salvation. We must read Matthew 7:21 and James 2:14 literally. Finally, I will share what Rick Joyner wrote in his book *The Call*, regarding what Jesus Christ said:

When my judgment comes upon the earth, I will send my messengers to teach my people the right way to live, so that they will not be destroyed. Time is urgent, so you must immediately obey my message that I give you. If you listen and yet do not obey, the punishment will be more severe. This is a righteous judgment. I require more from those who have received more...

This is a generation where knowledge is increasing. The knowledge of my people who know of my ways will also increase. Even though your generation has more knowledge than all other generations combined, people do not live according to their knowledge. The time has come when I will no longer tolerate those who do not obey me even though they say they believe me. I will remove among my people those who are lukewarm. Those who do not obey me do not really believe in me. They teach my people through their lives that it is okay to disobey me.[6]

Please take this word of the Lord seriously. I wish for both you and me that we would obey the word of the Lord without hesitation.

2. Owing greatly to Charles Finney.

I knew since I was young that faith without deeds is a false faith, and that with such faith no one can enter heaven. Still, because of my limited knowledge and wisdom, I had several questions about the doctrine of salvation for which I had no answers. I read many books in search of truth, but I could not discover the answers to my heart's questions. As I repeatedly faced failure, I became convinced that I would not be able to find answers through books or sermons, and I began to lose all hope. Then while I was reading Charles Finney's autobiography, I became very agitated. There the following words were recorded:

> My habit was to always study the gospel and its best applications. I do not set time and date to prepare my sermons. I constantly meditate on the truths of the gospel and how best to apply them. I go inside the people and find out what they need. Then under the light of [the] Holy Spirit, I choose the topic that will fill the immediate needs of these people. I meditate on the topic with focus and on Sunday morning, I pray about the topic. After I had saturated my heart with the topic, I pour it out to the people...
>
> I can say this seriously. Because I did not prepare my sermon manuscript, I was able to study much deeply about the topic. I needed to put my effort on becoming familiar with the topic, I needed to fill my heart with the topic, and then share the topic with the people. I only recorded brief words, which I did not repeat during my sermon from my sermon note.
>
> When I started preaching, I did not even record this much. For the first twelve years of my ministry, I did not even write down one word, and it was common for me to preach without any preparation except for what I had gained in prayer. I preached as the situation demanded, as [the] Holy Spirit gave me the passage and the topic in my heart. I do not know how I must preach if my sermons did not come from the inspiration. With conviction, I figured out what I had to say intuitively. And the thoughts, words, and examples rushed into me as fast as I could deliver them. When I first started recording the sermon outline, I did not do it before the sermon, but afterwards. I wanted to preserve the ideas

of that which I was receiving. But when I had to re-deliver the message, I had to re-create the points and add fresh new ideas given by [the] Holy Spirit.

I always receive the sermon topic while I am praying on my knees. And when [the] Holy Spirit gives me the sermon topic, I can barely record it as I tremble because of the big stimulation that I feel in my heart. These occurrences were common for me. When the topic is given to me that seemed to pierce my body and soul, I was able to readily come up with the summary that supports what [the] Holy Spirit has presented to me. Such sermons were delivered to people with mighty power.[7]

As I was reading Charles Finney's confession, my body shook with overwhelming emotion, because his testimony was very similar to my own experiences when the word came upon me. I knew from experience what Charles Finney was saying.

In that instant, I thought, *All this time I was disappointed when I tried to find the truth of salvation through books. Most preachers and authors were neither able to give me the answers to my questions, nor were even curious to know themselves. Here is a man who received the Word of God the same way that I receive the Word. Furthermore, he is a figure who was used by God as a representative in his generation, and I cannot even compare with him because he was a spiritual giant. Then, he must definitely have the answer that I am looking for.*

From then on, I went to a Christian bookstore and bought Charles Finney's books without even looking at the titles. My expectations were right on the mark. I was able to find satisfactory answers to my questions. As a result, my eyes became brighter, my understanding increased, and I was able to see clearly the meanings in the Bible.

If possible, I want to recommend that you read all of Charles Finney's books. It is not easy to read his books. It takes much more effort to read his books than others. Here, I would like to introduce a few important parts related to faith and obedience. In his book *True and False Repentance*, there is a sermon titled, "Justification by Faith." I would like to share some points from this sermon.

3. This is what Charles Finney said in his book.

Justification by faith does not mean that faith is accepted as a substitute for personal holiness, or that by an arbitrary constitution, faith is imputed to us instead of personal obedience to the law.

Some suppose that justification is this, that the necessity of personal holiness is set aside, and that God arbitrarily dispenses with the requirement of the law, and imputes faith as a substitute. But this is not the way. Faith is accounted for just what it is, and not for something else that it is not. Abraham's faith was imputed unto him for righteousness, because it was itself an act of righteousness, and because it worked by love, and thus produced holiness. Justifying faith is holiness, so far as it goes, and produces holiness of heart and life, and is imputed to the believer as holiness, not instead of holiness.[8]

In my past Christian walk, I have heard numerous preachers and saints who say, "The people in the Old Testament times had to follow the law to be saved, but today, how fortunate that we are saved by believing in Jesus!" They think that faith has replaced the law. They misunderstood Romans 10:4 which says, "Christ is the end of the law so that there may be righteousness for everyone who believes." This verse does not mean that faith has replaced the law, but rather, it means what John Stott has said: "Now not only righteousness, but sanctification is based on our faith in Jesus Christ, not based on the works of the law. In that way, Christ is the fulfillment of the law."[9] This statement does not mean that faith has replaced the law, but it implies that faith is the secret to obeying the law. That is why Paul says in Romans 3:31:

> Do we, then, nullify the law by this faith? Not at all! Rather, we uphold the law.

4. Charles Finney explains Paul's words.

> Their [the Jews] religious teachers taught them that they would be saved by obedience to the ceremonial law. And therefore, when Paul began to preach, he seems to have attacked more especially this error of the Jews. He was determined to carry the main question, that men are justified by faith in Jesus Christ, in opposition to the doctrine of the Scribes and Pharisees, that salvation is by obedience to law....And then certain individuals in the church laid hold of this doctrine and carried it to the opposite extreme, and maintained that men are saved by faith altogether, irrespective of works of any kind. They overlooked the plain principle, that genuine faith always results in good works, and is itself a good work.[10]

When the wrong doctrine invaded the church, James pointed out their misunderstanding regarding Paul's words.

He explained their error in this way:

> Was not our ancestor Abraham considered righteous for what he did when he offered his son Isaac on the altar? You see that his faith and his actions were working together, and his faith was made complete by what he did. And the scripture was fulfilled that says, "Abraham believed God, and it was credited to him as righteousness," and he was called God's friend. You see that a person is justified by what he does and not by faith alone.
>
> —JAMES 2:21–24

This epistle sounds like a contradiction to Paul's assertions. As a result, certain segments of the early church rejected this idea. They neglected the fact that the works spoken of by Paul and deeds mentioned by James are completely different in their meaning. Paul was speaking of works accomplished by legalistic motives. However, Paul also emphasized the essential elements of faith, which are the good deeds produced by faith. He was rejecting the opinion that sought to equate elements of righteousness with works based on legalistic motives. James taught that a person does not gain righteousness based on works or faith only, but on works and faith that combine together to form one entity. His teaching was the same as that of Paul. Paul's expression—that we gain righteousness by faith, which expresses itself in love—was the same idea. We must remember that we were speaking not about legalistic righteousness based on works, but biblical righteousness. Such biblical righteousness, or righteousness gained by faith, is based on God's forgiveness and acceptance.

The declaration that a person is made righteous through his faith and holiness does not mean that he is accepted because of the law, but that he is regarded as righteous because of his faith and deeds of faith. This is the method that God has chosen to justify a sinner. Faith is not the source of righteousness. That source lies in Christ. The method for sinners to be forgiven, accepted, and made righteous is this: when they repent of their sins and become holy, their past sins will be forgiven by Christ.

This is the biblical meaning of righteousness. Biblical righteousness is as Charles Finney said: repenting, believing, and thereby becoming holy through the forgiveness of Jesus. Of course I do not believe that righteousness is merely being forgiven of sin, as Finney and Professor Erasmus believed. As Jonathan Edwards and Pastor Kenneth Hagin have written, I believe that righteousness includes being attributed with the righteousness of Christ. What Finney has said about the method of receiving righteousness is fundamentally true. Righteousness is not given to those with intellectual faith who merely consent to the Christian doctrines, but to those who repent and become holy.

After reading this, some people might think, *I can understand repentance, but I never heard that we are not justified as righteous if we are not holy.* I want to answer this comment by quoting two scriptures.

> Now get up and stand on your feet. I have appeared to you to appoint you as a servant and as a witness of what you have seen of me and what I will show you. I will rescue you from your own people and from the Gentiles. I am sending you to them to open their eyes and turn them from darkness to light, and from the power of Satan to God, so that they may receive forgiveness of sins and a place among those who are sanctified by faith in me.
> —ACTS 26:16–18

> Do you not know that the wicked will not inherit the kingdom of God? Do not be deceived: Neither the sexually immoral nor idolaters nor adulterers nor male prostitutes nor homosexual offenders nor thieves nor the greedy nor drunkards nor slanderers nor swindlers will inherit the kingdom of God. And that is what some of you were. But you were washed, you were sanctified, you were justified in the name of the Lord Jesus Christ and by the Spirit of our God.
>
> —1 CORINTHIANS 6:9–11

Do you see? The Lord Himself told Paul that when he has faith, he will become holy, and Paul described the saved believers as being "washed, sanctified, and justified in the name of the Lord Jesus Christ and by the Spirit of God." Paul spoke of holiness before justification. What Finney said is not a wrong assertion. His words are true. Therefore, we must repent, believe, and become holy. Only then will we receive righteousness by the blood of Jesus.

That might be the most unfamiliar truth to some of you. Like all other truths mentioned in this book, I want to emphasize that this truth is not new. As proof, Bishop John Ryle in his book *Holiness,* wrote:

> People seemed to have forgotten that God has combined sanctification and justification. Of course, sanctification and justification are different from each other, but are intimately related to each other and cannot exist alone. Those who are justified are all made holy, and those who are holy are all justified. A person cannot separate what God has combined. If you do not possess the mark of sanctification, do not talk of your righteousness.[11]

In addition, Charles Hodge said in his book *The Way of Life*:

> We must always take into account the fact that holiness is absolutely essential...Holiness is necessary to salvation because salvation by definition is a change of heart. The reason why Jesus is our Savior is that He saves His people from sin. Therefore, people who do not become holy cannot be saved.
>
> To say that a person can remain in sin and still become saved is like saying that a person who is ill can at the same time be healthy. Such statement is contradictory. The state of being saved is the state of being holy. These two cannot be separated no matter how one tries. Salvation is not only rescuing a person from the penalty of sin, but the power of sin. Salvation is becoming free from the bondage of fleshly desires and evil intentions...This is salvation...
>
> No matter which denominations we belong to, no matter what privilege or professional knowledge we possess, if our heart and life are not holy, if our thought-life is not habitually controlled by the will of God, if we do not enjoy communion with God and do not wish to be conformed by the image of God, if we are not led by [the] Holy Spirit and do not show His fruit of love, joy, peace, patience, kindness, goodness, faithfulness, gentleness, and self-control, then we are not believers and we are not in the state of being saved.
>
> The Bible does not know of proud, selfish, jealous, and negative Christians. Christians are the ones who have received the holy calling, made clean by the name of the Lord Jesus and by the Spirit of God, and are made righteous. They are the holy saints in Christ Jesus.[12]

Lastly, Stephen Charnock wrote this in his book *New Birth:*

> If we are not born again, we definitely cannot receive God's righteousness. We are not justified before God because of the righteousness within us. But this does not mean that we completely rule out our righteousness when we are justified by God. We cannot be made righteous by our righteousness because it is too imperfect to fulfill the demands of the law.
>
> However, if we do not have righteousness within us, we cannot be made righteous before God. This is true because to say a wicked person who possesses the most corrupt nature is righteous is contradictory to God's wisdom and holiness.
>
> When we consider God's reputation, how can we expect God's forgiveness to those who are willfully, habitually, and stubbornly sinful? Even from an ethical point of view, the only person who deserves forgiveness is the sinner who has repented from his sins.
>
> Being made righteous and being born again cannot be separated, even though they are different. Justification is fulfilled in our relationship with God, while second birth is fulfilled within us practically. Union with Christ is the foundation of these. Christ is the attributing cause of justification and second birth.
>
> Justification is declared by the Father, while second birth is realized by [the] Holy Spirit. Justification is the declaration of the Father, and second birth is the work of [the] Holy Spirit.[13]

Relational change and practical change occur at the same time. We can see this truth when we read 1 Corinthians 6:11

carefully: "And that is what some of you were. But you were washed, you were sanctified, you were justified in the name of the Lord Jesus Christ and by the Spirit of our God."

I will explain more fully in the next chapter, but so that you will not have misunderstanding, I want to explain to you beforehand about holiness, which comes before being justified. Paul's mention of holiness in 1 Corinthians 6:11 is clarified when we realize that this holiness signifies the inner holiness that has not yet been realized outwardly. As Wesley Duewel expressed well, this holiness is not the sanctification that occurs progressively after we believe, but it is the initial stage of sanctification. The initial stage of sanctification is the change in our spirit that we experience instantly when we repent and are born again. Without such a change, repentance and second birth cannot take place. This change in our spirit is what Paul spoke of as holiness, and one cannot be made righteous without it. This is because justification is granted only to those who have repented, believed, and become born again.

5. Charles Finney addresses the function of faith.

What is the reason behind being made righteous by faith rather than by repentance, love, or some other grace?

> It is nowhere said that men are justified or saved for faith, as the ground of their pardon, but only that they are justified by faith, as the medium or instrument. If it is asked why faith is appointed as the instrument, rather than any other exercise of the mind, the answer is, because of the nature and effect of faith. No other exercise could be appointed. What is faith? It is that confidence in God which leads us to love and obey him. We are therefore justified by faith because we are

sanctified by faith. Faith is the appointed instrument of our justification, because it is the natural instrument of sanctification.[14]

Then what is the function of faith that allows it to become the medium of justification?

First, hear what Jonathan Edwards said:

> How this is said to be by faith *alone*, without any manner of virtue or goodness of our own. This may seem to some to be attended with two difficulties, *viz.* how this can be said to be by faith alone, without any virtue or goodness of ours, when faith itself is a virtue, and one part of our goodness, and is not only some manner of goodness of ours, but is a very excellent qualification, and one chief part of the inherent holiness of a Christian?... When it is said, that we are not justified by any righteousness or goodness of our *own*, what is meant is that it is not out of respect to the excellency or goodness of any qualifications or acts in us whatsoever, that God judges it meet that this benefit of Christ should be ours. It is not, in any wise, on account of any excellency or value that there is in faith, that it appears in the sight of God a meet thing, that he who believes should have this benefit of Christ assigned to him, but purely from the relation faith has to the person in whom this benefit is to be had, or as it unites to that mediator, in and by whom we are justified. [15]

Charles Finney presented another reason why faith was chosen as a vehicle of justification, and this is what he says:

What is faith? It is that confidence in God which leads us to love and obey him. We are therefore justified by faith because we are sanctified by faith. Faith is the appointed instrument of our justification, because it is the natural instrument of sanctification. It is the instrument of bringing us back to obedience, and therefore is designated as the means of obtaining the blessings of that return. It is not imputed to us, by an arbitrary act, for what it is not, but for what it is, as the foundation of all real obedience to God. This is the reason why faith is made the medium through which pardon comes.[16]

The two opinions seem different. However, they form one harmonious unity because Jonathan Edwards also said:

Holy Spirit finds it right that we compare the unity between Christ and a true believer with the following unity. The parts of the body united with the head; as the body parts are connected to the head, they participate in the life that is in the head. The branches united with the vine; the reason why the branches share in the life-giving fluid of the vine is because they are connected to the vine. A wife united with her husband; the reason why a wife enjoys all the husband's possessions is because of her relationship with her husband.[17]

We do not bear the fruit of obedience through our own strength, but like the branches bearing fruit, we bear fruit though Jesus Christ, the true vine. If branches were to bear fruit with the vine as the power source, they must remain connected to the vine. Faith plays such a role of connecting the believers to Jesus Christ. That is why faith was chosen as the vehicle of justification.

In other words, just as branches cannot bear fruit apart from the vine, we can never bear fruit if we do not remain in the Lord by faith. This is the absolute truth. If we remain in the Lord, we will automatically bear the fruit of obedience. Therefore, those who have faith but do not produce biblical obedience can never go to heaven. We must always have "the obedience that comes from faith" (Rom. 1:5).

6. Gaining a balanced understanding through the writings of Jonathan Edwards.

Since Sunday school, I believed James 2:14 literally:

> What good is it, my brothers, if a man claims to have faith but has no deeds? Can such faith save him?

Through reading Finney's books, I was clearly able to understand the role of faith in salvation. However, I still had one question deep in my heart.

> Was not our ancestor Abraham considered righteous for what he did when he offered his son Isaac on the altar? You see that his faith and his actions were working together, and his faith was made complete by what he did. And the scripture was fulfilled that says, "Abraham believed God, and it was credited to him as righteousness," and he was called God's friend. You see that a person is justified by what he does and not by faith alone. In the same way, was not even Rahab the prostitute considered righteous for what she did when she gave lodging to the spies and sent them off in a different direction?
>
> —JAMES 2:21–25

When I was explaining these verses, I taught that we can never be made righteous by merely consenting to the doctrines of Christianity, but we must have faith that leads to action. Of course, this is true. However, the act of sacrificing Isaac on the altar occurred thirty years after Abraham was credited as being righteous. And the act of giving lodging to the spies happened after Rahab had already possessed secret faith in her heart. Therefore, to teach from the very beginning that we must have living faith that leads to action felt somewhat inappropriate to me.

Then I came across Jonathan Edwards' *The Heart of Christianity*, which was translated relatively recently, and in it I found my long-awaited answer. Jonathan Edwards began his debate with these words.

> First, I believe that everyone will acknowledge this fact. You will all acknowledge that the word "faith" or "justified" used by the apostle James must be interpreted differently from the same word used by the apostle Paul. Even those who oppose us, not just ourselves, believe that the intent of the apostle James was not to contradict the teachings of the apostle Paul imparted to many churches regarding justification by faith.
>
> What will happen if we interpret the words *faith* or *justified* used by each of the apostles to mean the same thing? The apostles would then be precisely, directly and completely contradicting each other. Looking at the same thing, one would see it positively and the other would see it negatively.
>
> Therefore, we can conclude that the central point of the debate arising from the verses in James 2 can be summed up with the following question: "Of the words *faith* and *justified* used by the apostle James, which

word should we interpret differently from the meaning used by the apostle Paul?" We must answer this question in order to answer the opposing viewpoint.[18]

After posing this question, Jonathan Edwards insists that the word *justified* has different meanings from each other even though some people think that it is the word *faith*. Unfortunately, Jonathan Edwards is mistaken here. As I have said in the previous section of this chapter, the word *faith* used by James and Paul are different in meaning, just as the words *works* and *deeds* are different in meaning from each other. Verses 14 and 19 are the proof of this.

> What good is it, my brothers, if a man claims to have faith but has no deeds? Can such faith save him?
>
> —JAMES 2:14

> You believe that there is one God. Good! Even the demons believe that—and shudder.
>
> —JAMES 2:19

In James 2:24, it is written: "You see that a person is justified by what he does and not by faith alone." Just as Jonathan Edwards asserted, the word *faith* here can be seen as having identical meaning as the word *faith* used by Paul.

Therefore Jonathan Edwards' belief that only one of the words has a different meaning from the other is not correct. Still, I learned something important from reading his writings. That is, I learned that not only the words *faith*, *works*, and *deeds*, but also *justified* were used by James and Paul with different meanings.

Then in what way was the word *justified* used differently?

First, I want to continue quoting from Jonathan Edwards:

Being justified means that you are acknowledged and accepted. There are two ways a person can be acknowledged and accepted. One way is to be truly acknowledged as justified and another way is to be declared justified. The word *justified* includes both of these elements. Justification means that we are acknowledged and accepted by God the Judge, and this fact is also made clear by God's declaration or sentence to the world or through our conscience.

If the word *justification* is used in the former sense—meaning that God has truly acknowledged us—the evidence of our justification comes from whatever has made us righteous. However, if the word *justification* is used in the latter sense—meaning that God has declared us justified—then the evidence of our justification is all things that properly show that we are worthy to receive such acknowledgment.

In the former case, only faith and justification are involved, since only our faith causes us to be made righteous before God. In the latter case, however, all the facts that prove our right to become justified before God are related to justification. Therefore, if we understand justification by the latter definition, all other virtues besides faith must be related to justification, because all virtues, that is, holy deeds, prove that they are accepted before God and that we ourselves have the right to be acknowledged by God.[19]

Here Jonathan Edwards notes two different meanings in the words "being made righteous." One is being made righteous from the heart, and the other is being declared righteous in words. In everyday language, "being made righteous" can embrace both meanings. In other words, "being made righteous" can mean simply being acknowledged and accepted, or it can mean declared as accepted.

In everyday language "being made righteous" can be used one way or the other. This is true because both meanings are actually the same thing. If there is a difference, it is that the former meaning is internal, and the latter is an external expression of the internal fact.

Almost everyone is familiar with the following: if there are two concepts that are exactly the same in meaning except that one is an outward expression or declaration of the other, both of these concepts are described with one word. For example, take the word *judgment*. At times, this word means an opinion that we have formed in our mind, and at other times, it means an external testimony or declaration of what was formed in our mind. Likewise, words such as *justify, condemn, accept, reject, scorn, acknowledge,* and *deny* can mean an opinion formed in the mind, or they can mean an external expression of those inner opinions.

However, Jonathan Edwards saw the word *justified* as only a declarative expression. When we see the word *justified* as an outward declaration, we must also see that a person is not only declared righteous by faith, but also made righteous through his action. To prove a tree to be good, it is possible not only to examine it but also to see its fruit forming on the branches; likewise, a person can be proven righteous in the same way.

When we think about the intention of the apostle James, our opinion is strengthened. This was the error made by false teachers and opposed by the apostle James. They believed that to be saved, good deeds are not necessary. They believed that as long as they believed in God, in Christ as the Son of God, and were baptized, they were safe from damnation and could live however they chose. Such teaching led people astray. When we consider the background, the purpose of James's letter was to clarify the truth that opposed such an error.

Therefore, the words of James, "A person is justified by what he does" must be understood as "our deeds as evidence declare us justified at the judgment seat." This is a natural conclusion after an accurate meditation on the context, because James was emphasizing deeds as the necessary proof and mark of faith, thus proving faith as genuine. This is clear in the context. Look at James 2:18:

> Show me your faith without deeds, and I will show you my faith by what I do.

Therefore, the purpose of James is plain. It was to prove that faith without deeds is not a genuine faith; that was his intention when James wrote his letter.

Please listen carefully without misunderstanding. James never rejected the truth, "only by faith"! It was not his intention to assert that faith and obedience are both necessary to be justified. His intention was to prove that faith without deeds cannot be genuine. Therefore, although he emphasized that deeds are essential, he never rejected the truth that faith alone justifies.

There is a definite fact when we look at James's logic: the reason deeds are necessary for justification is that they are connected to our salvation in the same way that faith is. The apostle speaks of deeds, but only the deeds arising from faith. Basically, he is showing that to be justified, faith is the one and only condition. He is saying that there is nothing else that can justify us. If other things are mentioned as the condition of being justified, they are mentioned because there are many expressions and proofs of faith.

Again, "A person is justified by what he does" must be understood as "Our deeds only as evidence declare us justified at the judgment seat." This is confirmed in James 2:21:

> Was not our ancestor Abraham considered righteous for what he did when he offered his son Isaac on the altar?

Here, James is speaking of God's acknowledgment of Abraham's genuine faith when he offered his son Isaac, and His judicial declaration of Abraham's righteousness. Genesis 22:12 tells what God said to Abraham:

> Now I know that you fear God, because you have not withheld from me your son, your only son.

It was Abraham's one act of offering his son Isaac as a sacrifice that proved his genuine faith and made him righteous. When we look at the scripture that shows justification credited to Abraham, it is clear that this justification is granted as a result of his proven deed. In New Testament passages, Abraham's obedience is seen as a fruit and proof of his faith. Hebrews 11:17 says:

> By faith Abraham, when God tested him, offered Isaac as a sacrifice. He who had received the promises was about to sacrifice his one and only son.

Look at this verse. It clearly states that Abraham offered Isaac by faith. That means genuine faith was already in Abraham even before he offered Isaac. As a result of the faith he possessed, he was able to offer Isaac to God, who declared Abraham righteous when He saw his action. James, on the other hand, gives another illustration in James 2:25:

> In the same way, was not even Rahab the prostitute considered righteous for what she did when she gave lodging to the spies and sent them off in a different direction?

Here, the apostle James mentions about God's declarative judgment and acknowledgment of Rahab as a believer when He commanded Joshua to spare her from destruction involving Jericho. It is written in Joshua 6:25:

> But Joshua spared Rahab the prostitute, with her family and all who belonged to her, because she hid the men Joshua had sent as spies to Jericho—and she lives among the Israelites to this day.

The fact that Rahab hid the spies sent by Joshua was acknowledged as the proof and mark of her faith. Look at Hebrews 11:31:

> By faith the prostitute Rahab, because she welcomed the spies, was not killed with those who were disobedient.

Therefore, as I have said earlier, the justification of Rahab, which the apostle James mentions, signifies a declarative justification when God specially acknowledged her as a believer.

Please remember this: if we understand deeds as actions or expressions of faith, then our deeds are not disconnected from our justification. That is the reason a person is justified not by faith alone, but by what he does. In other words, a person is not only justified by faith within his heart, but by the actions that express his life of faith. This is just like the actions and movements of our bodies that express the life within us.

What I have been saying so far is a summary of what Jonathan Edwards wrote in his book. He further writes:

> People often present their opposition by saying that the doctrine of justification by faith encourages licentious behavior. But that is not true. The reason is that the biblical doctrine of justification by faith which excludes goodness and excellence is true and gospel-based, and it does not decrease the whole necessity and benefit of obedience. This fact was clearly demonstrated from what I was saying so far.
>
> Salvation is firmly related to obedience, just as damnation is firmly related to lack of obedience. Those who disobey despite the given opportunity to obey are damned as a result of their lack of obedience. Salvation is not only firmly related to obedience, but in many ways is based on obedience. Obedience is the way of salvation and a necessary preparation for salvation.
>
> Eternal blessings are given as a reward to obedience. In our conscience, His declaration of our righteousness at the last day all depends upon our obedience, which is the appropriate proof that we are in the state of being acknowledged as righteous. Moreover, God considers our obedience when He receives us as justified and the proper recipient of eternal life, and when he decides whether we are righteous or not. Therefore, our salvation depends wholly on our obedience as though we are made righteous according to our moral excellence in obedience.[20]

I will summarize what I have been sharing so you can own these truths in your heart. We are made righteous not by the works of the law, but by faith. Paul and James use the words *faith, works,* and *made righteous* differently. There is only one judgment; "judging in our hearts" and "declaring a judgment with our mouth" mean essentially the same thing. However, they describe two sides of one meaning. It is the same way with the phrase *made righteous.*

Paul used the phrase *made righteous* with the former meaning in mind, that is, internal righteousness. Paul's use of the phrase *made righteous* also means "God's external, judicial declaration of righteousness." However, in this instance, God has declared someone righteous based on His omnipotent knowledge of the person's heart, rather than seeing the proof of his righteousness in his actions. In this case, the only condition for being justified is having faith alone without biblical obedience, which is a seed in the heart that has not yet developed into fruit in the form of outward obedience. This faith does not merely consent to the doctrines of the gospel, but has received Jesus as King and Savior in the heart, and is solely relying on and trusting in the Lord for a new life. Therefore, the seed, or root, of obedience planted in the heart will definitely appear outwardly as fruit in due time. However, since there is no appearance of external deeds yet, we are first made righteous based on faith alone.

On the other hand, James used the phrase *made righteous* with the latter meaning in mind, that is, the external declaration of righteousness. In this case, biblical obedience as the proof of faith must appear with faith. That is why James says that a person is made righteous "not by faith alone but by what he does."

It is important to understand such distinction of faith

and justification, because it shows clearly that "justified by faith alone" and "faith without deeds cannot receive justification and salvation" are both biblical truths! Such distinction helps people to receive both truths easily in their hearts, so that their faith and Christian living are harmonious to each other. Therefore, even though it takes time and effort, we must understand these truths properly. I urge you to read Chapter 3 of this book over and over until you have comprehended its meaning thoroughly.

This is now my conclusion. People such as Jonathan Edwards and Charles Finney were in the center of revival. Yet, they not only experienced the Holy Spirit, but also saw clearly the truth about salvation revealed to them through the illumination of the Holy Spirit. That is why they were able not only to bring people into revival, but also to lead many people to true repentance and salvation.

I remember what someone had said, "Moody evangelized eighty thousand and Charles Finney evangelized fifty thousand. Yet, 80 percent of the people witnessed by Moody went back to the world, while 80 percent of the people witnessed by Finney held on to their faith."[21]

Soon the great revival will break out as prophesied by the prophets in the Bible. Ed Silvoso, one of the main leaders in the great revival of Argentina and the author of *Prayer Evangelism* and *That None Should Perish,* prophesied that "the revival in Korea will begin in Ulsan. In Ulsan, a revival such as that of Argentina will break out...God will use Ulsan along with other cities to bring about a great revival." [22]

Before, I did not understand why God would use Ulsan. Now I know. Great Faith Church, which possesses the truth of salvation, is in Ulsan. Five years before a great revival broke out in the Brownsville church in Pensacola, Florida,

God used Pastor David Yonggi Cho to prophesy that a great revival would break out in Pensacola and would spread to the rest of the country. The Brownsville church, said to be the place of origin that held the greatest revival in this century, believes the same doctrine of salvation as our church does.

Again, God will raise another great revival with Great Faith Church as the center. That is because God does not merely want another movement of the Holy Spirit or the gifts, but He earnestly desires that the illuminating truth of salvation will spread to other cities, nations, and the world. God does not want another huge number of converts through revival, but genuine Christians. That is the reason the Lord has chosen Ulsan as one of the originating centers of revival.

Hallelujah! I give all the glory to God. May His will be done quickly!

– Chapter 5 –

REBIRTH I

Now there was a man of the Pharisees named Nicodemus, a member of the Jewish ruling council. He came to Jesus at night and said, "Rabbi, we know you are a teacher who has come from God. For no one could perform the miraculous signs you are doing if God were not with him."

In reply Jesus declared, "I tell you the truth, no one can see the kingdom of God unless he is born again."

"How can a man be born when he is old?" Nicodemus asked. "Surely he cannot enter a second time into his mother's womb to be born!"

Jesus answered, "I tell you the truth, no one can enter the kingdom of God unless he is born of water and the Spirit. Flesh gives birth to flesh, but the Spirit gives birth to spirit. You should not be surprised at my saying, 'You must be born again.' The wind blows wherever it pleases. You hear its sound, but you cannot tell where it comes from or where it is going. So it is with everyone born of the Spirit."

–JOHN 3:1-8

THE FOUNDER OF The Salvation Army, General William Booth, pointed out six dangerous doctrines he observed in the Christian church of his generation:

1. Religion without the Holy [Spirit]
2. Christianity without Christ

3. Forgiveness without repentance
4. Salvation without regeneration
5. Politics without God
6. Heaven without hell[1]

Amazingly, these elements make up a far too accurate picture of today's church. Particularly dangerous and prevalent in today's church are the false messages of forgiveness without repentance and salvation without being born again. There are too many people in the church who are not born again. That is why one of the most needed sermons is one that leads people to be born again.

What Is Being Born Again?

We must know what being born again is not in order to understand what it is.

First, being born again is not the same as receiving forgiveness. Being born again is different from being made righteous. It does not mean receiving forgiveness of our sins through faith and being freed from judgment and condemnation.

Second, being born again does not mean a change in our status. Some people wrongly believe that being born again equals becoming a child of God. Having a new status as a child of God is a result of our being born again, but it is not being born again itself.

Third, being born again is not the same as being converted. Conversion occurs when we switch our religion. Just because someone switches his religion from Buddhism to Christianity does not mean he automatically becomes born again. The second birth is not merely conversion. It is not partial reformation or change, but a total, holistic change. That is why we call a person who is born again a "new creation" (2 Cor. 5:17), and not just a new mouth, or a new hand.

A pastor whom I respect, Reverend Kenneth Hagin, wrote in his book *The New Birth* regarding being born again.

> Registering and becoming a member of a church, water baptism, participating in a communion, fulfilling all the religious duties, intellectually consenting to the church, the tradition of faith, attending church, praying, reading the Bible, being ethical, polite, and charming, doing good deeds, working your best, and any other acts that people believe will save them—these things are not new birth. Nicodemus, who talked to Jesus about being born again, possessed most of the above-mentioned qualities. But Jesus still told him, "You must be born again."[2]

Therefore, the above things which I just mentioned are not the same as being born again. Then what is being born again?

1. Born again means "the rebirth of our spirit."

> Flesh gives birth to flesh, but the Spirit gives birth to spirit.
>
> —JOHN 3:6

Being born again does not mean that our flesh is born the second time, as Nicodemus mistakenly thought, but it means that our spirit is born anew. Reverend Kenneth Hagin said of human beings, "A person is a spirit, has a soul, and lives in a body," and explained that being born again is "the re-birth of the spirit of man."[3] Truly, to be born again means that our spirit is born again.

2. Born again means "the resurrection of our spirit."

> I tell you the truth, whoever hears my word and believes him who sent me has eternal life and will not be condemned; he has crossed over from death to life. I tell you the truth, a time is coming and has now come when the dead will hear the voice of the Son of God and those who hear will live.
>
> —JOHN 5:24–25

> As for you, you were dead in your transgressions and sins, in which you used to live when you followed the ways of this world and of the ruler of the kingdom of the air, the spirit who is now at work in those who are disobedient. All of us also lived among them at one time, gratifying the cravings of our sinful nature and following its desires and thoughts. Like the rest, we were by nature objects of wrath. But because of his great love for us, God, who is rich in mercy, made us alive with Christ even when we were dead in transgressions—it is by grace you have been saved.
>
> —EPHESIANS 2:1–5

Oswald Smith, in his book *The Gospel We Preach,* wrote that "Being born again means being transferred from death to life."[4] These are true statements. Being born again means that our spirit, which had died, is born again. As you well know, humankind experienced death of their spirit when they fell.

> But from the tree of the knowledge of good and evil you shall not eat, for in the day that you eat from it you shall surely die.
>
> —GENESIS 2:17, NAS

The death that God mentioned was not physical death, but spiritual death. If God had meant physical death, Adam and Eve's bodies would have died right way. The word *surely* makes the meaning clear that they would die in that instant. God also said, "In the day that you eat...," which meant that they would die that day. However, Adam and Eve's bodies did not experience death right away. Therefore, the death that God warned about was not physical death, but spiritual death.

After the fall, all human beings are born with dead spirits, even when their physical bodies are born alive. Jesus said, "Follow me, and let the dead bury their own dead" (Matt. 8:22). Paul said, "So I tell you this, and insist on it in the Lord, that you must no longer live as the Gentiles do, in the futility of their thinking. They are darkened in their understanding and separated from the life of God because of the ignorance that is in them due to the hardening of their hearts" (Eph. 4:17–18). Therefore, the spirit of human beings must live again, and this resurrection of the spirit is what is called born again.

3. Born again means "born of God."

> Yet to all who received him, to those who believed in his name, he gave the right to become children of God—children born not of natural descent, nor of human decision or a husband's will, but born of God.
>
> —John 1:12–13

Besides this passage, the phrase *born of God* appears many times in 1 John. *Born of God* means the same as *born again*. We can only be born again through God.

Like all births, our born-again experience brings us two

things: the first is life, and the second is nature. That is why many people have described being born again as inheriting the life and nature of God. As examples, T. L. Osborne defined being born again as "a glorious experience of receiving the character and life of Jesus Christ, the Son of God, who is born within you."[5] John Stott explained it as "a radical transformation of our character."[6]

The apostle John in 1 John 3:9 said, "No one who is born of God will continue to sin, because God's seed remains in him; he cannot go on sinning because he has been born of God." Here appears the phrase *God's seed*, which is choked with meaning. Those who are born again have God's seed within them. Because of God's seed they cannot go on habitually sinning.

Then what is God's seed? Like all life-forming seeds of plants and animals, God's seed also bears two things: one is life, the second is nature. Therefore, when we talk about born-again people who have God's seed in them, we mean that God's life and God's nature is within them. Having God's life and nature is an inevitable result of having been born of God.

4. Born again means "made holy by the Holy Spirit."

> I am sending them to you to open their eyes and turn them from darkness to light, and from the power of Satan to God, so that they may receive forgiveness of sins and a place among those who are sanctified by faith in me.
>
> —ACTS 26:17–18

> And that is what some of you were. But you were washed, you were sanctified, you were justified in the

name of the Lord Jesus Christ and by the Spirit of our God.

—1 Corinthians 6:11

For the unbelieving husband has been sanctified through his wife, and the unbelieving wife has been sanctified through her believing husband. Otherwise your children would be unclean, but as it is, they are holy.

—1 Corinthians 7:14

But we ought always to thank God for you, brothers loved by the Lord, because from the beginning God chose you to be saved through the sanctifying work of the Spirit and through belief in the truth.

—2 Thessalonians 2:13

Peter, an apostle of Jesus Christ, To God's elect, strangers in the world, scattered throughout Pontus, Galatia, Cappadocia, Asia and Bithynia, who have been chosen according to the foreknowledge of God the Father, through the sanctifying work of the Spirit, for obedience to Jesus Christ and sprinkling by his blood: Grace and peace be yours in abundance.

—1 Peter 1:1–2

Blessed and holy are those who have part in the first resurrection.

—Revelation 20:6

The holiness which appears in these scriptures is referring to being born again itself, or the result of being born again. *Bible Encyclopedia* well summarizes what born-again means: "New-birth is an act of God that makes people holy, while justification is an act of God that makes people righteous."[7] Truly being born again does not mean legal righteousness in which we are declared righteous, but true inward holiness through the work of God.

5. Born again means "the re-creation of man."

> Therefore, if anyone is in Christ, he is a new creation; the old has gone, the new has come!
>
> —2 CORINTHIANS 5:17

> Neither circumcision nor uncircumcision means anything; what counts is a new creation.
>
> —GALATIANS 6:15

> For it is by grace you have been saved, through faith— and this is not from yourselves, it is the gift of God— not by works, so that one can boast. For we are God's workmanship, created in Christ Jesus to do good works, which God prepared in advance for us to do.
>
> —EPHESIANS 2:8–10

The famous theologian James Packer said, "Regeneration, or new birth, is an inner re-creating of fallen human nature by the gracious sovereign action of the Holy Spirit."[8]

Also, the Indian saint Sundar Singh in his book *Reality and Religion* records his meditation on God, humanity, and nature, and describes the born again experience as follows:

> It is a well-known fact that a child takes his personality after his parents. A child is also influenced by the environment. He becomes influenced by his parents

whom he is constantly in contact with, and by other people around him. It is certain that a child who has bad parents and lives in a bad environment will become a bad person. Every circumstance around him prevents him from becoming a good person. So when such a child becomes a good person, this is a big miracle. Whether they are many or few, such miracles can be found. These miracles free a person from sin's bondage, make him a new creation, and prove that a hidden power exists. This is new birth, and the hidden power is [the] Holy Spirit.

In this world there are many criminals who will not be changed at all even after receiving a severe punishment from the government. No amount of parental love and friends' advice will change them. No methods of reformation have any effect upon them. Then one time, they are led to Christ, are immediately transformed, and become a new creation. A self-centered sinner becomes totally changed and lives for other people. A person who has been hurting and killing others becomes persecuted by others and is not even afraid of death. This is called new birth.[9]

The Book of Jeremiah records the following:

> This is the word that came to Jeremiah from the LORD: "Go down to the potter's house, and there I will give you my message." So I went down to the potter's house, and I saw him working at the wheel. But the pot he was shaping from the clay was marred in his hands; so the potter formed it into another pot, shaping it as seemed best to him.
>
> —JEREMIAH 18:1–4

The potter reshapes his marred pot into another one. Human beings are the pots that God has made with His own hands. However, due to their sin, they became broken and ruined. God, in His love, does not throw out his marred creation, but through "the finger of God" (Luke 11:20), which is the Holy Spirit, he reshapes us. This is being born again.

Thus far, I have explained what being born again is.

1. Born again is "the rebirth of the spirit."
2. Born again is "the resurrection of the spirit."
3. Born again is "born of God."
4. Born again is "made holy by the Holy Spirit."
5. Born again is "the re-creation of man."

I hope that now you have the right understanding of being born again, and that you truly are born again.

Why Do We Have to Be Born Again?

There are four reasons we need to be born again.

1. The Fall

Samuel Hopkins writes the reason for our new birth as follows:

> The only ground and reason of regeneration, or of the necessity of the regenerating influences of the Spirit of God, in order to men's converting and embracing the gospel, is the total depravity and corruption of the heart of man in his natural, fallen state.[10]

Our fallenness is the most important and real reason we must be born again. Genesis explains it clearly: on the sixth day of creation, "God created man in His own image" (Gen.

1:27). Since God is immortal, humans were also created as eternal beings that can live forever. They were spiritual beings endowed with intelligence, emotions, will, and freedom. The first humans were holy, just as God is holy. As God is love, humans were also full of love, the only principle that governed their nature, their way of thinking, language, and behavior. Since God is perfectly pure, they were also completely pure from all sinfulness. If human beings did not possess any of these characteristics, God would not have said, "It was very good" (Gen. 1:31) when He first created them.

St. Augustine said that even though all creation was created good, it was easy to become corrupt. Although human beings were created in the image of God, they were not created with immutability. Although they were given the ability to overcome tests, they were vulnerable to corruption. God informed and strictly warned them of this truth. Despite His warning, the first humans ate the forbidden fruit and fell.

As a result, His words, "When you eat of it [the fruit] you will surely die," became a reality, and death followed human beings. (See Genesis 2:17.) Physical death occurs when our body separates from our spirit; spiritual death occurs when our spirit separates from God. The first consequence of sin brought the separation of human spirit and God—the spiritual death. Human beings became miserable and impure, no longer the perfect image bearer of God. Moreover, they fell more and more into the image of Satan, full of pride and arrogance, and bore the image of corrupted animals, full of sexual desires and lusts.

After the fall, all descendants of Adam and Eve were born not bearing the image of God, but with the image of Satan, gripped with pride and arrogance, and with the image of fallen animals, displaying sexual desires and lusts. Therefore, all human beings who are born in sin must be born again. All born of woman also need to be born of the Holy Spirit. This is the first reason we need to be born again.

2. Holiness

John Wesley said, "New birth...is necessary for sanctification....New birth is a door and an entryway into sanctification. When we are born again, our sanctification—our internal and external holiness—is begun. From then on, we grow progressively into fullness of Christ, who is our head."[11]

In *At the Feet of the Master*, Sundar Singh records what Jesus spoke about being born again.

> It is foolish and irrational to think that without being born again, we can obtain salvation through our good deeds and self-effort. Worldly leaders and ethical teachers say "Be good by doing good." But I say, "Be good before doing good." Once a heart has been changed and reborn, good deeds are the natural results.
>
> It is the words of a foolish person who says that a bitter tree will bear sweet fruit when it bears enough fruit. A bitter tree can bear good fruit only when it has been grafted into the sweet tree. The vital ingredients and water from the sweet tree flow over to the bitter tree to completely change its constitution into sweetness.
>
> This is the "new creation" (2 Corinthians 5:17), which I have been speaking of. A sinner, no matter how good he tries to be, only produces evil results. But once he repents and becomes grafted, the old self dies and the new self is born. Through this salvation, the fruit

that is produced from the root of new life becomes good deeds.[12]

The apostle Paul wrote, "For we are God's workmanship, created in Christ Jesus to do good works, which God prepared in advance for us to do" (Eph. 2:10). Being born again means that we are created anew in Christ Jesus through the Holy Spirit so that we may do good works. Therefore, without being born again, no one can live righteous and holy lives.

The Word of God proves that only the born-again can become righteous and holy, for it is written: "For everyone born of God overcomes the world. This is the victory that has overcome the world, even our faith. Who is it that overcomes the world? Only he who believes that Jesus is the Son of God" (1 John 5:4–5). Therefore, we must be born again.

3. Happiness

"The fruit of righteousness will be peace; the effect of righteousness will be quietness and confidence forever" (Isa. 32:17). But "there is no peace...for the wicked" (Isa. 48:22). "There will be trouble and distress for every human being who does evil" (Rom. 2:9) because his wickedness will punish him and his rebellion will rebuke him. (See Jeremiah 2:19.) Thus his sin is "evil and bitter" (Jer. 2:19). That is why Paul reveals that "there will be terrible times in the last days" (2 Tim. 3:1), and points out many sins that brought about terrible bitterness.

Sin causes bitterness and pain, and as the End Times draw near, such phenomenon will only increase. To be happy, a person must be rid of his sins and become holy. This is only possible after he has been born again. John Wesley said:

For the same reason, except he be born again, none can be happy even in this world. For it is not possible, in the nature of things, that a man should be happy who is not holy. Even the poor, ungodly poet could tell us, *Nemo malus felix*: "no wicked man is happy." The reason is plain: All unholy tempers are uneasy tempers: Not only malice, hatred, envy, jealousy, revenge, create a present hell in the breast; but even the softer passions, if not kept within due bounds, give a thousand times more pain than pleasure. Even "hope," when "deferred," (and how often must this be the case!) "maketh the heart sick;" and every desire which is not according to the will of God is liable to "pierce" us "through with many sorrows:" And all those general sources of sin—pride, self-will, and idolatry—are, in the same proportion as they prevail, general sources of misery. Therefore, as long as these reign in any soul, happiness has no place there. But they must reign till the bent of our nature is changed, that is, till we are born again; consequently, the new birth is absolutely necessary in order to happiness in this world, as well as in the world to come.[13]

Therefore, being born again is truly necessary if we want to live a happy life on earth.

4. Heaven

There is a famous saying, "If we are born once, we die twice, but if we are born twice, we die once." If a person is born one time from his mother, he will experience physical death and then his second death when he is thrown into hell. (See Revelation 21:8.) A person who is born twice as a result of being born again may experience physical death, but will never face the second death of hell. He will live forever in heaven. The Bible clearly teaches us that only a person who is born again will go to heaven. This is one ultimate reason we must be born again.

> I tell you the truth, no one can see the kingdom of God unless he is born again.
>
> —JOHN 3:3

Here, the word *see* translated from the Greek *adon*, does not merely mean to look at a matter or phenomenon, which in Greek is *blepho*, but it means "to experience," "to participate," or to "realize." Therefore, this verse signifies participating in the kingdom of God.

> I tell you the truth, no one can enter the kingdom of God unless he is born of water and the Spirit.
>
> —JOHN 3:5

> Praise be to the God and Father of our Lord Jesus Christ! In his great mercy he has given us new birth into a living hope through the resurrection of Jesus Christ from the dead, and into an inheritance that can never perish, spoil or fade—kept in heaven for you.
>
> —1 PETER 1:3–4

As written, only the born-again can go to heaven. To go to heaven, you must be born again. Do you realize that only a life of God can exist in heaven? Natural life has no place there. The life given to a fish allows him to live only in the water. The life of birds makes it possible for birds to exist in the air. In the same way, the life of God is the only appropriate life that can live in heaven. Therefore, if you want to live in heaven, you must be born again of the water and the Spirit and receive the life of God while you are on Earth.

How Can You Be Born Again?

We must be born again. How can we be born again? In John 3:5 Jesus reveals that we must be born again "of the water and the Spirit." This is true, but verses 9–15 are more helpful for those who want to be born again:

> "How can this be?" Nicodemus asked.
>
> "You are Israel's teacher," said Jesus, "and do you not understand these things? I tell you the truth, we speak of what we know, and we testify to what we have seen, but still you people do not accept our testimony. I have spoken to you of earthly things and you do not believe; how then will you believe if I speak of heavenly things? No one has ever gone into heaven except the one who came from heaven—the Son of Man. Just as Moses lifted up the snake in the desert, so the Son of Man must be lifted up, that everyone who believes in him may have eternal life."
>
> —JOHN 3:9–15

Here, Jesus presents faith as the way to being born again. When one is born of the water and the Spirit, the Spirit represents the role that God plays, and faith, which Jesus says is the way to being born again, is the role that human beings play. Therefore, faith is the answer to those who want to be born again.

We are born again by faith. When we believe, the Holy Spirit causes us to be born again. Therefore, we must believe. Then what kind of faith are we talking about that is required for new birth?

Even in his own land and among his own people, he
was not accepted. But to all who believed him and
accepted him, he gave the right to become children
of God. They are reborn! This is not a physical birth
resulting from human passion or plan—this rebirth
comes from God.

—John 1:11–13, nlt

Please read these verses carefully. In verse 11, Jesus is
shown to be King because the land of Israel is "his own land"
and the Israelites are "his own people." Verse 12 shows what
it means to receive Him. Faith is not simply acknowledging
or knowing about Jesus, but receiving Jesus. And one must
receive Jesus not only as a Savior, but as the Master or King.
Verse 13 shows that only those who have received Him are
born again because it is written that they are "born of God."
The phrase "born of God" is another expression for being
born again, and it appears frequently in 1 John. New birth
comes only from God.

Do you know why I am pointing out this truth? It is because
of popular assertions such as the following. Many people like
to compare being born again with a baby being born into
the world. When a baby is being born, is it the baby who is
laboring to come out, or is it the mother? It is the mother
who is laboring to give birth, and the baby does nothing to
come out of the womb. In the same way, there is nothing we
can do to be born again. That is God's job.

There is certain truth to this statement, but not the whole
truth. There is a part that we must play in order to be born
again, and our part is to have faith. Can faith automatically
happen to us when we just sit around? Of course not! We
do not have faith automatically. If we want to have faith,
we must go to church and listen to the Word of God (see

Romans 10:17), renounce sin in our lives, and pray to God with active will. If we do not do these things, we cannot have faith, and therefore, we cannot be born again.

A. W. Tozer pointed out an important truth in his excellent book *The Root of the Righteous:*

> The converted man is both reformed and regenerated. And unless the sinner is willing to reform his way of living he will never know the inward experience of regeneration. This is the vital truth which has gotten lost under the leaves in popular evangelical theology[14]

Samuel Hopkins wrote similarly in his essay "Regeneration and Conversion."

> Means are necessary in order to conversion, or the exercise of faith and holiness, without which men cannot be saved. He, therefore, who lives and dies in the neglect of the use of means must perish. The use of means, then, is of as great importance to men as is their salvation; and the motives and encouragement to a constant attendance on them, in this view of the matter, are equal to the importance and worth of salvation. [15]

Also, T. L. Osborne wrote in his book *The Secret of Being Reborn:* "In being born again, there must be an internal change that turns away from sin and a change of purpose through willful decision."[16] Therefore, we must renounce all sin and have an active will to obey God.

Is active will all that is necessary? No. We must actively utilize the method of grace—the vehicles of the Bible, sermons, confession, prayer, et cetera, that make faith and new birth possible.

Thomas Manton pointed out well that our seeking God through utilizing the various methods of grace is a preparation stage in the process of rebirth. He said that human beings are completely incapable, but they must use external methods.[17] In his writing, he wrote that although humans cannot change themselves, there are four reasons why they should use the methods of grace.

1. It is because we are frail.

Those who want to receive God's grace must seek it earnestly. We never seek God's help earnestly unless we are convinced through our own experience, that we are weak. When a person tries to lift a burden that is too heavy for him, that is when he will seek help.

2. It is to alleviate our guilt.

There is no excuse for people who do not use the methods of grace. It is clear that we are lazy and lack self-will, not lacking power, if we do not try to come out of a sinful state. We like to be bound by sin, and we shut off ourselves. So we "do not consider [ourselves] worthy of eternal life" (Acts 13:46), and sentence punishment upon our own souls.

3. It is because there is no hope without using the vehicle of grace.

If we don't use the methods of grace, we cannot hope on anything. "How can they hear without someone preaching to them?"(Rom. 10:14). If we want to meet God and Christ, it must be this way; grace comes from God. However, reading the Word of God and praying are methods that God has chosen. Just because grace comes from God and not ourselves, we must not give up on these methods.

4. It is because we can experience salvation through the vehicles of grace.

God can meet us through these methods. These are God's conventional practices of free grace. It is beneficial to test this general hope. "Pray to the Lord. Perhaps he will forgive you for having such a thought in your heart" (Acts 8:22). Pray even when it is unsure. This is His conventional method of meeting those who are seeking God.

My beloved friend Thomas Manton teaches us why there are so few born-again people in the church. Few people kneel before the sovereignty of God. So many people come to church on Sunday mornings, but they grumble and daydream during sermons, and they neither repent from their sins nor kneel before God and pray for their salvation.

Of course, rebirth is God's work. He will meet those who come to worship faithfully, listen carefully to the sermons, read and meditate on the Bible, confess all their known sins, work on reforming themselves, and pray. That is why Jesus said, "Enter through the narrow gate (Matt. 7:13)" and "From the days of John the Baptist until now, the kingdom of heaven has been forcefully advancing, and forceful men lay hold of it" (Matt. 11:12). Therefore, we must not be passive, but active. We must not be lazy, but diligent. We must seek God continually, and until we receive the kingdom, we must use the methods of grace to lay hold of it.

Now you do not have to wait under the persimmon tree for the persimmon to fall to the ground because you know the way to be born again. Now do those deeds. Now actively use the methods of grace so that you will launch an attack toward heaven. Be diligent to enter through the narrow gate so that you may lay hold of the kingdom. Let us meet one another in the kingdom in the future.

— Chapter 6 —

REBIRTH II

Dear children, do not let anyone lead you astray. He who does what is right is righteous, just as he is righteous. He who does what is sinful is of the devil, because the devil has been sinning from the beginning. The reason the Son of God appeared was to destroy the devil's work. No one who is born of God will continue to sin, because God's seed remains in him; he cannot go on sinning, because he has been born of God. This is how we know who the children of God are and who the children of the devil are: Anyone who does not do what is right is not a child of God; nor is anyone who does not love his brother.

—1 JOHN 3:7-10

IT IS SAID that George Whitfield preached on John 3:3 more than three hundred times. One day someone came and asked him, "Why do you preach so much that unless you are born again, you cannot see the Kingdom of God?" George Whitfield looked straight at him and replied, "It is because you must be born again."[1]

How about you? Are you sure you are born again? I wish that all of you were born again, because if you are not, you cannot enter God's kingdom.

How Do You Know You Are Born Again?

By anyone's standard, Nicodemus was an excellent, model Jew. He was probably well acknowledged and respected by the people, but he was not born again. In the same way, there are many people today who are religiously faithful and sincere, appear to be a child of God, and yet, are not born again. Therefore, we must not just assume the fact, but must seriously examine whether we are truly born again.

How can we tell whether we are born again? For those who want to find out, I encourage them to read 1 John. In 1 John, we can discover five direct scriptural verses that speak of whether a person is a true born-again believer.

> If you know that he is righteous, you know that everyone who does what is right has been born of him.
>
> —1 JOHN 2:29

> Dear children, do not let anyone lead you astray. He who does what is right is righteous, just as he is righteous. He who does what is sinful is of the devil, because the devil has been sinning from the beginning. The reason the Son of God appeared was to destroy the devil's work. No one who is born of God will continue to sin, because God's seed remains in him; he cannot go on sinning, because he has been born of God. This is how we know who the children of God are and who the children of the devil are: Anyone who does not do what is right is not a child of God; nor is anyone who does not love his brother.
>
> —1 JOHN 3:7–10

Dear friends, let us love one another, for love comes from God. Everyone who loves has been born of God and knows God.

—1 JOHN 4:7

For everyone born of God overcomes the world. This is the victory that has overcome the world, even our faith. Who is that overcomes the world? Only he who believes that Jesus is the Son of God.

—1 JOHN 5:4–5

We know that anyone born of God does not continue to sin; the one who was born of God keeps him safe, and the evil one cannot harm him.

—1 JOHN 5:18

Please don't pass these verses lightly, but use the Word of God to honestly examine your true spiritual state. Then you will clearly be able to find out whether you are born again.

The Bible teaches that as one important proof of one's new birth, there must be an ethical change, or the transformation of one's character and lifestyle. Today however, there is a tendency for many to replace this biblical teaching by relying on logical conclusions based on various scriptures. That is very dangerous. A. W. Tozer pointed out this evil tendency in his book *Born After Midnight:*

> In an examining room, the following is the conversation between the examiner and the examinee.
>
> "Do you wish for the Lord to accept you as a child of God?"
>
> "Yes."
>
> "All right, then you must read this."

"I will never drive away those who come to Me."

"Do you believe this?"

"Yes."

"Well, if Jesus does not drive you away, what will He do?"

"I think Jesus will accept me."

"That's right. Now, He has accepted you. You are His child. Won't you confess this fact to other people?"

The perplexed examinee who has been seeking is now forced to smile and testify to other people that he has been reformed by Christ. Although he had been seeking the truth sincerely, he is led astray. He became the victim of spiritual logic. His conviction lies upon a shaky syllogism. There is no testimony, no immediate knowledge, no encounter with God, and no internal transformation.[2]

In reality, many people find their assurance of salvation through such syllogism, but this is wrong.

John Stott said that if the believer should "continue in sin, it would indicate that he has never been born again,"[3] Therefore, we must objectively discern whether we are born-again through our fruits. In the Bible, we can discover an interesting passage that symbolizes this truth.

The Gileadites captured the fords of the Jordan leading to Ephraim, and whenever a survivor of Ephraim said, "Let me cross over," the men of Gilead asked him, "Are you an Ephraimite?" If he replied, "No," they said, "All right, say 'Shibboleth.'" If he said, "Sibboleth," because he could not pronounce the word correctly, they seized him and killed him at the fords of the Jordan. Forty-two thousand Ephraimites were killed at that time.

—Judges 12:5–6

The Hebrew word *shibboleth* means "an ear of grain." As "an ear of grain" distinguishes between grain and chaff, the *shibboleth* was used to separate true Canaanites from the Gileadites who faced their death at the fords of Jordan by the judge.

The allies of Jephthah who pronounced *shibboleth* correctly represent grain, the faithful crop, and symbolically represent the fruitful friends of Christ. The enemies of Jephthah who pronounced *sibboleth* with a harsher accent represent chaff, which is empty inside. They are like the hypocrites who have the appearance of religion but are fruitless in real life. In the same way, we can see the true and the false people by looking at their fruit. We must discern whether a person is born again only by his fruit.

In his book, *The Dynamics of Spiritual Growth*, John Wimber wrote:

A few years ago, a new believer shared his testimony of many changes in his life after his repentance. He used to visit the same bar every day after work not so much to drink, but to socialize. The first Monday after he had turned away from his old life, he went to the bar as usual and his friends asked him how he was. After ordering one beer, he shared how he accepted Jesus into his life. There was cold silence, and unable to endure it any longer, he walked out of the bar. A few days later, he could not stand the smell of smoke, the beer did not taste the same as before, and the obscene language felt awkward to him. During the middle of the week, he realized that he did not fit into his social circle anymore, and wanted to know how his evil desires were so quickly restrained. "That is easy," I told him. "You have been born again. You are a new creation with a new heart and new hope. Now your old habits will not be enjoyable to you."[4]

What an inspirational illustration! But do not assume that born-again experiences will always occur radically and suddenly. Some people experience their new birth in a quiet and unobtrusive way. These people may not even realize that they were born again. Frequently, these people were brought up in a Christian background. However, even in these cases, one thing must be certain: they have been freed from sin, they are a new creation, and are living in obedience to God presently. If this is true, there is no doubt of their new birth. However, if a person is still living in sin, he is not born again.

I must repeat what I have said once more. A born-again person must have changes in his heart and will. However, being born again is different from being sanctified. Therefore, do not think that the proof of new birth, the fruits in life, will be perfect.

First John 3:9 states, "No one who is born of God will continue to sin, because God's seed remains in him; he cannot go on sinning, because he has been born of God." John said that a person who is born again does not sin. But this does not mean that a born-again person will never sin or cannot sin. In the same letter, John wrote:

> If we confess our sins, he is faithful and just and will forgive us our sins and purify us from all unrighteousness. If we claim we have not sinned, we make him out to be a liar and his word has no place in our lives. My dear children, I write this to you so that you will not sin. But if anybody does sin, we have one who speaks

to the Father in our defense—Jesus Christ, the Righteous One.

—1 JOHN 1:9–2:1

We have heard two truths so far: "A person who is born
again cannot sin" and "A person who is born again can sin,
and in that case must confess his sin." What is the exact standard? This is the standard:

For sin shall not be your master, because you are not
under law, but under grace.

—ROMANS 6:14

At times, even born-again Christians commit sin. However,
sin cannot dominate them. They will regret what they have
done, confess their sins, and then they will obey God again.
If you are that kind of a person, you are definitely born again.
However, if you only confess your sin, but go on to live in the
sin, you are not born again.

There is something we must understand in order to accurately examine ourselves. That is, the changes in our life after
being born again occur not after a long time has passed, but
right after our new birth. Charles Spurgeon said, "Newness
of life—what does it mean? It means this. When we are born
again, and believe in the Lord Jesus Christ—which things
take place at the same time—we receive a life which we never
before possessed. We begin to feel, to think, and to act as we
never did before." [5] Therefore, it does not take a long time after
new birth to live a transformed life, as many people assume.
Rather, a person can live a transformed life the moment he
is born again. I believe that we must not compromise this
truth, but hold firmly to it. If we forget this truth, people
who are not born again will be able to say, "I am born again,

but it's just that my faith is immature." As a result, what John said in his epistle regarding the touchstones of new birth will become useless, and the spirit of deception will operate in their lives. Therefore, we must never compromise this truth, but firmly hold on to it.

Rebirth and Justification— Which Comes First?

I say this often, but after the Reformation, faith was emphasized while repentance was de-emphasized; justification was highlighted while rebirth was downplayed. Concerning the safety of our souls, this is very dangerous. I will explain why this is dangerous.

When humanity fell as the result of original sin, there were two problems faced by humans: the first was guilt, and the second was internal decay. A human being who commits sin must pay the penalty for sin. Also, because of internal decay caused by the original sin, it is necessary for people to be free from the bondage of sin. The original sin caused these two problems, guilt and internal decay. Salvation resolved these two problems. Therefore, there are two elements that are needed for human beings to receive salvation. That is, salvation consists of two elements—rebirth and justification.

Human beings need justification because of guilt. They also need rebirth because of internal decay. In his book, *The New Birth*, Pastor Kenneth Hagin wrote: "For human beings to be saved, somebody must pay the penalty of their sin and give a new nature."[6]

Stephen Charnock wrote:

> Seek it [rebirth], for it is as necessary as justification. You should therefore seek it with as high an esteem

of it as you have of pardon, none but would desire pardon of sin. You must be as desirous of the regeneration of your nature; they are equally necessary. Those who will not have an inherent righteousness can never expect an imputed righeousness from Christ; he never came to that end. Two things happened to us by the fall: another state and another nature; the regaining of the former must be equally sought with the latter...[7]

Also, John Ryle wrote:

It is a subject of the utmost importance to our souls. If the Bible be true, it is certain that unless we are "sanctified," we shall not be saved. There are three things, which, according to the Bible are absolutely necessary to the salvation of every man and woman in Christendom. These three are: justification, regeneration, and sanctification. All three meet in every child of God—he is both born again, and justified, and sanctified. He that lacks any one of these three things is not a true Christian in the sight of God, and dying in that condition will not be found in heaven and glorified in the last day.[8]

And, Sundar Singh, the Indian saint, wrote about salvation in this way: "The forgiveness of sins does not mean full salvation, for that can only come with perfect freedom from sin."[9]

Sundar Singh received this idea from the Lord while he was directly fellowshipping with Him. While he was praying in the woods, he met the Lord, who appeared to him. The conversation he had with the Lord is written in his book *At the Feet of the Master*.

As an example, there was a hallucinating, pneumonic patient, and next to his bed lay some fruit and a knife. One day, his friend visited him, and without realizing it, the patient cut his friend's throat with the knife and killed him. As a result, he was sentenced to be executed at five o'clock that afternoon. His friends and relatives went to the king, begging for his pardon because the patient could not be responsible for his own actions. When they had returned with the pardon, he was already dead with pneumonia. His crime was due to his illness. Even though he had received forgiveness for his sin, his illness, which caused him to sin, could not be cured. The king's forgiveness could not help the man because he could only be saved when he was cured of his illness. Jesus was incarnated in order to save those who believe and repent from the disease of sin, to rescue them from the penalty of death, and to eliminate the result and cause of sin. That is how a person avoids destruction, escapes from death, and becomes an heir of eternal life.[10]

I will summarize what I have been saying like this. Salvation is like a coin, in that it has two sides: one side is justification, and the other side is rebirth. If we look at just one side, it looks as though this is all there is to salvation. In reality, we cannot have salvation if we have just one side. We must have both sides of salvation. Let us go a little further with this metaphor. If salvation is like two sides of a coin (justification and rebirth), which is the head and which is the tail?

Long ago I bought a book in a Christian bookstore, titled *The New Birth* by Stephen Charnock. He wrote the longest book on rebirth in the entire history of the Christian faith. He wrote five books just on the topic of rebirth.

Honestly, I think it is unnecessary to write that long on the topic of rebirth. At the time, I no longer had the desire to read books on salvation, including the topic of rebirth! Only seven years ago, I would have bought any and all books related to salvation. Now the situation was different, because I had sufficiently studied about salvation and thought I possessed great knowledge on that topic.

Despite this fact, I bought that book. As I was reading the table of contents, the subtitle "No Justification Without Rebirth" came to my eyes.

Generally, in my sermons there are many special contents that other preachers do not talk about, and I do not talk about anything odd because the contents are strictly biblical. Therefore, there is no problem for those people whose hearts are open and who listen with an unprejudiced attitude. But it is a sad fact that not everyone's heart is open. That is why even though I could express myself with my own words, I usually borrow words from famous seminary scholars and Christian leaders. I do this so that people will easily accept the truths without being suspicious and rejecting them. In many cases, I read books not to learn something new, but to collect enough materials for testifying to the truths effectively. That is the reason I bought Stephen Charnock's book.

As I had predicted, I found that there was unnecessary and lengthy information while I was reading the book. This is the weakness of the sermons by Puritan preachers. I am not saying that this book has no value, because I believe that it is a valuable book simply because of its excellent point on "no justification without rebirth."

I had already known this truth long ago, but it is a hard sermon to preach because many seminarians and pastors are ignorant of this truth. Those who listen are also seriously prejudiced against this truth. Gladly though, Stephen Charnock wrote that without rebirth we can never receive justification from God. We do not receive justification from God because of our own righteousness. But we do not completely exclude our righteousness when we receive God's justification. We cannot be justified by God because of our own righteousness because our righteousness is imperfect and cannot satisfy the requirement of God's law.

However, if there is no righteousness in us, we cannot receive God's righteousness either. That is because to take most wicked and corrupt people and consider them righteous is contradicting God's wisdom and holiness.[11]

When we consider God's reputation, how can we expect that He will forgive someone who stubbornly and willfully sins? Even from an ethical perspective, it is only appropriate to forgive the sinner who has repented and turned away from evil ways. Therefore, if we are not born again, we can never expect ourselves to be justified. In addition, we will not find any proof within us that we have been justified. If we say someone is justified before he is born again, we are saying he was made righteous before he was born.

Perhaps there may be some preachers who will be opposed to this sermon. Those who possess some knowledge of the Bible may feel confused because of Romans 4:1–8:

> What then shall we say that Abraham, our forefather, discovered in this matter? If, in fact, Abraham was justified by works, he had something to boast about— but not before God. What does the Scripture say? Abraham believed God, and it was credited to him as righteousness.
>
> Now when a man works, his wages are not credited to him as a gift, but as an obligation. However, to the man who does not work but trusts God who justifies the wicked, his faith is credited as righteousness. David

says the same thing when he speaks of the blessedness of the man to whom God credits righteousness apart from works:

Blessed are they whose transgressions are forgiven, whose sins are covered. Blessed is the man whose sin the Lord will never count against him.

Most preachers who preach on this passage assert that even though we do not live righteously, God will consider us righteous based on our faith in the blood of Christ when we believe in Jesus Christ. They will say this is justification, thinking that this truth has been resurrected through the Reformation. However, orthodox belief is having the opinion that conforms to biblical teaching, not to the teachings of reformers.

Many people read this passage through the lens of prejudice. That is why in their eyes, they see this passage and think it is talking about what they already believe. However, in this passage, sins and transgressions are the unrighteous acts before faith, not the disobedience of believers. In other words, the sins and transgressions that Paul mentions are past sins, not the present, stubborn sins in which believers are bound. Therefore, this passage does not mean that God will automatically grant righteousness based on the blood of Jesus to those who are presently in bondage of sin. To prove this point, let us read David's psalm, which Paul used to prove his point:

Blessed is he whose transgressions are forgiven, whose sins are covered. Blessed is the man whose sin the LORD does not count against him and in whose spirit is no deceit. When I kept silent, my bones wasted away through my groaning all day long. For day and night your hand was heavy upon me; my strength was sapped as in the heat of summer. Then I acknowledged my sin to you and did not cover up my iniquity. I said, "I will confess my transgressions to the LORD"—and you forgave the guilt of my sin.

—PSALM 32:1–5

Is this the picture of a person who is living in sin and yet holding on to God's mercy and grace? Definitely not! Even though David had committed the terrible sins of adultery and murder, he repented and turned from his sins. Paul used this passage to prove his point in Romans 4. Therefore, it is wrong to assume that Paul is asserting that God grants righteousness to someone based on the blood of Christ when he is living in sin.

This kind of assertion cannot be harmonious even with the rest of the Bible. As an example, I ask, how do we receive justification? We receive justification by faith. Then what comes before faith? Repentance. Then what is repentance? It is cutting off one's sins. Therefore, such an assertion cannot be justified. We can tell this by just thinking about what faith is. What is faith? Is it simply consenting to biblical doctrines? No. That is a belief held by demons. (See James 2:14, 19.) Faith is accepting Jesus as King and Savior and relying wholly on Jesus to obey His Word. Therefore, such an assertion does not honestly follow the truth of the Bible, but sees the opinion of reformers as the absolute, biblical truth.

Now, I want to suggest that you meditate on the following verses. Then you will truly understand that justification without rebirth—justification without internal change—is unbiblical.

And that is what some of you were. But you were washed, you were sanctified, you were justified in the name of the Lord Jesus Christ and by the Spirit of our God.

—1 Corinthians 6:11

But we ought always to thank God for you, brothers loved by the Lord, because from the beginning God chose you to be saved through the sanctifying work of the Spirit and through belief in the truth.

—2 Thessalonians 2:13

This is the covenant I will make with the house of Israel after that time, declares the Lord. I will put my laws in their minds and write them on their hearts. I will be their God, and they will be my people. For I will forgive their wickedness and will remember their sins no more.

—Hebrews 8:10, 12

Peter, an apostle of Jesus Christ, To God's elect, strangers in the world, scattered throughout Pontus, Galatia, Cappadocia, Asia and Bithynia, who have been chosen according to the foreknowledge of God the Father, through the sanctifying work of the Spirit, for obedience to Jesus Christ and sprinkling by his blood: Grace and peace be yours in abundance.

—1 Peter 1:1–2

Above all, please pay special attention to Titus 3:5–7:

He saved us, not because of righteous things we had done, but because of his mercy. He saved us through the washing of rebirth and renewal by the Holy Spirit, whom he poured out on us generously through Jesus Christ our Savior, so that having been justified by his grace, we might become heirs having the hope of eternal life.

Have you meditated on these verses? Then see if you can answer the following question. Out of rebirth and justification, which comes first? Clearly, rebirth occurs first. Of course, rebirth and justification do not occur at two different times; they happen almost at the same time. Therefore, there is no such thing as receiving justification but not rebirth, or vice versa. Logically speaking, rebirth always occurs before justification. Justification is never the first step.

Why is that fact so important? Why did I take time to explain this fact? It is because we must understand this fact clearly to be able to proclaim the truth of salvation. To put it severely, many preachers possess the tongue of a snake. Snakes have tongues that split at the end. Pastors are like snakes with a split tongue when they preach on Romans 4, saying, "It is necessary to have faith alone. We are not saved by works," and then preach on James 2 and say, "Faith alone is not enough. We must show our deeds." Between these two sermons, the saints become lost and perplexed. The more serious fact is that preachers lack coherent understanding of the gospel and end up saying two different things. The saints do not receive their sermons at face value when they hear sermons on living faith with deeds. They merely believe that the preacher is emphasizing good deeds. The reason preachers make such a mistake is that they do not have a correct understanding of Romans 4:1–8. In other words, they miss the clear biblical truth of "no justification without rebirth" due to their doctrinal prejudice. Therefore, we must understand this truth correctly.

Why Can't We Go to Heaven Without Being Born Again?

Only those who are born again can go to heaven. Those who are not born again can never enter heaven. (See John 3:5.) This is a basic truth known to believers of Jesus Christ. However, have you thought about why those who are not born again cannot go to heaven?

Most people think this way: God permits born-again believers to go to heaven, but God forbids those who are not born again from entering heaven by putting angels at the gate. This is a fleshly, or earthly, way of thinking. This is not a heavenly way of thinking.

Sundar Singh wrote his masterpiece, *At the Feet of the Master.* In the book, he says that Jesus told him the following:

> When land animals and birds live with humans for a long time, and then return to their species, they are not welcomed, but rather, attacked and killed. The reason is that their living habits and behaviors have changed as a result of living with and befriending humans for a long time. Since even animals do not welcome into their society those that have been domesticated by humans, how can heavenly angels and saints welcome those who have been fellowshipping with wicked people? It is not that angels and saints do not love sinners, but only that sinners cannot live with harmony in such a holy environment called heaven. Even on earth, sinners hate to be among the saints, so how can they be expected to be their eternal friends? For them, heaven will seem like hell and they will feel terrible living in it.
>
> Do not think that God or angels throw sinners out of heaven. God, who is love, never throws anyone into hell.

He will never do that eternally. It is the foolish living of sinners that puts them in hell. Before a person ends his life, he will approach toward heaven or hell. Heaven or hell has already been built in his heart. Therefore, those who want to avoid eternal pain must sincerely repent from all sins and give their heart to me. Then he will become an eternal citizen of heaven through my abiding presence and the fellowship of the Holy Spirit.[12]

Another excellent book by Sundar Singh, *Meditations on Various Aspects of the Spiritual Life*, records the testimony of his visit to heaven. In this book, there is an important testimony with the subtitle "A Wicked Man Permitted to Enter Heaven."

Once in my presence a man of evil life entered at death into the world of spirits. When the angel and saints wished to help him he at once began to curse and revile them, and say, "God is altogether unjust. He has prepared heaven for such flattering slaves as you are, and casts the rest of mankind into hell. Yet you call Him Love!" The angels replied, "God certainly is Love. He created men that they might live forever in happy fellowship with Him, but men, by their own obstinacy, and by abuse of their free will have turned their faces away from Him, and have made hell for themselves. God neither casts any one into hell, nor will He ever do so, but man himself, by being entangled in sin, creates hell for himself. God never created any hell."

Just then, the exceedingly sweet voice of one of the high angels was heard from above saying, "God gives permission that this man may be brought into heaven." Eagerly the man stepped forward accompanied by two angels, but when they reached the door of heaven, and saw the holy and light-enveloped place and the glorious and blessed inhabitants that dwell there, he began to feel uneasy. The angels said to him, "See how beautiful a world is this! Go a little farther, and look at the dear Lord sitting on His throne." From the door he looked, and then as the light of the Sun of Righteousness revealed to him the impurity of his sin-defiled life, he started back in an agony of self-loathing, and fled, with such precipitancy, that he did not even stop in the intermediate state of the world of spirits, but like a stone he passed through it, and cast himself headlong into the bottomless pit.

Then the sweet and ravishing voice of the Lord was heard saying, "Look, My dear children, none is forbidden to come here, and no one forbade this man, nor has any one asked him to leave. It was his own impure life that forced him to flee from this holy place, for, 'Except a man be born again he cannot see the kingdom of God'" (John 3:3).[13]

In church history, Sundar Singh, the Indian saint recognized as a man of faith, had the most mystical experiences, visiting heaven many times in the spirit. According to oral tradition, he was in heaven after about twenty minutes of prayer. In his book Sundar Singh contains the following story:

One day, while he was in heaven in the spirit, he asked the angels and saints, "Do the dead receive judgment as they wait in a line?" They replied, "No, the souls who left their bodies instantly understand everything that happened to them in life. They receive judgment because they remember everything. When the light of heaven shines upon the wicked, they realize that they cannot live with saints and angels. They see that everything in heaven is inappropriate for them and request to leave this place. God does not throw them out of heaven. Heaven does not have walls and gates where one receives a pass to heaven. The pass to heaven is the life that they lived on earth."

They also told him, "People who are born of God find comfort in heaven, but not so the ones who were not born of God. This is the true judgment, and it occurs every day. Judgment is not the action and result which God brings upon us, but it is internally within us. The last judgment is the final result, and it is the time when the servants of God will be lifted up before all creation."[14]

People who do not understand call Sundar Singh a mystic. However, just as Paul, who had many mystical experiences, is not a mystic, Sundar Singh is not a mystic either. Sundar Singh loved the Lord, was holy, and prayed a lot. That is why he received much revelation as Paul and John did. The revelations that Sundar Singh received coincide with the views of God's people. Before him, many giants of faith spoke of the same thing.

For example, Bishop John Ryle said, "...if we die spiritual we shall rise spiritual, if we die carnal we shall rise carnal, and if we are to be made fit for heaven, our natural hearts must be changed now on earth." [15]

Charles Finney wrote in his book *True and False Repentance*:

All was done for you that God could wisely do; all that Christ could do; all that the spirit of God could consistently do: but all was vain: all came to naught and availed nothing because you would not forego your sins--would not renounce them, even for everlasting life. And now will heaven let you in? No. Nothing that worketh abomination can by any means go in there.

Besides, it would not be for your own comfort to be there. You were never quite comfortable in spiritual society on earth; in the prayer meeting you were unhappy. As one individual said here: "O, what a place this is! I cannot go across the street without being spoken to about my soul. How can I live here?"

Let me tell you—it will be just as bad—nay much worse for you in heaven. That can be no place for you, sinner, since you hate worst of all things on earth, those places and scenes which are most like heaven.[16]

Stephen Charnock wrote sufficiently on the necessity of rebirth for the state of glory (heaven):

A wicked man would meet with hell in the midst of heaven as long as he carries his own rack within him, boiling and raging lusts in his heart, which can receive no contentment without objects suitable to them, let the place be what it will. Heaven, indeed, is not only a place, but a nature; and it is a contradiction to think that any can be happy with a nature contrary to the very essence of happiness.[17]

One day, one of the Pharisees asked Jesus, "When will the kingdom of God come?" The Lord replied, "The kingdom of God does not come with your careful observation, nor will people say, 'Here it is,' or 'There it is,' because the kingdom of God is within you." (See Luke 17:20–21.) Jesus is not denying that the kingdom of God does not actually exist. Rather, He is only describing the beginning and characteristics of the kingdom of God.

As the Lord pointed out, the kingdom of God truly is within a person. Hell is also within a person. In Acts 16, Paul and Silas were beaten and thrown into a dirty and smelly prison by the magistrates even after they had preached the gospel and performed the good deed of casting out a demon. Captured in a foul cell full of vile language and the curses of the prisoners, bodies sore and bleeding, this place was like hell. However, rather than groaning, complaining and feeling miserable, Paul praised God, because although his body was in a jail, heaven was in his heart. Even though our bodies may be sick and our environment is desolate, we are happy when heaven is in our heart.

The same is true in the opposite case. There are people who are miserable and even commit suicide while living in a good, wealthy environment. From these examples, we know that heaven and hell are internal states. Therefore, just going to heaven does not make a person happy. Even if the person goes to heaven, he will never be happy when his heart is in hell. This is because, as Paul said, "The kingdom of God is not a matter of eating and drinking, but of righteousness, peace and joy in the Holy Spirit" (Rom. 14:17). In other words, if righteousness is not formed in us through the Holy Spirit, there are no peace and joy. Just as God proclaimed in Isaiah that "there is no peace…for the wicked" (Isa. 48:22), the peace and joy of heaven are built upon the foundation of righteousness. Therefore, those who have not been "created…anew…[to] do good things" (Eph. 2:10, NLT) can never be happy even if they go to heaven.

Those who are not born again cannot be happy even if they

go to heaven. This truth has special value because it eliminates any justifiable excuses on the part of sinners. In general, when biblical repentance, faith, and salvation are carefully explained, some sinners stumble because they cannot get rid of their distorted perceptions and prejudices, while others become shocked and try hard to become genuine Christians. However, not all of them will become Christians. Some of them truly receive salvation and become children of God; others merely know the truth and struggle inside, but do not become born again because of their disobedience to God and retain a rebellious lifestyle. In the latter case, they slowly turn against God as time passes.

Why did God make the way of salvation so narrow? Why does God so strictly require repentance, faith, and rebirth as a requirement for salvation? If only He had lowered the standards of salvation! Why does He make people suffer as a result of such a high standard?

If you allow such thoughts to enter your mind, the following deception will arise: "Really? Can salvation really be that hard to obtain? Perhaps our pastor does not know anything and has appointed a high standard so that he would give us a hard time. Other pastors do not preach this way. Yeah, I'm sure I must be right in thinking this way. I am right."

Please be careful. For such people, the devil has gained access to their mind and is deceiving them, because they did not respond right away to the light of truth that shone on them. Paul warns in 2 Thessalonians 2:11–12:

> For this reason God sends them a powerful delusion so that they will believe the lie and so that all will be condemned who have not believed the truth but have delighted in wickedness.

This word of God is true. In reality, the deception will operate in those who love unrighteousness. Therefore, be careful that this warning does not apply to you.

The truth that I just shared is extremely effective in rooting out doubts and rebellion. Charles Finney, in his excellent book *Experiencing Revival,* wrote about this.

> God has greater mercy and love than all human beings and desires to comfort the sinners. But God will never compromise when it comes to the method of solution for sinners. God never changes. God knows that there is no method that is more effective than this for sinners, because there is nothing that can make sinners happy if they do not repent from their sins. Therefore, God never relents in this matter.[18]

He also asserted the following in his book *God's Love for a Sinning World:*

> The conditions for the salvation of souls are not opinionated. All the conditions are absolutely necessary. Each condition is needed and that is why each of them was revealed to us. God requires these conditions to be met because without them, He cannot save souls. Our heart and life must be purified and holy. The reason is not because God arbitrarily decided upon these conditions by Himself, but if these conditions are not met, we cannot be happy. Without them, we cannot enjoy heaven, nor enter it. Therefore, we are purified by our faith in Christ, and are completely saved by this faith. No other deeds can make us pure or save us.[19]

As Finney mentioned, the conditions or standards for

salvation were not determined arbitrarily. They were chosen because they were needed as the minimum requirement for salvation. Anyone who believes differently regarding the conditions of salvation is deceived by Satan.

Think about it. God had to give up His Son in order to save us. Jesus had to pour out His blood and water as He hung on the cross to save us. God wanted to save us that badly. Does it make sense that God maliciously raised the standard for salvation, even though He had the choice to lower it, so that people may not be saved? That can never be. Therefore, we must know that God requires these conditions of salvation because they are absolutely essential.

The conditions of salvation were appointed to meet the needs of salvation, and were not by God's sovereignty. How can we rebel against God saying that He is not fair? We can never do that. That is an irrational behavior. Therefore, we must make every effort to get rid of our rebelliousness and willingly fulfill the conditions of salvation.

The Spirit of Deception Is Widespread in Today's Churches

The Bible mentions the "spirit of falsehood" (1 John 4:6) or the "deceiving spirits" (1 Tim. 4:1).

What is the identity of these spirits? Revelation 20:10 mentions "the devil, who deceived them." Therefore, the devil and his demons are the deceiving spirits. The first deception occurred when the devil deceived Eve.

> But I am afraid that just as Eve was deceived by the serpent's cunning, your minds may somehow be led astray from your sincere and pure devotion to Christ.
> —2 CORINTHIANS 11:3

However, the devil's deception did not stop then. The devil continues to deceive people even to this day. In Genesis, the devil used a serpent. Today, he deceives using "money" (1 Tim. 6:10), various "evil desire[s]" (James 1:14), "miraculous signs" (Rev. 19:20), and mostly cult beliefs.

> Jesus answered: "Watch out that no one deceives you. For many will come in my name, claiming, 'I am the Christ,' and will deceive many. You will hear of wars and rumors of wars, but see to it that you are not alarmed. Such things must happen, but the end is still to come. At that time many will turn away from the faith and will betray and hate each other, and many false prophets will appear and deceive many people."
>
> —MATTHEW 24:4–6, 10–11

> The Spirit clearly says that in later times, some will abandon the faith and follow deceiving spirits and things taught by demons. Such teachings come through hypocritical liars, whose consciences have been seared as with a hot iron.
>
> —1 TIMOTHY 4:1–2

> Many deceivers, who do not acknowledge Jesus Christ as coming in the flesh, have gone out into the world. Any such person is the deceiver and the antichrist. Watch out that you do not lose what you have worked for, but that you may be rewarded fully. Anyone who runs ahead and does not continue in the teaching of Christ does not have God; whoever continues in the teaching has both the Father and the Son. If anyone comes to you and does not bring this teaching, do not

take him into your house or welcome him. Anyone
who welcomes him shares in his wicked work.

—2 JOHN 7–11

The cult leaders are soul hunters. They are deceivers. Therefore, we must not invite cult evangelists into our homes, or
even greet them. In other words, we must not show actions
that encourage them in any way.

But Satan does not only use cult members to deceive souls.
As instruments of deception, he even uses many pastors who
are passionate soul lovers, have good intentions, and yet have
insufficient understanding of the gospel. Satan's deception is
spread not only in cult meeting places, but also even in the
house of God, the church, where various worship services
are being offered. Some people might exclaim, "No way!" at
my statement. They might look at me with suspicious eyes.
However, my assertion coincides with the writers of the
Bible, and it is a very biblical one. As proof, Paul warned the
church, not the cult members, of deceptions that can occur
among believers.

> Do you not know that the wicked will not inherit the
> kingdom of God? Do not be deceived: Neither the
> sexually immoral nor idolaters nor adulterers nor male
> prostitutes nor homosexual offenders nor thieves nor
> the greedy nor drunkards nor slanderers nor swindlers
> will inherit the kingdom of God.
>
> —1 CORINTHIANS 6:9–10

> Do not be deceived: God cannot be mocked. A man
> reaps what he sows. The one who sows to please his
> sinful nature, from that nature will reap destruction;

the one who sows to please the Spirit, from the Spirit will reap eternal life.

—GALATIANS 6:7–8

But among you there must not be even a hint of sexual immorality, or of any kind of impurity, or of greed, because these are improper for God's holy people. Nor should there be obscenity, foolish talk or coarse joking, which are out of place, but rather thanksgiving. For of this you can be sure: No immoral, impure or greedy person—such a man is an idolater—has any inheritance in the kingdom of Christ and of God. Let no one deceive you with empty words, for because of such things God's wrath comes on those who are disobedient.

—EPHESIANS 5:3–6

As the above verses illustrate, Paul wrote to churches not to be deceived. Paul had to exhort them because there were deceptions and lies that actually existed in the church. Such deceptions occur more frequently today.

Just as Paul did, the apostle John saw the danger of deception in the church. Inspired by the Holy Spirit, he wrote 1 John, which tells how one can come out of deception by examining oneself. Here is one prime example from the following passage:

Dear children, do not let anyone lead you astray. He who does what is right is righteous, just as he is righteous. He who does what is sinful is of the devil, because the devil has been sinning from the beginning. The reason the Son of God appeared was to destroy the devil's work. No one who is born of God will continue to sin, because God's seed remains in him; he cannot go on sinning because he has been born of God. This is how we know who the children of God are and who the children of the devil are: Anyone who does not do what is right is not a child of God; nor is anyone who does not love his brother.

—1 John 3:7–10

John points out something very important in this passage, that a serious deception related to rebirth was at work in the church of his day. Many people were under the delusion that they were born again even though they were living in sin. However, I see the same thing in today's church. The serious deception regarding rebirth is working powerfully in our modern church. Do you not see the spirits of deception that are active in the church? Of course, I do not see the spirits themselves with my eyes, but I see their activities very clearly. The spirits of deception created the lie that is very familiar to our ears: *Salvation is by faith; rewards are by deeds. Salvation is by faith only. Therefore, we can receive at least the shameful salvation as long as we believe even though we are living in sin.*

Such statements have become like one of the traditional truths in the church. This is not the truth. Despite that fact, this lie acts squarely like a truth in the church. If you are one of those people who mistakenly took these statements as truth, I would like you to compare them with the warnings of the apostles that I mentioned previously. Then, you will immediately see that this statement cannot be in harmony with the assertions of Paul and John. Moreover, these statements do not agree with the Lord's words: "Not everyone who says to me, 'Lord, Lord,' will enter the kingdom of heaven, but only he who does the will of my Father who is in heaven" (Matt. 7:21); and James's words: "What good is it, my brothers, if a man claims to have faith but has no deeds? Can such faith save him?" (James 2:14). These statements are a false teaching created by the spirits of deception that are at work in the church. This is the clearest proof that spirits of deception are at work in the church.

There are many cult activities in our nation of Korea. One cult calls itself a "salvation sect." Previously, the ringleader of this sect was Shin Chan Kwon, but now Ok Su Park is a bigger problem; he leads meetings with the title, "Forgiveness of sin, the secret of rebirth." Even though this cult says many things regarding rebirth, cult members have no concept of rebirth in their teachings. Rather, extreme and heretical ideas comprise their main teachings. They say that upon believing in Jesus, all past, present, and future sins are forgiven; therefore, there is no need for confession or repentance; they will go to heaven no matter how they live. This is a clear Antinomianism heretical teaching.

They would ask, "Are you born again? When were you born again? Do you know the year, month, and day of your rebirth?" If a person cannot immediately answer, they would tell him that he was not saved. This is how they deceive people. However, it is not important or necessary to know when we have been saved. Stephen Charnock wrote:

> Here is comfort in the ignorance of the time of the new birth. "Except a man be born again," not except he know the time of his being born again; the want of the knowledge of the time has troubled some, but it is no matter for the time, if we find the essential properties; our happiness is secured by the essence, not by the circumstance.[20]

Therefore, what is important in relation to rebirth is not

the time, but the state. Even if we do not know the time of our rebirth, we are born again if our present state is that of the born again. On the other hand, even if a person knows the time of rebirth, he is not born again if his present state does not coincide with the biblical state of the born again. Consequently, we must discern the existence of rebirth through the fruit that Jesus mentioned.

Now I will state the conclusion. I want to say a few words of exhortation. First, I would like to say a word of exhortation to all readers, and then to those who are not born again, and lastly to those who are born again.

1. I want to exhort all readers to give thanks to God for being in this light.

In his pamphlet "New Birth," Pastor Kenneth Hagin grieved that "so many people had wrong teachings regarding the experience of rebirth and will never be saved when they die." [21]

As the Lord said, both will fall into a pit if a blind man leads a blind man. How many of you received a clear knowledge of rebirth through this teaching?

Jesus warned, "Do not give dogs what is sacred; do not throw your pearls to pigs. If you do, they may trample them under their feet, and then turn and tear you to pieces" (Matt. 7:6). The words that you read in this book are a "holy pearl." You must realize the value of these words, and then give thanks to God.

2. For those who are not born again, I want to exhort you not to say, "Come back tomorrow" to the Holy Spirit who is knocking on your heart right now.

Stephen Charnock said that if we are not genuine Christians, we are better off not having been born. And the only way to being a genuine Christian is by being born again.

What else can I say? This is the basic truth. Charnock also said, "There is not a man but has, or once had, the strivings of this Spirit with him. There are the knockings of Christ by his Spirit at the door..."[22]

This is also true. I believe that this is the day He visits you. (See 1 Peter 2:12.) Right now, God is inviting you to salvation. He is suggesting, "Give Me your heart. Then I will give you My kingdom." Therefore, I wish that you hold on to this opportunity.

Stephen Charnock presented four reasons you must be born again immediately when God exhorts you.

- Being born again early contributes to glorifying God.

- Being born again brings many benefits to us.

- It is most foolish to lay aside rebirth.

- The longer it takes, the harder it is to be reborn.

In explaining the last one, he said something important.

> In regard of spiritual judgments, which will make it impossible. Such judgments upon men that sit under the gospel, and admit not the influence of it, are more frequent than is usually imagined, though they are not so visible. Open sins God punishes many times by visible judgments, but wilful unregeneracy by spiritual.[23]

Spiritual judgment actually exists. The Bible is full of warnings regarding spiritual judgment. These are few passages:

The L ORD said to Samuel, "How long will you mourn for Saul, since I have rejected him as king over Israel?"

—1 S AMUEL 16:1

I snatched you from the power of Egypt and from the hand of all your oppressors. I drove them from before you and gave you their land. I said to you, "I am the L ORD your God; do not worship the gods of the Amorites, in whose land you live." But you have not listened to me.

—J UDGES 6:9–10

O Jerusalem, Jerusalem, you who kill the prophets and stone those sent to you, how often I have longed to gather your children together, as a hen gathers her chicks under her wings, but you were not willing. Look, your house is left to you desolate.

—M ATTHEW 23:37–38

I tell you, not one of those men who were invited will get a taste of my banquet.

—L UKE 14:24

So I declared on oath in my anger, "They shall never enter my rest."

—H EBREWS 3:11

Afterward, as you know, when he wanted to inherit this blessing, he was rejected. He could bring about no change of mind, though he sought the blessing with tears.

—H EBREWS 12:17

We cannot know when a person will die, but as these verses show, not all people who are alive can repent. Some people are rejected by God while they are living. That is, they may be alive, but they no longer have the opportunity to repent. This is spiritual judgment. Such judgment occurs to those who do not repent despite their many spiritual benefits through the gospel.

> Then Jesus began to denounce the cities in which most of his miracles had been performed, because they did not repent. "Woe to you, Korazin! Woe to you, Bethsaida! If the miracles that were performed in you had been performed in Tyre and Sidon, they would have repented long ago in sackcloth and ashes. But I tell you, it will be more bearable for Tyre and Sidon on the day of judgment than for you. And you, Capernaum, will you be lifted up to the skies? No, you will go down to the depths. If the miracles that were performed in you had been performed in Sodom, it would have remained to this day. But I tell you that it will be more bearable for Sodom on the day of judgment than for you."
> —MATTHEW 11:20–24

Likewise, there is a great danger of receiving spiritual judgment if a person does not repent after having enjoyed much spiritual privilege.

3. For those who are born again already, I want to exhort to you to remember that your spirit is born again, but not your flesh.

> So I say, live by the Spirit, and you will not gratify the desires of the sinful nature. For the sinful nature desires

what is contrary to the Spirit, and the Spirit what is
contrary to the sinful nature. They are in conflict with
each other, so that you do not do what you want.

—Galatians 5:16–17

Dear friends, I urge you, as aliens and strangers in the
world, to abstain from sinful desires, which war against
your soul.

—1 Peter 2:11

Therefore, we must beat our bodies and make them a slave
as Paul did. (See 1 Corinthians 9:27.) Some people believe
that we will automatically live according to God's Word after
we become born again. That is an erroneous thinking. John
Stott wrote in his book *Christ the Controversialist:*

To say that sanctification is the natural result of rebirth
is different from saying that it is the automatic result.
Those who are truly reborn can act thoughtlessly,
commit a grave sin, fail in human relationships, and
have problems in their marriage. This was true in the
lives of New Testament believers, and is still true in
the lives of our own Christian friends and of our own
lives. That is why the epistles contain detailed ethical
teachings—regarding restraining our tongue, living
diligently to earn our own bread, being honest, fair,
hospitable, forgiving, and kind, having sexual purity,
and having mutual duties in the relationships between
husband and wife, parent and child, and master and
slave. Were not the people who received the apostles'
exhortations born-again Christians? That is right. They
were born-again people! However, the apostles did not
naturally assume that they were holy. They fulfilled

holiness through detailed teachings and exhortations, role models and prayers.[24]

Truly, sanctification is the natural result of rebirth, but it is not the automatic result. New birth is when the spirit is born, and like the flesh, it is born not partially, but with a full form. However, it is born as a baby. Therefore, as babies grow, our spirit must grow. That means we need to diligently come to worship, eat the Word of God, and pray. We must give generously to God, be faithful in service, and eager to evangelize. That is how we become a young adult, and then a father, like the apostle Paul. Ultimately, we must be like Christ, becoming perfect like our heavenly Father.

Chapter 7

THERE IS NO SUCH THING
AS SHAMEFUL SALVATION!

By the grace God has given me, I laid a foundation as an expert builder, and someone else is building on it. But each one should be careful how he builds. For no one can lay any foundation other than the one already laid, which is Jesus Christ. If any man builds on this foundation using gold, silver, costly stones, wood, hay or straw, his work will be shown for what it is, because the Day will bring it to light. It will be revealed with fire, and the fire will test the quality of each man's work. If what he has built survives, he will receive his reward. If it is burned up, he will suffer loss; he himself will be saved, but only as one escaping through the flames.

–1 CORINTHIANS 3:10-15

THIS IS A passage that both Protestants and Catholics misunderstand. Catholics present this passage as the basis for the idea of purgatory. They assert that those who are not saved will go to purgatory to be purified in the flames before receiving salvation. However, this passage cannot be the basis for the idea of purgatory. The reason is the following:

1. The topic in the passage is in reference to the connection between church workers and their doctrines, and is not related to regular saints.

2. The word *flames* in the passage refers to judgment flames, not purifying flames.

3. Paul is asserting that salvation is gained with great difficulty, as though "escaping through the flames"; he is not saying that salvation is obtained through the process of purification by fire. Therefore, this passage is unrelated to the idea of purgatory.

On the other hand, many Protestants mistake this passage to be referring to shameful salvation. This is how they think: *People who believe in Jesus and live in obedience to His Word will receive their reward and glorious salvation. However, even if they have not lived according to the Word, those who believe in Jesus will at least gain shameful salvation.*

But this is what Jesus said:

> Not everyone who says to me, "Lord, Lord," will enter the kingdom of heaven, but only he who does the will of my Father who is in heaven.
> —MATTHEW 7:21

And this is what James said:

> What good is it, my brothers, if a man claims to have faith but has no deeds? Can such faith save him?
> —JAMES 2:14

Therefore, what the Protestants believe regarding this passage comes from error. Despite this, many people still believe this error based on 1 Corinthians 3:10–15. That is why I would like to demonstrate first that this passage is not referring to shameful salvation, explain what it actually means, and lastly, prove that shameful salvation does not exist.

The Passage Is Not About Believers' Deeds and Their Judgment

Without thinking, too many people consider this passage to be referring to Christians' deeds and God's judgment of them, but that is not true. The analogy of deeds and judgment is recorded in Matthew 7:24–27:

> Therefore everyone who hears these words of mine and puts them into practice is like a wise man who built his house on the rock. The rain came down, the streams rose, and the winds blew and beat against that house; yet it did not fall, because it had its foundation on the rock. But everyone who hears these words of mine and does not put them into practice is like a foolish man who built his house on sand. The rain came down, the streams rose, and the winds blew and beat against that house, and it fell with a great crash.

Jesus' analogy begins with the word *therefore*. Thus, we know that this analogy is the conclusion of His prior words. What are His prior words? From a broad perspective, it is the Sermon on the Mount. Therefore, this analogy is Jesus' conclusion of the whole Sermon on the Mount. The crowd heard this sermon. The fact that they heard it does not make them saved. The ones who live according to the Sermon on the Mount will have eternal life. The ones who hear the sermon and do not put it into practice will be destroyed. From a narrow perspective, however, the teaching that comes right before this analogy is the famous passage from Matthew 7:21–23:

> Not everyone who says to me, "Lord, Lord," will enter
> the kingdom of heaven, but only he who does the will
> of my Father who is in heaven. Many will say to me
> on that day, "Lord, Lord, did we not prophesy in your
> name, and in your name drive out demons and perform
> many miracles?" Then I will tell them plainly, "I never
> knew you. Away from me, you evildoers!"

Therefore, what Jesus is saying through this analogy is clear. No matter how much we confess our faith (v. 21), no matter how much we act like prophets, cast out demons, and perform miracles (vv. 22–23), no matter how much we listen to God's Word and understand it, even if we heard through Jesus Himself, we will be judged, destroyed, and thrown into hell if we do not live by the Word.

No one can change these words. These are the Lord's own words—conclusive, representative words out of His many sermons. In the introduction and body of the sermon, a preacher can use other words or illustrations to expand his point. However, he cannot say anything else in the conclusion. Therefore, this passage is a literal, definite truth.

How can we use a passage from the apostle Paul's epistle to refute what Jesus Himself taught through the analogy of the wise and foolish builders? No, that cannot be. If Paul wrote something other than what Jesus said, he is wrong. We must not interpret the Bible in such a way. One passage in the Bible never contradicts another passage. This is not the correct, biblical interpretative method. Again, I must clearly emphasize that the passage in this chapter is not about believers' deeds and God's judgment of them. Saint Augustine wrote in his book *Confessions:*

Faith without deeds is dead, and cannot save a person. According to certain people's belief, if a person is baptized in Christ, does not depart from the church because of heresy, and does not forsake the name of Christ, even if he is living in sin... even if he continues to live in sin until he dies, he is still saved... But such belief stems out of a kind of humanistic, merciful feeling, and is a departure from the truth. Because when I read the Bible, it gives a totally different answer.[1]

I once wrote a book titled *The Enchiridion on Faith, Hope, and Love* about this topic, and, with the help of God, I worked my best and clarified from the Bible what Paul has sufficiently described as the faith that can save us in the following verse:

> For in Christ Jesus neither circumcision nor uncircumcision has any value. The only thing that counts is faith expressing itself through love.
>
> —GALATIANS 5:6

However, if faith acts evil and not good it demonstrates what James said: "Faith by itself, if it is not accompanied by action, is dead" (James 2:17). James also said, "What good is it, my brothers, if a man claims to have faith but has no deeds? Can such faith save him?" (James 2:14).

Furthermore, if an evil man can be saved by his faith, demonstrating what Paul meant when he said, "He himself will be saved, but only as one escaping through the flames" (1 Corinthians 3:15), then faith without deeds can save a person, and the apostle James's words are false. Paul's words elsewhere would then also be false.

Do you not know that the wicked will not inherit the kingdom of God? Do not be deceived: Neither the sexually immoral nor idolaters nor adulterers nor male prostitutes nor homosexual offenders nor thieves nor the greedy nor drunkards nor slanderers nor swindlers will inherit the kingdom of God.

—1 CORINTHIANS 6:9–10

If simply believing in Jesus can save those who continue in evil, how can these words be true, that they cannot inherit the kingdom of God?

Therefore, the passage in the chapter is not referring to the relationship between deeds and salvation. We must acknowledge this fact clearly and get rid of any distorted views on this passage. Only without a distorted bias can we understand the Bible clearly. Only then can the truth be seen. Therefore, I wish that you would throw away any biases regarding this passage.

The Passage Is About Christian Workers and Their Judgment

This passage does not explain the relationship between deeds and salvation. Then what is the true meaning of the passage? I would like to introduce you to what the commentaries say about this passage.

In *1 Corinthians*, a commentary written by Charles Hodge, it is written:

> Since the context is talking about the Christian workers, Paul is giving them a warning (verse 10). They must be careful of the materials they use to build the temple. It is required that they prove themselves loyal

as well as diligent. If they do not use appropriate material, they will lose their reward. Only truth can be used to develop Christian character and build the church.[2]

The *Hokma Comprehensive Commentary* speaks about verse 10: "The topic that is being dealt with in the verse is in reference to church workers and their doctrines, and is not about regular saints."[3]

In *The Grand Bible Commentary*, it is written: "In the passage, Paul presents through the analogy of builders that Christ is the one and only foundation of the church, and the correct attitude that Church leaders should possess. In the passage, Paul depicts Christ as the foundation, Paul himself as the foundation builder, and the other leaders as the ones who build on top of the foundation."[4]

Lastly, Dr. David Lowley in his *Tyrannus Expository Commentary Series,* wrote: "Here Paul is developing a topic on the responsibilities of ministers (8). Even though it is true that the Corinthian saints were expected to serve other saints after receiving at least one spiritual gift or power, here Paul's interest lies in leaders in ministry such as Apollos or himself (3:5, 21–22)...At the judgment day, Christ will judge the quality of his servants' power (2 Corinthians 5:10). This judgment does not deal with the free gift of salvation (Rom. 6:23), or personal deeds (Eph. 2:8–9), but is regarding Christian service, and will be judged not by its quantity, but its quality."[5]

Therefore, the reward mentioned in the passage is not related to deeds. As verse 8 says that "each will be rewarded according to his own labor," it is referring to the reward of ministry. It is not about the relationship between deeds and salvation, but about the relationship between ministry and reward. Then what kind of ministers will be rewarded?

> If any man builds on this foundation using gold, silver, costly stones, wood, hay or straw, his work will be shown for what it is, because the Day will bring it to light. It will be revealed with fire, and the fire will test the quality of each man's work. If what he has built survives, he will receive his reward. If it is burned up, he will suffer loss; he himself will be saved, but only as one escaping through the flame.
>
> —1 CORINTHIANS 3:12–15

Likewise, to receive a reward we must build the church not using wood, hay, or straw, but using gold, silver, and costly stones. Of course, it is not saying that to receive a reward, we must build an external, fancy church building. Jesus expressed negativity toward Herod's temple. Then what does this statement really mean?

1. Gold, silver, and costly stones represent correct doctrinal truths in the hearts of people, while wood, hay, or straw represent erroneous doctrines.

Charles Hodge said that gold, silver, and costly stones are pure truths of God, while wood, hay, and stubble are false teachings. He wrote, "Paul warns all teachers against building, even on the true foundation, with wood, hay, and stubble. He reminds them that God's temple is sacred; that it cannot be injured with impunity, and that those who inculcate error instead of truth, will, in the great day, suffer loss..."[6]

> And the words of the LORD are flawless, like silver refined in a furnace of clay, purified seven times.
>
> —PSALM 12:6

They are more precious than gold, than much pure gold; they are sweeter than honey, than honey from the comb.

—PSALM 19:10

The law from your mouth is more precious to me than thousands of pieces of silver and gold.

—PSALM 119:72

Do not give dogs what is sacred; do not throw your pearls to pigs. If you do, they may trample them under their feet, and then turn and tear you to pieces.

—MATTHEW 7:6

Therefore, God's Word is spiritual gold, silver, and costly stones. Like a person who appraises gold, silver, and costly stones carefully, ministers must discern God's Word carefully. When Paul wrote to Timothy, he exhorted, "Do your best to present yourself to God as one approved, a workman who does not need to be ashamed and who correctly handles the word of truth" (2 Timothy 2:15). Therefore, ministers must discern God's Word correctly. They must not "peddle the word of God for profit" (2 Cor. 2:17). If they do, they are not discerning the Word of God correctly. "On the contrary, in Christ [they must] speak before God with sincerity, like men sent from God" (2 Cor. 2:17); that is the only way they will receive a reward from the Lord.

2. Gold, silver, and costly stones represent good motives of the builders, while wood, hay, or straw represent impure motives.

Recently, this century's greatest evangelist Reinhard Bonnke, who led a six-day evangelistic crusade and had three million forty thousand people convert, wrote:

> Some preach Christ "out of envy and rivalry, but others in love," said the apostle (Philippians 1:15–16). What drives us? We can preach to assert ourselves, for self-gratification, to satisfy our egos, jockeying to be centre stage, or even for money. It may well serve our own ends but like wood, hay and stubble it will fail the test of fire in the judgement to come (1 Corinthians 3:12–13). If we do it for him, as his voice and his hands, with his love in our eyes, we already have our reward—his "well done" in our soul.[7]

This is a true statement. Hebrews 6:10 records, "God is not unjust; he will not forget your work and the love you have shown him as you have helped his people and continue to help them." In addition, in 1 Corinthians 13:1–3, it is written:

> If I speak in the tongues of men and of angels, but have not love, I am only a resounding gong or a clanging cymbal. If I have the gift of prophecy and can fathom all mysteries and all knowledge, and if I have a faith that can move mountains, but have not love, I am nothing. If I give all I possess to the poor and surrender my body to the flames, but have not love, I gain nothing.

Therefore, we must receive Paul's loving exhortation and be loyal to do God's work with a pure motive of love.

3. Gold, silver, and costly stones represent the builder's continuous effort, while wood, hay, or straw represent temporary, valueless effort.

Wood, hay, and straw easily change and disappear, but gold, silver, and costly stones do not change so easily and disappear. Some people are loyal, but only during one period of time. Their loyalty is based on emotion, not will. These people cannot receive a reward from the Father at the end.

> Therefore, my dear brothers, stand firm. Let nothing move you. Always give yourselves fully to the work of the Lord because you know that your labor in the Lord is not in vain.
>
> —1 Corinthians 15:58

> Be faithful, even to the point of death, and I will give you the crown of life.
>
> —Revelation 2:10

The apostle Paul confessed in 2 Timothy 4:6–8: "For I am already being poured out like a drink offering, and the time has come for my departure. I have fought the good fight, I have finished the race, I have kept the faith. Now there is in store for me the crown of righteousness, which the Lord, the righteous Judge, will award to me on that day—and not only to me, but also to all who have longed for his appearing."

Our calling is like a marathon race. A marathon runner must run at a constant, persistent speed in a 42.195 kilometer race. If he runs speedily at one point as if in a 100 meter race, and then pauses to take a long nap like a rabbit, how can he receive his prize? He cannot be a winner. Therefore, we cannot be fickle; we must be loyal with perseverance.

4. Gold, silver, and costly stones represent true believers in the church, while wood, hay, or straw represent church members who are not born again.

In the following passage, the image of gold, silver, and costly stones that represent the church built by a minister is reminiscent of the New Jerusalem.

> And he carried me away in the Spirit to a mountain great and high, and showed me the Holy City, Jerusalem, coming down out of heaven from God. It shone with the glory of God, and its brilliance was like that of a very precious jewel, like a jasper, clear as crystal.
> —REVELATION 21:10–11

> The wall was made of jasper, and the city of pure gold, as pure as glass. The foundations of the city walls were decorated with every kind of precious stone. The first foundation was jasper, the second sapphire, the third chalcedony, the fourth emerald, the fifth sardonyx, the sixth carnelian, and the seventh chrysolite, the eighth beryl, the ninth topaz, the tenth chrysoprase, the eleventh jacinth, and the twelfth amethyst. The twelve gates were twelve pearls, each gate made of a single pearl. The great street of the city was pure gold, like transparent glass.
> —REVELATION 21:18–21

New Jerusalem is the heaven in which we will live in the future, and this is the description of the church when the new heaven and new earth arrive. This fact cannot be doubted when we look at Revelation 21:9–10:

> One of the seven angels who had the seven bowls full
> of the seven last plagues came and said to me, "Come, I
> will show you the bride, the wife of the Lamb." And he
> carried me away in the Spirit to a mountain great and
> high, and showed me the Holy City, Jerusalem, coming
> down out of heaven from God.

This New Jerusalem is made up of gold and various kinds of precious stones. Likewise, the Lord wants to build the church on earth with gold, silver, and costly stones. In other words, He wants the church to be made up of genuine believers who possess precious faith. (See 2 Peter 1:1.)

Historically the Old Testament tabernacle represents the house made of gold, silver, and costly stones. Now, we believers are the temple. Therefore, we must each become a precious stone house in a spiritual sense. We must become a dwelling place for the Lord, who is the King of kings.

When we see the church this way, the number of believers is not the problem. A minister must make each Christian a genuine believer with precious faith. By preaching the gospel in a correct way, ministers must develop genuine believers in their church. That is the only way believers will receive God's reward.

And, although this passage is for full-time ministers such as Paul and Apollos, it also applies to lay ministers. You will not receive a reward just because you serve as a Sunday school teacher or a small group leader. You must build the house using gold, silver, and costly stones, not wood, hay, or straw. In other words, you must discern the Word of God correctly, labor with a pure motive of love, be persevering and loyal, and help the souls under your care to become genuine believers. Only then, you will receive a great reward from the Lord.

Now I must tell you this. Although I made four interpretations regarding the two types of building materials so that I would give a lesson, the most appropriate interpretation based on the context is actually the first one. That is, gold, silver, and costly stones represent correct doctrines planted in people's hearts by the builder, and wood, hay, and straw represent wrong doctrines.

The Bible teaches that those who build the house using wood, hay, or straw "will suffer loss; he himself will be saved, but only as one escaping through the flames" (1 Cor. 3:15). However, such ministers who receive salvation with little to no reward—like a person who barely escapes from a burning house—are not ministers who did not live by the Word of God, as many people assume; they are ministers who, though not cult leaders, did not teach the Word correctly.

Please heed my words carefully. If these ministers not only taught the Word incorrectly, but also did not live according to the Word, they will not even escape the flames of fire to receive salvation. They would be thrown into the fires of hell. As Jesus said, heaven is only for the one "who does the will of my Father who is in heaven" (Matt. 7:21). Therefore, it is false to believe, using this passage as proof, that everyone who has faith in Jesus but neglects to live by His Word will go to heaven.

5. Shameful salvation does not exist.

There are many people in the church who mistake this passage to mean shameful salvation. Many people believe the following: A person who believes in Jesus and obeys His Word will receive a reward and glorious salvation. Even if they did not obey His Word, they will at least receive shameful salvation as long as they believed in Jesus.

This is false. This kind of salvation does not exist, because heaven is only for those who do the will of the Father. Therefore, the ones many believe to receive shameful salvation are actually those who will end up in hell.

Even the term *shameful salvation* is problematic. In a certain sense, this is an unbiblical term. Of course, those who receive little to no reward in heaven may feel relatively shameful. In that sense, it is not impossible to call their salvation shameful.

However, many people today believe that shameful salvation is given to those who believe in Jesus but do not live according to His Word, not merely to those who do not receive a reward in heaven. This is definitely a wrong belief.

> As the Scripture says, "Anyone who trusts in him will never be put to shame."
>
> —ROMANS 10:11

As the verse declares, those who believe in Jesus will never be put to shame. At the judgment seat, it is not that some who receive salvation will be glorious while others are shamed. As Scripture says in 1 Corinthians 15:41–42, everyone will be glorious, but each person's glory will be different from the others: "The sun has one kind of splendor, the moon another and the stars another; and star differs from star in splendor. So will it be with the resurrection of the dead."

Long ago, when I shared this during a prayer meeting, one deacon asked, "What will happen to the thief who was on the right side of Jesus?" I think you will be curious to know the answer, because people who teach about shameful salvation regularly use this illustration to prove their point.

This is their assertion: It is wrong to believe that only those with living faith will go to heaven. Look at the thief on the right side of Jesus. He repented on the cross and believed in Jesus. However, he did not do any good deeds. Despite that fact, Jesus promised him that he would be with Him in paradise that very day. Therefore, we will go to heaven without any good deeds as long as we believe in Jesus.

At first glance, this sounds right. But this is false. To understand, we must know the true meaning of repentance. The thief on the right side of Jesus repented from his sins. I am sure everyone will agree with that.

What is repentance? Many people think that repentance is cutting off sin. This is partially true, but not completely true. As Matthew 3:8 records, we must "produce fruit in keeping with repentance."

The Greek word for repentance is *metanoia,* and it means "change of heart" or "change of mind." Repentance is changing one's heart and mind. This is repentance, which naturally and inevitably leads to a change of behavior and speech—the fruit of repentance.

John Stott wrote about the psychology of the genuine change that follows repentance:

> Let me be more explicit about the forsaking which cannot be separated from following Jesus Christ. First, there must be a renunciation of sin. This, in a word, is repentance. It is the first part of Christian conversion. It can in no circumstances be bypassed. Repentance and faith belong together. We cannot follow Christ without forsaking sin. Repentance is a definite turn from every thought, word, deed and habit which is known to be wrong. It is not sufficient to feel pangs of remorse or to make some kind of apology to God. Fundamentally, repentance is a matter neither of emotion nor of

speech. It is an inward change of mind and attitude towards sin which leads to a change of behavior. [8]

Let us consider the thief on Jesus' right side as we remember the above words. What do you think? Do you think that the thief had no change of heart? No, he definitely had a change of heart. In the Bible, both thieves mocked Jesus. Then the thief on Jesus' right side had a change of heart, saying, "We are punished justly, for we are getting what our deeds deserve. But this man has done nothing wrong" (Luke 23:41). Then he cried out sincerely to Jesus, "Jesus, remember me when you come into your kingdom" (Luke 23:42). How did his attitude change all of a sudden? It is because his heart and mind changed. The fact that he experienced true repentance through a change of heart can be glimpsed from his faith in Jesus, who was hanging on the cross.

Many people did not believe Jesus when He was proclaiming the Word and performing amazing miracles in front of a crowd, but the thief believed Jesus, who, just like him, was hanging on a cross and dying a gruesome death as a criminal. What do you think? Is this possible without a change of heart? This is only possible to someone who had a change of heart!

Paul wrote in Romans 12:2: "Be transformed by the renewing of your mind." Therefore I can say with confidence that if the thief's execution was suspended and he were given the opportunity for a new life, he would never have lived as he did in the past, because his heart was renewed.

However, unlike the thief, there are too many people who do not cut off their sins and do not show fruit in keeping with repentance even after weeks, months, and years of believing in Jesus. And foolishly they say that they will at least receive shameful salvation because the thief on Jesus' right side received salvation. Their thinking is truly irrational because these two situations are clearly different. Therefore, the thief on the right side of Jesus is not a true example of shameful salvation.

As long as we are on this subject, I would like to say one more thing. There are three verses that people use as their basis for asserting the doctrine of shameful salvation. The most representative one is the example of the thief on Jesus' right side, and the other one is our passage in this chapter. The last one is from 1 Corinthians 5:1–5 (NAS):

> It is actually reported that there is immorality among you, and immorality of such a kind as does not exist even among the Gentiles, that someone has his father's wife. You have become arrogant, and have not mourned instead, in order that the one who had done this deed might be removed from your midst. For I, on my part, though absent in body but present in spirit, have already judged him who has so committed this, as though I were present. In the name of our Lord Jesus, when you are assembled, and I with you in spirit, with the power of our Lord Jesus, I have decided to deliver such a one to Satan for the destruction of his flesh, so that his spirit may be saved in the day of the Lord Jesus.

When I was a youth president in a church, the pastor in charge over us preached this message: *Even if you commit sexual immorality, your body will be rejected, but your spirit will go to heaven. Once a person is saved, he will go to heaven no matter what kind of sin he commits.* I remember that he also said, "The bodies of Israelites who disobeyed God in the wilderness and were killed, and even the bodies of Korah,

Dathan, and Abiram, who were swallowed up by the earth, are destroyed, but their spirits received salvation."

A few years ago, I heard the same preaching. A pastor who was the head of a mission organization came to preach in Ulsan. Since I had a positive opinion of the mission organization, I attended the meeting with expectation with several of my church members. In the middle of a sermon, he asked the saints, "Where did the Israelites go who died in the wilderness? Did they go to heaven or hell?" When the saints replied that they went to hell, he argued, "No, they went to heaven." At that moment, I thought to myself, *How could he make such a groundless assertion? Has he not read 1 Corinthians 10 and Hebrews 3?* I am not saying this to criticize my high school pastor or the head of the mission organization. From what I know, they are wonderful people, but it is clearly true that their thinking is wrong. Why did these two people end up having such a wrong view? They mistook the words from 1 Corinthians 5:5 (NAS):

> I have decided to deliver such a one to Satan for the
> destruction of his flesh, so that his spirit may be saved
> in the day of the Lord Jesus.

These words do not signify that the flesh will be destroyed but the spirit will receive salvation. A prominent seminary scholar, Lenski, said that the Bible does not mention anything about the flesh and spirit being separated to receive salvation and destruction. They are both saved or both destroyed. These words also do not signify that the believer will be assured of salvation, despite his sin of sexual immorality with his stepmother.

What does this passage mean? Since long ago, there have been two predominant interpretations regarding the phrase, "deliver such a one to Satan." One interpretation is that this phrase refers to excommunication; the other is that Paul is commanding that the man be surrendered to Satan for his benefit. Those who agree with the first interpretation assert that handing the man over to Satan means the same as "put[ting] out of...fellowship the man who did this" (vs. 2). They believe that the Corinthians were negligent of excommunicating such evildoers, and that Paul is determined to do so.

Moreover, they assert that "delivering a person to Satan" is an appropriate expression for excommunication since the world belongs to Satan, and putting someone out of fellowship means throwing them out of the kingdom of Christ into the kingdom of Satan. (See Colossians 1:13.) On the other hand, the logic behind the second interpretation—that "delivering a person to Satan" means more than excommunication—is as follows:

- The Bible clearly reveals that physical calamities will follow people as a result of Satan's operations.

- Satan was granted the ability to impose such calamities through miracles (Acts 5:1–11, 13:9–11; 2 Corinthians 13:10).

- First Timothy 1:20 seems to signify the same meaning when Paul handed Hymenaeus and Alexander over to Satan so that they will not blaspheme.

- There is no evidence that the Jews of that time used the phrase to signify excommunication, so it is unlikely that Paul's readers would have understood the phrase that way.

- Looking at the way the phrase was used in the epistle, excommunication did not seem to have the power to destroy the flesh.

Therefore, most commentary writers agree that the apostle's frightening phrase "deliver such a one to Satan" signifies handing a person to a certain physical calamity. Therefore, it is most natural to see that the word *flesh* in the phrase *destruction of the flesh*, does not represent sinful nature as some people assert, but signifies the body. What is the reasoning behind Paul's harsh punishment? The root of his action lies in love, not anger, because such a punishment is given to cause the sinner to repent. Therefore, verse 5 does not mean that a person's spirit will be saved even though his body will be destroyed; rather, it means that the purpose of punishment lies in love.

I would like to give an illustration. In Pastor Kenneth Hagin's book *The Art of Prayer* the following testimony appears:

Thirty years ago, I went over to a bedridden person to pray for healing. But I could not say the word *heal*. Instead of saying "heal him," I was only able to say "O Lord, bless this man." My tongue could not say the word *heal* because I could not control my tongue. I asked, "Lord, why could I not pray for this man's healing? He's not ready to die at his age. The Lord promised at least seventy to eighty years for us to live." (Psalm 91 says "With long life will I satisfy him." If we are not satisfied with seventy to eighty years of life, He will lengthen our years until we are satisfied.)

But this is what the Lord said. "Yes, but he was born again thirty-six years ago, and I have been waiting for the last thirty-six years for him to renounce his sin. [Think how much our God is patient and long-suffering.] For the last thirty-six years, he did not live righteously for longer than two weeks. That is why I judged him and handed his body over to Satan to be destroyed, so that his spirit may receive salvation in the day of the Lord Jesus." [His words are from 1 Corinthians 5:5.]

Then the Holy Spirit told me, "You cannot pray for his healing, but this is what you can do. Put your hand on him and pray that he may receive the fullness of the Holy Spirit. Then his remaining days will be better than his beginning." I told him as the Lord told me. The moment I put my hand on his forehead he began to pray in tongues. Then I left him. When I came back a month later, he was dead. The people told me that he sat on his bed, praying and praising in tongues for three days and nights, and then went to be with the Lord gloriously. That was God's perfect will for him. It was better than going to hell.

I drove back on the highway, crying and singing. "Grace, grace, God's grace, God's grace is greater than all our sin."[9]

Listen to this testimony carefully. The Lord gave his flesh over to Satan because if he continues to live in sin he would not be able to avoid destruction. That is why, by delivering him to Satan to become physically ill, He gave him the opportunity to repent and prepare for heaven.

Do not be mistaken. Just because this man lived healthily and then died in sickness—that is, his flesh was destroyed—does not mean that he avoided hell to go to heaven. He had the opportunity to repent while he was lying in bed; he did not waste the opportunity, but repented and went to heaven. What Paul was doing in 1 Corinthians is exactly the same thing. Therefore, this verse shows that without repentance, which means cutting off our sin, we cannot go to heaven. It is foolish to use this verse as an evidence to say that we can receive shameful salvation even if we did not live according to the Word.

I will say the conclusion now. What do you think is the most important word for Christians today? I believe it is Colossians 3:1–2:

> Since, then, you have been raised with Christ, set your hearts on things above, where Christ is seated at the right hand of God. Set your minds on things above, not on earthly things.

For many people today, the purpose of life is on things below. This of course is true not only of nonbelievers, but also of believers. Christians must be pilgrims. Why are many Christians not coming to their senses? Instead, they madly seek after the things below while being indifferent to the things above. I believe one of the reasons is that they received wrong teaching and were made to believe that shameful salvation exists. Many people go to church but live in sin, thinking their salvation is guaranteed. Having false assurance, they want to enjoy earthly things now.

As I have stated, there is no such thing as shameful salvation. What I mean is, there is not a kind of salvation where one only believes without obeying the Word of God and still goes to heaven. We must think again. We must renounce the sin that we hold on to before it is too late, and we must obey God. Our purpose of life must change. Paul said in 1 Thessalonians 5:23:

> May God himself, the God of peace, sanctify you through and through. May your whole spirit, soul and body be kept blameless at the coming of our Lord Jesus Christ.

Of course we will go to heaven if we are holy. We will go to heaven even though we are not completely blameless. However, are we not ashamed if going to heaven is our only purpose? We must make it our goal to become perfectly holy. We must put all our effort into becoming more and more blameless and spotless, just like Jesus Christ.

Let us restore the lost biblical purpose and standard, which the apostles and saints of the New Testament held on to in their lives.

– Chapter 8 –

THE KINGDOM THAT ONLY THE VICTORIOUS CAN ENTER

*But thanks be to God, who always leads us in triumphal proces-
sion in Christ and through us spreads everywhere the fragrance of
the knowledge of him.*

–2 CORINTHIANS 2:14

IN THIS PASSAGE, Paul gives thanks to God.

First of all, the important word in this verse is *triumphal.*
It is important to be triumphant. The more important word,
however, is *always,* because if we are not always triumphant,
the result is that we have lost. The phrase that is even more
important is *in Christ,* because it shows the secret to victory.
However, for people living today I believe the most important word is *us,* because we have the unconscious tendency to
ascribe this experience only to Paul. However, this is not just
Paul's personal experience. It is *our* experience.

Don't mistake the word *us* to mean *all of us.* I wish that
were so, but it is not. *Us* does not refer simply to the Corinthian church or Great Faith Church. It refers to the genuine
church, not the external church. There are many people who
belong to the external church but not the genuine church. In
other words, there have always been chaffs, weeds, and goats
in the church. Even the twelve disciples had Judas Iscariot
among them. Therefore, this is a regular phenomenon.

I would like to tell a story. When I was in seminary, I

mostly read the Bible. I had to change the cover of my Bible three times and mend several interior pages with Scotch tape. That's how diligently I read the Bible. I was known as the Bible scholar among the seminary students. During this time of my devotion to the Bible, I began to earnestly read other Christian books.

At the time, I had a powerful leading of the Holy Spirit to read Christian books. Because of the Spirit's guidance, I began to dedicate myself to reading Christian books. In the first three years, I read two or three books in a week. Sometimes I read two or three books in a day. I can no longer read that much, because there are no more books that I want to read. Of course there are many books, but not many books worth reading! I have already read all the standard Christian books, so now I regularly go to the bookstore to find something to read that was published that month. I discovered an important fact while I was spending time in the bookstore. I found that the messages before and after the nineteenth century were different. Before the nineteenth century, the famous theologians and preachers, beginning with the Puritans, emphasized self-examination. The Puritans did not immediately baptize a person after conversion. They observed the person for three months to ensure that he had truly repented, renounced sin, and was obeying the Word continuously by faith. After the observation, only when they felt convicted that his faith was genuine did they give him baptism. After the nineteenth century, the message that emphasized the importance of self-examination left the pulpit. In place of self-examination, what materialized was the message of the assurance of salvation.

Of course, there were those who broke the tradition by focusing on self-examination, such as Dr. Lloyd-Jones. But these days, there are not many preachers who sufficiently emphasize self-examination as the Bible does. On the contrary, there are many people who do not confirm the biblical truth of repentance, faith, and rebirth with impartial attitude, instead planting false assurance of salvation to people based on superficial syllogism. This is a frightening snare for souls!

Many of you have the assurance of salvation. Of course, there are those who have assurance because they truly are saved, but there are many people who have this assurance even though they are not saved. People in the latter group believe that they will go to heaven. However, if they do not discern their true spiritual state and genuinely repent and turn from sin, they will be thrown into hell. They will be like those in Matthew 7:22–23 who went to hell even though they had the assurance of salvation. For this reason, I always preach this message wherever I go. Therefore, I wish that if you have assurance of salvation, you will read this book more carefully.

Christians Are Victorious Ones

Many people are living in a delusion. They believe that mature Christians who are filled with the Holy Spirit are the victorious ones, and the immature Christians are not victorious. But that is not true. All Christians are victorious because they all possess the faith that overcomes the world. Genuine faith overcomes the world. This is seen in the following scriptural passage:

> For everyone born of God overcomes the world. This is the victory that has overcome the world, even our faith. Who is it that overcomes the world? Only he who believes that Jesus is the Son of God.
>
> —1 JOHN 5:4–5

Here, the phrase *born of God* means "people who are born again." *Everyone* means there is no exception! In Greek the word *everyone* is *pan* (i.e., "all"), and is in neutral form. Up to this point, John wrote in the masculine form, but suddenly switches to a neutral noun. This means that the word is a general and universal principle. Charles Finney said firmly: "You cannot fail to observe that this is a universal proposition—all who are born of God overcome the world—all these, and it is obviously implied none others. You may know who are born of God by this characteristic—they overcome the world." [1] Therefore, it is not true that some Christians overcome the world, while others do not. All who are born again overcome the world. They overcome the world by faith. Those who do not have faith cannot overcome the world. That is why Paul said, "Without faith it is impossible to please God" (Heb. 11:6). John asked rhetorically, "Who is it that overcomes the world?" (1 John 5:5).

Then what is the meaning of *the world*? This world is different from the world mentioned in the famous verse John 3:16. In John 3:16, the world represents sinful humanity. Here, it means something different. We must read 1 John 2:15–17 in order to figure out what he meant by *the world*.

> Do not love the world or anything in the world. If anyone loves the world, the love of the Father is not in him. For everything in the world—the cravings of sinful man, the lust of his eyes and the boasting of what he has and does—comes not from the Father but from the world. The world and its desires pass away, but the man who does the will of God lives forever.

In the beginning of this passage, it is written, "Do not love the world or anything in the world" (v. 15). Therefore, the world is the subject we must not love. We must love God and our neighbors. Therefore, God and neighbors are not the world. Our enemies, persecutors, and evildoers are not the world because they are the subjects of our love. However, Christians have subjects of hatred.

That is, Christians have subjects we must hate. In 2 Timothy 3:2–4, Paul revealed them as self, money, and pleasure. Therefore, it is not wrong to say that the world represents selfishness, greed, and sexual immorality. The next verse shows the more specific meaning of the world: "For everything in the world—the cravings of sinful man, the lust of his eyes and the boasting of what he has and does" (1 John 2:16).

To give you an analogy, the world is a kingdom. It is the "kingdom of darkness" (Col. 1:13, NLT). The king in this kingdom is what Jesus called "the prince of this world," who is Satan. (See John 12:31, NLT.) In this kingdom called "the world," there are soldiers who fight to expand the kingdom. In the kingdom of the world, "the cravings of sinful man, the lust of his eyes, and the boasting of what he has and does" make up its army, navy, and the air force. They attack constantly to defeat the people of God's kingdom. Therefore, these (Satan's) troops are "the world" that we must fight and triumph against. In other words, the enemies that we must fight against are "the cravings of sinful man, the lust of his eyes, and the boasting of what he has and does." It is clear what it means to overcome the world. It means defeating our sinful cravings, the lust of our eyes, and the boasting of what we have and do. When these three tempt and attack us, we must not succumb to them, but defeat them by counterattack. As it is recorded in Colossians 3:5, we must "put to death, therefore, whatever belongs to your earthly nature: sexual immorality, impurity, lust, evil desires and greed, which is idolatry." We must crucify and kill them. This is what it means to overcome the world.

> For everyone born of God overcomes the world. This is the victory that has overcome the world, even our faith. Who is it that overcomes the world? Only he who believes that Jesus is the Son of God.
>
> —1 JOHN 5:4–5

When we had only a vague idea of what "the world" meant, this passage was not very shocking. However, when the meaning of "the world" becomes clear, this passage will be very shocking to many people. That is because those who have not overcome their sinful cravings, lust of their eyes, and the boasting of what they have and do, are not truly born again and are not the children of God. This teaching may sound unfamiliar to you. However, this is not a new teaching. As proof, I will give you several examples.

John Wesley said, "Peace and victory over sin are essential to faith in the Captain of our salvation." [2]

John Ryle said, "Reader, one great lesson I wish you to learn this day is this—that if you would prove you are born again and going to heaven, you must be a victorious soldier of Christ. If you would make it clear that you have any title to Christ's precious promises, you must fight the good fight in Christ's cause, and in that fight you must conquer."[3]

D. L. Moody said, "Let no one believe that just going to church will be enough. The fact that you go to church will not save you. The problem is this. 'Are you overcoming the world? Or is the world overcoming you?'"[4]

One time, I paid a visit to a deacon in our church. She had studied in seminary, and posted a very gracious writing on the wall. I felt a deep affinity for the writing as I read it, so I wrote it down. The words were from the world famous theologian and commentary writer William Barclay.

> In Christianity there are two essentials. One is victory, and the other is persevering loyalty. In Christian life, there is no one-time victory over sin. The victory comes through a lifetime loyalty that defies all the attacks of sin. Christian life is not a battle. It is a long journey.

Therefore, to say that a person is not born again if he cannot overcome sin is not a strange assertion. But we must be careful as we digest this word. This does not mean that a person who is born again never commits sin.

As an analogy, the believer's life is like a boxing match. Is the boxer who is the victor never punched? Yes, he is punched. However, he punches more than he gets hit. That's why he is the winner. The life of a born-again believer is just like that. Born-again believers do sin; however, they are more victorious than defeated. That is why even the believers with weak faith can win by one point even though they may not achieve a total knockout. This is explained wisely by Charles Finney.

> He who does not habitually overcome the world is not born of God. In saying this, I do not intend to affirm that a true Christian may not sometimes be overcome by sin; but I do affirm that overcoming the world is the general rule, and falling into sin is only the exception.[5]

Based on this truth, I want to ask you two questions. My beloved friend, are you an overcoming one? In the life of sin, are you winning at least by a point even though you may not achieve a complete knockout? If you can answer yes to these questions, you are a Christian. Therefore, you can be assured of your salvation. If you cannot say yes you are not a Christian, because God's Word says that Christians are victorious.

There Is a Promise for Those Who Overcome

A few years ago on Korean Thanksgiving Day, I met my sister-in-law and her husband. They were living in Ulsan and then moved to DaeGu, so they did not find a home church for a while. Then they decided to remain with one church because of a letter sent to them. The pastor of her church had written a book titled, *Pastor, Write a Letter on Monday.* That church was a unique church that had a revival because of the pastor's continuous letters. My sister-in-law and her husband suggested to me, "Pastor, why don't you write a letter, too?" When I heard that, I thought, *That is a good idea!* I thought so because there is no religion like Christianity that achieved great history through letters.

As you know, two-thirds of the New Testament is letters. All of Paul's writing is letters. Paul did not write a book. He only wrote letters. Peter, James, John, and Judas all wrote letters. From Romans to Revelation, all are letters.

That's not all. Our Lord Jesus wrote a letter, too. Some people think that Jesus only wrote two things—the Ten Commandments and all the charges for her accusers on the ground for the woman caught in adultery. That is not true. Jesus wrote seven letters, but they were not addressed to His mother, Mary, His adoptive father, Joseph, or to His four brothers. He wrote them to the church, because the church is His bride, and all His heart is for His bride.

Jesus' letters are recorded in Revelation 2–3. Out of these seven letters, I want to look together at the ones He wrote to Ephesus and Smyrna. The letter written to His bride in

Ephesus is vehement. It does not seem like a love letter, because the Ephesian bride had a waning of the heart and lost her "first love." However, the Lord's letter to His bride in Smyrna seems like a love letter. You can feel His warmth and tenderhearted love, because the church in Smyrna was going through much hardship.

If Jesus were to write a letter to you today, what kind of letter would He write? Would it be vehement or warm? I pray that you will receive a warm, tenderhearted letter.

As we read Jesus' letters, we discover two distinctive common characteristics in His letters to all seven churches. The first common characteristic is the sentence, "He who has an ear, let him hear what the Spirit says to the churches" (Rev. 2:7). Of course, this word can mean "to listen carefully to the previously given compliment, rebuke, or exhortation," but to me, it feels like Jesus is saying that He has an important declaration to make and that the church should listen carefully and take heed. They seem like preparatory words given to the people so they would focus before an important announcement is made.

The second common characteristic is the important announcement itself, the promise to those who overcome. I believe that there are many misunderstandings regarding this promise. This generation is a generation of misunderstandings. Just as the Sadducees were "in error because [they did] not know the Scriptures or the power of God" (Matt. 22:29), many people today have many misunderstandings and prejudices of the gospel. Jesus' promise to those who overcome is one of those misunderstood verses.

Many people wrongly think that what Jesus promised was a reward, not heaven. Perhaps it is because of the nuance of the words *those who overcome*. In this instance, what Jesus promises is not a reward but heaven. Look at Revelation 2 to find out whether this is true.

> He who has an ear, let him hear what the Spirit says to the churches. To him who overcomes, I will give the right to eat from the tree of life, which is in paradise of God.
>
> —REVELATION 2:7

Jesus promised to the church in Ephesus that those who overcome will be given the fruit from the tree of life to eat. The exact opposite verse is probably found in Revelation 22:19:

> And if anyone takes words away from this book of prophecy, God will take away from him his share in the tree of life and in the holy city, which are described in this book.

Therefore, this is not the promise of a reward, but of heaven, which is salvation itself.

> He who has an ear, let him hear what the Spirit says to the churches. He who overcomes will not be hurt at all by the second death.
>
> —REVELATION 2:11

This verse is clearer. Do you know what "second death" signifies?

> The lake of fire is the second death. If anyone's name was not found written in the book of life, he was thrown into the lake of fire.
>
> —REVELATION 20:14–15

> But the cowardly, the unbelieving, the vile, the murderers, the sexually immoral, those who practice magic arts, the idolaters and all liars—their place will be in the fiery lake of burning sulfur. This is the second death.
>
> —REVELATION 21:8

Shockingly, what is promised to the church in Smyrna is simply an avoidance of hell. This is not the promise of a reward. It is the promise of salvation. We can draw a very important truth from this. That is, not everyone who goes to church will go to heaven.

Jesus did not write a letter to a world organization. He wrote it to the church in Ephesus. He did not promise the fruit from the tree of life in the paradise of God to all the believers in Ephesus, but only to those who overcome. Therefore, only those who overcome can go to the paradise of God. Only those who overcome can eat from the tree of life. As a result, only the victorious will have eternal life.

The same truth goes to the church in Smyrna. Jesus did not promise salvation from second death, which is hell, to all the people in the church. Only those who overcome were given this blessed promise. Therefore, those who overcome will not be thrown into hell. They will go to heaven. But those who do not overcome will go to hell. They will be destroyed because either they were not born again, or if they were, they became decayed.

At this time I imagine in my heart that Jesus is writing a letter to your church. Of course, I cannot know the detailed contents of that letter. But I think I know generally what it would say. First, He would introduce Himself with grand, profound words. Then the Lord would find reasons to compliment your church. Afterward, He would rebuke its wrongdoings and give overall exhortations. Jesus would write a solemn expression:

> He who has an ear, let him hear what the Spirit says to
> the churches.
>
> —REVELATION 2:7

Next, He would promise His kingdom not to all the believers in the church, but only to those who overcome. Therefore, I hope you will not be satisfied with just attending your church. Do not be satisfied until you have overcome. That is the only way to avoid the punishment of hell and inherit heaven.

Only Those Who Overcome Can Enter Heaven

Let us find Revelation 21, and read verses 1–5 aloud:

> Then I saw a new heaven and a new earth, for the first heaven and the first earth had passed away, and there was no longer any sea. I saw the Holy City, the new Jerusalem, coming down out of heaven from God, prepared as a bride beautifully dressed for her husband. And I heard a loud voice from the throne saying, "Now the dwelling of God is with men, and he will live with them. They will be his people, and God himself will be with them and be their God. He will wipe every tear from their eyes. There will be no more death or mourning or crying or pain, for the old order of things has passed away." He who was seated on the throne said, "I am making everything new!" Then he said, "Write this down, for these words are trustworthy and true."

Now try to reduce the above passage into a word. What would it be? It would be heaven. Here John is describing heaven.

The following verses record those who will receive this

blessed kingdom as an inheritance. Who do you think they would be? Please say your answer and then confirm it by reading the verses:

> He said to me: "It is done. I am the Alpha and the Omega, the Beginning and the End. To him who is thirsty I will give to drink without cost from the spring of the water of life. He who overcomes will inherit all this, and I will be his God and he will be my son."
>
> —REVELATION 21:6–7

Likewise, only those who overcome will inherit heaven, as promised beforehand by Jesus in Revelation 2–3. Then who will go to hell?

In verse 8, a list of people who will be thrown into hell is recorded. Do not read the Bible yet, and answer the next question. There are eight types of people recorded in verse 8. Who do you think the first type is?

Most people would probably say unbelievers, or idolaters, or heretics. But they are wrong. Unbelievers are listed second, idolaters eighth, and heretics last when they are included with the liars. (See 1 John 2:18–22.) Surprisingly, the first people listed to go to hell are the "cowardly." Specifically, who are the cowardly?

Once a television drama titled "Han Myung Hee" was broadcasted in Korea, and it became nationally popular. In the drama, Han Myung Hee makes a "death list" after careful consideration. The first one on the list is the prime minister named Kim Jong Suh. The crown prince nods his head in agreement. The next one on the list is the second prime minister. The crown prince turns the page. In that moment, his face turns livid because included on the list is his younger brother's name.

I think Revelation 21:8 is God's death list. When "the unbelieving...the liars" appear on the list, Christians nod their head. They think it is obvious that these people should be included. If they understood this passage accurately, they would be shocked, and their faces would turn livid to find the cowardly on the list. It is because these people went to church with us and were called brother or sister by us.

"On what basis do you say such a thing?" you might ask. This is the basis: the unbelievers, idolaters, and heinous sinners are not afraid of God's judgment because they do not believe it exists. Of course, when they stand before the judgment seat, their hearts will melt in fear, and their knees will knock together as they tremble. They will be filled with enormous fear. Will the unbelievers in verse 8 continue to be unbelieving at the judgment seat? Will the idolaters and heinous sinners continue to commit idolatry and wickedness at the judgment seat? No, they are committing sins presently as they live on the earth. Likewise, the cowardly are those people on the earth who are presently cowardly. Then why are they cowardly? There are two reasons.

First, and this may sound odd, but they are cowardly because they believe.

> You believe that there is one God. Good! Even the demons believe that—and shudder.
>
> —JAMES 2:19

Here, it is written that even the demons believe. How nice it would be if God did not exist as unbelievers think; they are being deceived by the demons. God does exist, and the demons know it. They used to be angels before they became corrupt. They served God and saw Him face-to-face. Therefore, they cannot help but believe in the existence of God.

Also, they know that the Bible is the truth. After their corruption, they have survived to this day and have witnessed all the events that are recorded in the Bible. Therefore, they know that the Bible is true.

Also, they know that Jesus is the Messiah. When Jesus appeared to a demon-possessed man, they said, "I know who you are—the Holy One of God!" (Mark 1:24). Because of jealousy, they are working to prevent people from believing in Jesus.

They know that there is judgment, heaven, and hell. That is why they were fearful and asked Jesus, "Have you come to destroy us?" (Mark 1:24). Moreover, heaven is where they used to reside, and hell is where their colleagues are now. Therefore, they cannot help but believe in the existence of heaven and hell. The demons believe in all this.

Now, I want to tell you something very important. Today, many people think, *I believe that God is the only true God. I believe the Bible is the perfect truth. I believe that Jesus is the only Savior, and I believe in the existence of God's judgment, heaven, and hell. Therefore, I am a saved believer. I will go to heaven.* But the important fact is that demons also believe in all this. Therefore, this kind of faith cannot bring salvation. If these people with such a faith go to heaven, then demons will also go to heaven. Therefore, no one can ever go to heaven with this kind of faith.

Beloved, it is not a lie that even demons believe; the Bible says so. This kind of faith cannot bring peace to demons. Rather, they are filled with fear as a result of their belief. There are many Christians who are just like them. It would be better if they just cannot believe, but they believe that God exists, the Bible is the truth, Jesus is the Messiah, and there is judgment and afterlife. They believe all this 100 percent, but they cannot cut off from their sin. They know that it is not right, but they go on being enslaved by sin. That is why death makes them fearful, Jesus' Second Coming makes them fearful, and hell also makes them fearful.

Such people did not receive the spirit of adoption. They have received a spirit that makes them slaves again to fear. (See Romans 8:15.) They are still under the law, and not under grace. These people are like the ruler whom Jesus spoke about; they are not far from heaven, but they are not the people of heaven yet. Unfortunately, they are like those whom the author of Hebrews warned: "Since the promise of entering his rest still stands, let us be careful that none of you be found to have fallen short of it" (Heb. 4:1). Therefore, if they die in this state, they will go to hell.

The second reason the cowardly are fearful is that even though they have faith, they do not have love. They have speculative faith, not the faith that expresses itself through love. The only faith that saves us is "faith expressing itself through love" (Gal. 5:6), but their faith does not express itself through love. If they had love, they would not become cowardly, because John testified that there is no fear in love. "Perfect love drives out fear" (1 John 4:18). If they had true love, they would have become joyful and glad. This truth is shown in the apostle Peter's writing:

> Though you have not seen him, you love him; and even though you do not see him now, you believe in him and are filled with an inexpressible and glorious joy.
>
> —1PETER 1:8–9

Here, people have "faith that expresses itself through love," not just speculative faith. They are not fearful. They are joyful and glad. Therefore, the reason our false brothers and sisters are fearful is because their faith is merely a speculative faith, not the kind of faith that expresses itself through love.

I want to point out one more fact before I state my conclusion. The cowardly will go to hell. But not only will they go to hell, but they will go to the most frightening part of hell, because Jesus said, "That servant who knows his master's will and does not get ready or does not do what his master wants will be beaten with many blows" (Luke 12:47).

In verse 8, the only people who knew the master's will and did not get ready were the cowardly. The others did not know, and because of that, they did not get ready. However, the cowardly knew but did not act upon their knowledge. Therefore, in hell they will be in a position to be envious of unbelievers, idolaters, and heretics. With this thought in mind, Jesus said, "And you, Capernaum, will you be lifted up to the skies? No, you will go down to the depths. If the miracles that were performed in you had been performed in Sodom, it would have remained to this day. But I tell you that it will be more bearable for Sodom on the day of judgment than for you" (Matt. 11:23–24). Therefore, it is natural for the cowardly to be afraid. If we are going to believe in Jesus, we must not believe in Him half-heartedly, but decisively and thoroughly. We must not be lukewarm when living our Christian life. We must become the people of hot, passionate faith.

Now is my conclusion. I told you three things:

1. Christians are victorious ones.
2. There is a promise for the victorious ones.
3. Only the victorious can go to heaven.

Therefore, we must become the victorious ones. How can we become victorious? We cannot do it with only our determination and effort.

In 2 Corinthians 2:14 Paul spoke of being "in Christ." Also, John asked rhetorically, "Who is the one who overcomes the world?" (1 John 5:5). Therefore, we must believe in Jesus to be victorious. There is one thing that is strange, however. That is, there are many people among us who believe, yet do not experience victory. Why is that? It is because their faith is not the biblical faith.

Then what is the kind of faith that is required of us specifically in the Bible? This is a very important question, so I will explain in detail.

When humanity became corrupt, human beings were confronted with two problems. One was guilt, and the other was inner decay. First, the human beings who commit sin must pay the penalty for their sin. Second, they become enslaved to sin because of their internal decay, the natural outcome of being corrupt. That is why God worked out two things through Jesus in order to save humanity. God sent Jesus to the world with God's wisdom and God's power.

With God's wisdom, Jesus solved the problem of humanity's guilt. This is how He did it. Because God is love, He desires to save human beings. At the same time, He is just and therefore must judge human beings. So the destruction of humans was inevitable. Humanity really had no hope. However, through God's wisdom, Jesus solved the problem. By giving Himself as a sacrifice of atonement, He satisfied the justice of God while materializing God's love at the same time.

However, there is one more remaining problem: inner decay. Because of inner decay, human beings, like the people who fell deeply into the mire, cannot free themselves from sin by their own strength. They are dragged by sin because it dominates them, but Jesus came with God's power to solve the problem. With that power, Jesus rescues us from the domination of sin, setting us free (John 8:34–36). This is what the Bible refers to as salvation (Matt. 1:21).

Let us summarize what I have been saying. Human beings disobeyed God's commandment and became corrupt. The corruption brings forth the two problems of guilt and inner decay. What solves these problems is salvation. So Jesus came to the earth to save people from their sin by solving the problem of guilt with God's wisdom, and the problem of inner decay with God's power.

So what must we do to experience our own salvation? We must believe in our Savior Jesus. We must believe Jesus not only with God's wisdom, but also with God's power. In today's church, most people believe in Jesus' work of redemption on the cross; they merely believe Him with God's wisdom. Unfortunately, out of these people, a large number of them do not believe in God's power to free them from sin. That is why many say they believe, yet are still being dragged by their sin, thus remaining in dead faith that has no deeds. Of course, the result is their destruction. (See James 2:14.)

Do you know when people change? Do they change when they hear the Word? Do they change when they pray a lot? No, the Word and prayer alone do not change a person. The exact moment when a soul becomes a victorious Christian is when, while listening to the Word or praying, he ends up believing the power of God that saves him from sin. It is when the person believes not with his head, but with his spirit. That is when the sin's grip is loosed and the person is free. Hallelujah!

Therefore, at this time, fix your eyes on Jesus, "the author and perfecter of our faith" (Heb. 12:2). Do not just acknowledge how powerful sin is, but believe and rely upon the power of Jesus Christ, which is far mightier. Then, every Christian will become a victorious one.

– Chapter 9 –

JE-E-SUS!

As the Scripture says, "Anyone who trusts in him will never be put to shame." For there is no difference between Jew and Gentile— the same Lord is Lord of all and richly blesses all who call on him, for "Everyone who calls on the name of the Lord will be saved."

–ROMANS 10:11-13

OUT OF ALL the sermons I preached, I think this sermon title is the most original and unique. And it has the most beautiful title. As I sat down to prepare for my sermon, I immediately thought, *I must preach a series of sermons using this title! It is the most becoming title!*

After I led a revival meeting at the Bi-Sul-San Prayer Center, one general principle was impressed on my heart, and that is: Sermons are for testifying Jesus Christ. They are for drawing people to Jesus.

Sermons are not seminars, eloquent speeches, or one-man-shows. Moreover, sermons are not simply for interpreting and teaching the content of the Bible. Of course we preach on the Bible. Despite that, we preach Jesus, not the Bible. The Bible is a record and proof about Jesus. That is true for the New and the Old Testament. (See John 5:39.) However, the Bible is not the Savior; Jesus is. We must believe in Jesus, not the Bible. In other words, rather than believing in the Christian doctrines which the Bible presents, we must personally and directly believe in Jesus Christ of whom the Bible testifies. This is true faith and is the only secret to victory. It is what the world needs for life itself. They need Jesus—the way, the truth, and the life.

Preachers must testify the living Jesus who "is the same yesterday, today, and forever" (Heb. 13:8, NLT), and not preach about Jesus. They must focus the people's attention on Jesus. This is the goal of preachers. Recently, the Holy Spirit increased that realization about sermons deep in my spirit. As my realization increased, I deeply felt the desire to lift up Jesus and testify only about Him in my sermons.

For two months the Holy Spirit gave me a continual burden to prepare the sermon on the necessity of only believing in Jesus and calling on His name using the scripture, "Everyone who calls on the name of the Lord will be saved" (Acts 2:21). I knew that this sermon was necessary for many people and that it would be beneficial to them. I felt that this message should not be delivered only once, but that it should be a central message that I would deliver in other places.

There was one little problem. The focus of the sermon was clear, but I did not have the detailed guide from God, as I had with other sermons. Then two days ago on a train ride, the Holy Spirit began to speak to me while I was listening to Pastor Stephen Hill's sermon. The Holy Spirit spoke to me about the sermon's point and framework. At the time, I did not have a pen, so I got out of the train and bought a pack of pens from a stationery shop. I ripped off the last page of the train schedule bulletin and began to write. This sermon is based on that memo. I am going to preach the Word using the following order:

1. Calling on the name of the Lord—What does it mean to call on the name of the Lord?

2. Those who call on the name of the Lord—That is, who needs to call on the name of the Lord?

3. Salvation that comes to those who call on the name of the Lord—I will explain about the salvation that definitely happens to those who call on the name of the Lord using specific illustrations.

Calling on the Name of the Lord

Everyone who calls on the name of the Lord will be saved.

—ROMANS 10:13

The most important thing in this world is salvation. Without salvation, everything is futile, even if a soul gains the whole world. We receive salvation only when we call on the name of the Lord. Salvation belongs to those who call on His name. Therefore, we must call on the name of the Lord! Then what does it mean specifically to call on the name of the Lord?

I want to say, first, that we do not call on the name of the Lord in a negative way. There is something that people mistakenly believe as calling on the name of the Lord. I will tell you three specifically.

First, calling on the name of the Lord does not mean repeating after a confessional prayer and acknowledging that Jesus is the Lord.

That if you confess with your mouth, "Jesus is Lord," and believe in your heart that God raised him from the dead, you will be saved. For it is with your heart that you believe and are justified, and it is with your mouth that you confess and are saved.

—ROMANS 10:9–10

Many people use this scripture as a basis for leading converts to repeat a confessional prayer. Of course, this is a worthy and important act.

As you know, confessional prayers are generally offered when there is an assurance of salvation. After a confessional prayer, people say, "Now you are saved. Have assurance of salvation." But just because someone repeated a confessional prayer does not mean that he is really saved. If he confessed that Jesus is Lord (not simply a Savior) as the Bible demands, and acknowledged His Lordship with his heart (not just with his mouth), he is saved. But if the person did not do that, he is definitely not saved.

Romans 10:9–10 states that confessing with the mouth that Jesus is Lord during the confessional prayer is very important, and the passage is deeply related to our main verse today. The chapter verse, "Everyone who calls on the name of the Lord," goes further than that. It has a more extended meaning. Simply put, confessing Jesus as Lord signifies a sincere resolution to obey the Lord's will and live for Him from then on. The resolution alone does not actually make it possible to happen. There is something that makes the resolution possible. It is calling on the name of the Lord. So the act of calling on the name of the Lord is based on the confession that Jesus is the Lord, but it goes beyond just the confession. These two acts are a little different from each other.

Secondly, calling on the name of the Lord does not mean acknowledging oneself to be a Christian and referring to Jesus as the Lord.

In the four gospels, many people called Jesus the Lord, but of these people, many were not saved. Likewise, many people in the church these days are not saved, and yet refer to Jesus as the Lord out of habit. That is why Jesus warned:

Not everyone who says to me, "Lord, Lord," will enter the kingdom of heaven, but only he who does the will of my Father who is in heaven. Many will say to me on that day, "Lord, Lord, did we not prophesy in your name, and in your name drive out demons and perform many miracles?" Then I will tell them plainly, "I never knew you. Away from me, you evildoers!"

—MATTHEW 7:21–23

It is obvious that calling on the name of the Lord does not mean this.

On the other hand, there are people with genuine faith who live according to God's will and refer to Jesus as Lord. This is a good thing. However, this too does not mean the same as calling on the name of the Lord.

Thirdly, calling on the name of the Lord does not mean repeating, "Lord, Lord, Lord!" at a revival meeting. Please do not misunderstand what I say. I am not saying that calling on the name of the Lord and this act are always different. At times, these two acts are one and the same thing. But in many cases, they are totally different. Then when are they the same and when are they different? The answer depends on whether internal elements are present in both. Therefore, please judge for yourselves after listening to the explanation.

Before I answer, I will give you a hint. Those who call on the name of the Lord will be saved. Therefore, after repeating "Lord, Lord, Lord!" and if there is no salvation (answer), then this prayer is not calling on the name of the Lord. When you call on the name of the Lord, you always receive salvation (answer).

I just told you what "calling on the name of the Lord" is not. Then now, what specifically is calling on the name of the

Lord? First, calling on the name of the Lord is the same thing as faith, but expressed differently.

> As the Scripture says, "Anyone who trusts in him will never be put to shame." For there is no difference between Jew and Gentile—the same Lord is Lord of all and richly blesses all who call on him, for, "Everyone who calls on the name of the Lord will be saved."
>
> —ROMANS 10:11–13

Please read this passage carefully again, paying attention to the line of thought. Then you will realize that "anyone who trusts in him" in verse 11 and "everyone who calls on the name of the Lord" in verse 13 are used in the same way. In this context, those who call on the name of the Lord are those who trust in Him.

I will prove this truth more easily and clearly. How do we receive salvation? Yes, by faith. Is that true? Can we be saved by other means? No, absolutely not. Then what is the result of calling on the name of the Lord? You will be saved. Therefore, calling on the name of the Lord means none other than having faith.

Next, "calling on the name of the Lord" is faith, but it is a faith that is being demonstrated—it is a prayer of faith. As I said before, calling on the name of the Lord is faith, but it is not the faith that is in your heart. Rather, it is the faith that is outwardly being expressed through your voice. In other words, it is the faith that is being demonstrated in the present.

Let us find out what things in our heart are being expressed and demonstrated through our calling the name of the Lord. This is very important because this explains the real substance of our faith, and evaluates whether or not our repeating "Lord, Lord, Lord!" is the same as our calling on the name of the Lord.

1. Through calling on the name of the Lord, the first internal element that is expressed is the despair of our own selves.

In order to truly believe in Jesus, we must realize our own sin. However, there is something more important than realizing our own sin. That is, we must realize our inner decay.

> Can the Ethiopian change his skin or the leopard its spots? Neither can you do good who are accustomed to doing evil.
>
> —JEREMIAH 13:23

> By their fruit you will recognize them. Do people pick grapes from thornbushes, or figs from thistles? Likewise...a bad tree bears bad fruit...a bad tree cannot bear good fruit.
>
> —MATTHEW 7:16–18

> He went on: "What comes out of a man is what makes him 'unclean.' For from within, out of men's hearts, come evil thoughts, sexual immorality, theft, murder, adultery, greed, malice, deceit, lewdness, envy, slander, arrogance and folly. All these evils come from inside and make a man 'unclean.'"
>
> —MARK 7:20–23

> Therefore no one will be declared righteous in his sight by observing the law; rather, through the law we become conscious of sin.
>
> —ROMANS 3:20

> As for you, you were dead in your transgressions and sins, in which you used to live when you followed the ways of this world and of the ruler of the kingdom of the air, the spirit who is now at work in those who are disobedient. All of us also lived among them at one time, gratifying the cravings of our sinful nature and following its desires and thoughts. Like the rest, we were by nature objects of wrath.
>
> —EPHESIANS 2:1–3

As the previous verses, as well as other passages of Scripture reveal, human beings are internally decayed, and can never extricate themselves from the domination of sin by their own strength, effort, and determination. In short, humans are slaves of sin. In order to be saved, we must thoroughly realize the moral bankruptcy which we have inherited from Adam since birth. And then, there must be a bold turnabout from the effort of law to faith in Christ. We must express this turnabout through our calling on the name of the Lord.

2. Through calling on the name of the Lord, the second internal element that is expressed is faith in the Lord's power to save.

Jesus Christ is the wisdom of God and the power of God. Especially, Jesus has the power to free people from their sins.

> Jesus replied, "I tell you the truth, everyone who sins is a slave to sin. Now a slave has no permanent place in the family, but a son belongs to it forever. So if the Son sets you free, you will be free indeed."
>
> —JOHN 8:34–36

Here, the son referenced in verse 35 signifies a true believer who had been set free from the domination of sin, and "the Son" in verse 36 signifies Jesus Christ. Jesus frees us from our condition of slavery of sin, that is, from domination of sin. He turns us into God's children. This is Jesus' work as Savior, and this is the Lord's power to save. Believing in Jesus does not merely mean believing in the power of His blood. It means believing and relying on the Lord's power to free us from sin. We must believe in the Lord's power to save us from sin. By calling on the name of the Lord, we must entrust ourselves to Him.

3. Through calling on the name of the Lord, the third internal element that is expressed is humility.

This is an extension of the first element. We are people who are internally decayed. Human hearts are deceitful and corrupt beyond belief. Therefore, we have nothing to boast about ourselves.

The most appropriate place of the Lord is at the right hand of God, which is the place of power. For us, however, the most appropriate place is the place of humility. Of course, in Christ we have received an honorable status, allowing us to sit with Jesus in heaven. (See Ephesians 2:6.) Although that is true, our most appropriate place is that of humility. It is the most appropriate place for us forever. We must be humble after victory, and we must be humble after receiving our crown. As recorded in Revelation, we must cast down our crown at the Lord's feet and exalt and worship the Lord only. (See Revelation 4:10.) Those who call on the name of the Lord genuinely have this humility deep within them.

4. Through calling on the name of the Lord, the fourth internal element that is expressed is the heart of total reliance on the Lord.

Humility was the extension of the first element, and this is the extension of the second element of believing in the power of the Lord. Some people may ask, how are believing in the Lord's power and relying on the Lord different? There is a difference. The second element means believing firmly from the heart that the Lord has the power to rescue and set us free from the sin that is controlling us, as well as all other sins. The fourth element goes beyond believing in His power; it is longing for, seeking after, and relying upon that power. That is the difference.

Beloved, within the act of calling on the name of the Lord, which is the true expression and demonstration of faith, are these four elements. The biblical meaning of calling on the name of the Lord is when we feel total despair and impotence in our self-effort and determination, have faith in the power of the Lord to save us, and humbly cry out to God with a heart of total reliance. When we call on the name of the Lord with such a heart, the act of salvation always takes place. Therefore, I wish that you would call on the name of the Lord right now.

Those Who Call on the Name of the Lord

Today, those who need to call on the name of the Lord do not do so. The cost is horribly frightening, because the result is eternal destruction. Therefore, out of my deep desire for people to avoid God's terrifying judgment, I want to describe those people who need to desperately call on the name of the Lord.

1. Those who are not yet saved must quickly call on the name of the Lord.

Beloved, do you want to be saved? Then you must not remain still. God has resolved that the ones who will be saved are those who call on the name of the Lord. Therefore, you must call on the name of the Lord so that you will be saved.

In the Old Testament Book of Ezekiel, God made a blessed promise:

> For I will take you out of the nations; I will gather you from all the countries and bring you back into your own land. I will sprinkle clean water on you, and you will be clean; I will cleanse you from all your impurities and from all your idols. I will give you a new heart and put a new spirit in you; I will remove from you your heart of stone and give you a heart of flesh. And I will put my Spirit in you and move you to follow my decrees and be careful to keep my laws.
>
> —EZEKIEL 36:24–27

Afterward, this is what God said:

> This is what the Sovereign LORD says: Once again I will yield to the plea of the house of Israel and do this for them.
>
> — EZEKIEL 36:37

This is what Jesus said to the Samaritan woman as He evangelized to her:

Jesus answered her, "If you knew the gift of God and who it is that asks you for a drink, you would have asked him and he would have given you living water."

—JOHN 4:10

Therefore, our salvation lies upon our calling on the name of the Lord. Call on the name of the Lord, then you will receive the Holy Spirit, and you will have a new spirit! Your heart will become soft, and you will be able to live by the Lord's law and commandments. Call on the name of the Lord! Then you will be released from the sins of alcoholism, drug addiction, pornography, hatred, rage, lying, greed, unforgiveness, and all other sins that enslave you, and you will have miraculous freedom.

Beloved, I wish I could do this for you if I can. But this is something that cannot be done by someone else. No matter how much a parent loves his child and a married couple love each other, they cannot eat food or go to the bathroom for the other person. When his beloved wife is about to give birth and in terrible pain, she needs to push with all her strength so that the baby will come out; he cannot do it for her by clenching his own fist. In the same way, no one can call on the name of the Lord for someone else. You must do this yourself. Therefore, I wish that you would make your decision and call on the name of the Lord with a sincere heart.

2. Those who believed and then became corrupted must quickly call on the name of the Lord.

There are people who have called on the name of the Lord in the past and have experienced salvation and freedom from sin. Like the proverbs quoted by Peter: "'A dog returns to its vomit,' and 'A sow that is washed goes back to her wallowing in the mud,'" (2 Pet. 2:22) there are people who have gone back to their old ways.

In the past they rejoiced because they were free from the domination of sin, but now the sin dominates them again. Before, their hearts were filled with the peace that came from the Lord, but now their spirits are empty and anxious again. Before, the Lord abided in their hearts, and they felt His sweet presence. Now they cannot feel His presence at all. Are you one of them?

Please remember that even if you attend church, pay tithes, pray, and serve, but your condition is like this, you have become corrupted. Examine yourself carefully, and you will find a habitual sin in your life.

What sin is that? I will tell you. That sin is the one Jesus warned about: "If your hand causes you to sin, cut it off. It is better for you to enter life maimed than with two hands to go into hell, where the fire never goes out" (Mark 9:43). That sin is the one that Jesus warned about: "And if your foot causes you to sin, cut it off. It is better for you to enter life crippled than to have two feet and be thrown into hell" (Mark 9:45). That sin is what Jesus warned about: "And if your eye causes you to sin, pluck it out. It is better for you to enter the kingdom of God with one eye than have two eyes and be thrown into hell, where 'their worm does not die, and the fire is not quenched'" (Mark 9:47–49). Please do not be self-deceived by seeing God's kindness only, but as Paul exhorted, see God's kindness and sternness. (See Romans 11:22.) Be fearful, and cut off your sin.

At this time, some might want to say, "I want to cut off this sin, too. I want to go back to my previous state of freedom and happiness. But I cannot do it. The power of sin is too strong for me. I cannot but be dragged by this sin."

This is what I want to say to them in reply: I heard that many people take cold medication diligently, thinking it is worthwhile, but pharmacists do not prescribe it for their own children. Even if they do, they only prescribe a small portion, because they know that cold medications are harmful for the body. They let their children fight the virus without medication or with a very small amount of medication. After hearing that, I took cold medication only twice when I caught a cold, and won the fight over the virus on my own. After a while, the same cold symptoms visited me. I did not despair because I went back to my sick condition even after I fought and won the virus. Instead, I just took the medication, then I got over the cold and became healthy again.

You must have a hint of why I am saying this. Beloved, do not despair because you are in a corrupted state. How were you able to come out of sin before? You had to call on the name of the Lord. Therefore, do not despair, but call on the name of the Lord again. Then sin's bondage will be broken, and you will be free again.

3. Those who desire to live in holiness continuously must call on the name of the Lord without ceasing.

I want to remind you of an important truth.

> I am the true vine, and my Father is the gardener. He cuts off every branch in me that bears no fruit, while every branch that does bear fruit he prunes so that it will be even more fruitful. You are already clean because of the word I have spoken to you. Remain in me, and I will remain in you. No branch can bear fruit by itself; it must remain in the vine. Neither can you bear fruit unless you remain in me. I am the vine; you are the branches. If a man remains in me and I in him, he will bear much fruit; apart from me you can do nothing. If anyone does not remain in me, he is like a branch that

is thrown away and withers; such branches are picked up, thrown into the fire and burned.

—JOHN 15:1–6

This passage shows that a once-saved person can be rejected, while at the same time, saying that just as a branch remains in the vine, we must remain in Jesus until the end.

Now those who had been scattered by the persecution in connection with Stephen traveled as far as Phoenicia, Cyprus and Antioch, telling the message only to Jews. Some of them, however, men from Cyprus and Cyrene, went to Antioch and began to speak to Greeks also, telling them the good news about the Lord Jesus. The Lord's hand was with them, and a great number of people believed and turned to the Lord. News of this reached the ears of the church at Jerusalem, and they sent Barnabas to Antioch. When he arrived and saw the evidence of the grace of God, he was glad and encouraged them all to remain true to the Lord with all their hearts.

—ACTS 11:19–23

In the city of Antioch, many new believers came to be as a result of outreach. Hearing the news, the apostles sent Barnabas to them. What entreaty did Barnabas make to these new believers? He exhorted them "to remain true to the Lord with all their hearts." The reason for that was, as the analogy of the vine and the branches shows, if they did not remain in the Lord, they could not bear fruit. Such "branches" will be thrown into the fire of hell.

> For as in Adam all die, so in Christ all will be made
> alive. But each in his own turn: Christ, the firstfruits;
> then, when he comes, those who belong to him.
> —1 CORINTHIANS 15:22–23

This is a decisively important word. Who will be lifted up when Jesus returns to the earth again? Who will be resurrected and receive heaven as inheritance? Paul's answer is: "When he comes, those who belong to him." Pay attention to Paul's expression. Paul did not say, "Those who belonged to him before." He said, "When he comes, those who belong to him." This means that until the day the Lord comes, we must continuously belong to him in order to inherit God's kingdom.

Then some may ask, "Pastor, are you saying that those who have been grafted in to Christ can be broken off from Christ?" Of course, that is what I am saying; unlike some doctrines, the Bible says that. The analogy of the true vine clearly shows that truth. Paul said in Romans 11:

> If the part of the dough offered as firstfruits is holy, then
> the whole batch is holy; if the root is holy, so are the
> branches. If some of the branches have been broken off,
> and you, though a wild olive shoot, have been grafted in
> among the others and now share in the nourishing sap
> from the olive root, do not boast over those branches. If
> you do, consider this: You do not support the root, but
> the root supports you. You will say then, "Branches were
> broken off so that I could be grafted in." Granted. But
> they were broken off because of unbelief, and you stand
> by faith. Do not be arrogant, but be afraid. For if God
> did not spare the natural branches, he will not spare you
> either. Consider therefore the kindness and sternness of

God: sternness to those who fell, but kindness to you,
provided that you continue in his kindness. Otherwise,
you also will be cut off.

—ROMANS 11:16–22

Also, this is what Paul said in his letter to the Galatians:

Behold I, Paul, say to you that if you receive circumcision, Christ will be of no benefit to you. And I testify
again to every man who receives circumcision, that
he is under obligation to keep the whole law. You have
been severed from Christ, you who are seeking to be
justified by law; you have fallen from grace.

—GALATIANS 5:2–4, NAS

Likewise, today there are people who used to remain in
Christ, but are now severed from Him. They are like the
Galatian believers who did not rely on the grace of God in
Christ, but on the works of the law.

Please do not mistake my word. Paul is not saying that
because salvation comes from God's grace we can be saved
by relying on the blood of Christ and still live any way we
like. That is never true. We can immediately see that by
reading the subsequent verses in Galatians 5:16–24. Then
what is Paul saying? He is saying that we must not rely on our
strength but solely on Christ's, not only in regard to forgiveness of sin, but also in regard to our fight against sin. That
is the only way we will be victorious and actually remain in
Christ.

Paul says in Romans 11 that we remain in Him by faith.
That is true. We remain in Christ by faith, and only by faith
can we continue to remain in Him. As I said earlier, calling
on the name of the Lord signifies demonstrative faith. When

Christ returns to the earth, only those who remain in Him will be lifted up. Therefore, we must constantly call on the name of the Lord. That is the only way we will triumph over sin and remain in Christ until the end.

Salvation Comes to Those Who Call on the Name of the Lord

Do you know what the word *gospel* means? Of course there are many conditions required in salvation, but unlike the law, the gospel is not a heavy burden. The gospel means literally good news.

Why is the gospel good news? It is because the gospel is about Jesus, and Jesus is the power of God for our salvation. To experience the power of the gospel, what must we do? It is simple: we must call on the name of the Lord. All those who call on the name of the Lord can experience the power of the gospel.

Because this is so simple, many people do not believe this fact. They think, *No, that cannot be,* but it is true. I myself experience this power of the gospel. I will not tell you my testimony because there are better testimonies that more dramatically show God's power of salvation to those who call on the name of the Lord. Just as there are many people who are saved, there are many testimonies of the Lord's power of salvation to those who call on His name. I want to introduce a few of them here.

The following happened while the famous evangelist T. L. Osborne was leading a meeting in the southern city of Netherlands, The Hague. The meeting took place in a huge outdoor plaza called Maribeld, and each night more than one hundred thousand people gathered in it. One hotel owner who had antipathy toward Christianity became curious by the large number of people, and he attended the meeting.

On the day he attended, Osborne spoke on the simple and artless power of prayer and that we must pray honestly and sincerely in the Lord's name to receive a new life and be born again—that is, he spoke on the necessity of prayer. Toward the end of the sermon, Osborne once again emphasized that "everyone who calls on the name of the Lord will be saved" (Romans 10:13). Afterward, he had the public pray aloud together. When the hotel owner saw the people praying, this is what the he thought: *Are the masses gone mad? How could they all go wrong? What are they doing?*

Then he began to change his mind. "I never prayed in my life even once. I bragged about that all my life. But if I were to pray for the first time, this is the best opportunity. I will pray as the preacher showed us. If God exists God will answer His believers!"

Then he held his hands together in front of his chest, closed his eyes, and began to pray. At that moment, the presence of God, which he could not resist, came over him. He became gripped by fear. He wanted to look up to the sky all of a sudden. When he looked up, Jesus Christ was standing there. Panicked, he tried to hide, but he could not move as though bound by something.

Jesus fixed His fiery eyes upon him without a word. He knew that with His eyes, Jesus was seeing right through all his past sins, words of blasphemy against God, and his obscene talk. He felt as though all his past life scenes were displayed in front of Jesus, and because of that, he was filled with fear and trembling. He felt deep shame and guilt in front of Jesus over his wicked lifestyle. The tears that fell from his eyes made his eyes bulge as he repented from his sin before Christ.

Then, Christ touched his soul, and the face of Jesus Christ had a smile filled with love and compassion toward him. At that moment, he realized that all of his sins were forgiven, and amazing joy and comfort flooded over his heart.

With the strength left from his body, he plopped down on the ground and wept with joy. All the people around him were praising the Lord with a loud voice. He felt heaven in that place. That day, he was born again and became a new creation. Jesus came into his heart. Overjoyed, he went toward the podium. He wanted to tell what happened to his friend, but he could not talk because of his tears.

Hallelujah! Praise the Lord who is our Savior!

In 1968, a seventeen-year-old boy named Larry was admitted to Mother Francis Hospital in Tyler, Texas. His family was extremely wealthy. The size of his house was five thousand square feet. He had the second floor all to himself, which consisted of two bedrooms, two bathrooms, and a study room. Despite his good environment, he began to utter nonsense and became mentally ill, because everything he possessed was external, not internal to him.

When he was hospitalized, he was given four sedatives every four hours. As a result, he was barely conscious and at times, did not recognize people.

Then one day in his hospital room, he knelt down and cried out to God. "Jesus! Jesus! Merciful Jesus!" It was not a formal, religious prayer. He simply cried out to God, weeping and repeating the name of God over and over again.

At that time, he heard a voice speaking to his soul within him. "Now you are My son. You will spread My message in this generation. You will be My mouth and My worker." The voice said that he would become well and go home. True enough, he became completely well and left the mental hospital. Currently, he is faithfully serving God through a nationwide prayer movement.

Dr. Larry Lea wrote many books, one of which is titled *Wisdom—Don't Live Life Without It*. The following testimony is in the book. After being saved, the first person Larry Lea evangelized was a man named Jerry Howell. Jerry was a hippie and a drug addict. He was also a keyboardist for a rock-and-roll band. Before salvation, the most important goal in life for Jerry was to sit in the backyard counting the blades of grass, and struggling hard not to have a nervous breakdown. Then one day, Larry Lea called him up and said, "Jerry, I will be preaching tonight. I would like for you to come with me to New London Baptist Church and play the organ for our worship."

Jerry was surprised and asked, "You want me to come to church with you, Pastor?"

Larry Lea said, "Yes, I need your help."

Jerry said, "I don't know any of those songs, really."

Larry Lea said, "Play the hymn 'Amazing Grace.'"

Finally, Jerry consented to coming. That night around midnight after the worship service was over, he asked, "Pastor, can you tell me about Jesus?" Larry Lea immediately began to testify about Jesus. Around four o'clock in the morning, Jerry asked, "Then how do I receive salvation?" At that moment, Larry Lea realized that he did not know how to explain how one receives salvation, and he told him what he knew.

"Well, Jerry, go home and read Matthew 5 to 7 and cry out, 'Jesus! Jesus! Jesus!' When something comes up in your heart, then you will know that you are saved."

Jerry did as he was told. He took the Bible and read the three chapters of Matthew, crying out to God. At that moment, the Lord saved him.[1]

A while ago, Pastor Stephen Hill, who was famous for the great revival in the Pensacola church, came to our nation in the city of Inchun. I attended the meeting and received much blessing through his sermon. Among his sermons, the most impressive and memorable was his testimony about how he received salvation by calling out to God.

The detailed content of his testimony is written in his book, *The Pursuit of Revival.* I want to introduce what he said. I want you to know that he was a drug addict for several years before he was saved.

> On October 25, 1975, a frightening spirit of death came to take me away eternally. For four days from Saturday to Tuesday, I had an intense fit and the dark cloud of death surrounded the room. Mother watched me day and night, but I needed greater power to overcome this hellish hour...
>
> On Tuesday morning of October 28 at 10:50 a.m., while I was languishing in bed, I heard a knock on the door. I did not want to see anyone, but at the same time, I needed someone's help desperately. The sound heard from outside the door seemed that Mother had let in a young man from out of town who wanted to see me.
>
> "Mrs. Hill, may I see Steve? I have something I need to say to him."
>
> Feeling hopeless at my condition, Mother answered, "I don't know why Steve is like this, but he is desperately ill. I cannot give him any help, but please come in to help him."
>
> Mother invited him into my room. He came near to me and said, "Steve! Before, you didn't want to see me, but when I heard that you were sick, I wanted to come and see you. Of course, I cannot help you, but

here is someone who came along with me to be your great strength. His name is Jesus. Jesus is here with you right now. My most precious Friend is here to help you right now."

Tainted by fifteen years of rebellion, tears that had been corked up in a bottle poured down my cheeks. Sadness and pain flowed out along with my tears. The power of evil was still oppressing me, and my body was still in a fit. My mind was still clouded with confusion. But one thing changed. Now I knew that someone who can help me is here. I did not want to play any more religious games. I just wanted to receive Jesus' help by clinging to Him. "All my life, I never believed in Jesus. I never prayed once to God, but how can I feel that Jesus is alive?"

"Steve! Only know this. Jesus is here in this room right now. And when you call out to Him, He will come near. You don't have to pray fancy prayers. Jesus already knows your heart. Just call out 'Jesus! Jesus!'"

When I called out "Jesus!" I felt hope which I had never felt before rising up. Fear and confusion disappeared slowly as I lay in bed looking up at the ceiling. I kept yelling, "Jesus! Jesus! Jesus!"

It was the strangest sensation. Peace which I had never felt before began to surge into my body, overflowing within me. Powerful force flooded in like a river, dispelling the shadows of darkness. I kept screaming out louder, "Jesus! Jesus! Jesus!" The more I raised my voice, the greater freedom I felt. My fit stopped altogether. The power of darkness had scampered out with a tail between its legs. The walls that had risen up and down unevenly became straight again.

At this time, I felt the room filled with a different power. I knew that some beautiful divine force had come in. My young visitor did not have to explain this phenomenon. I felt the presence very vividly. Jesus Christ came and gave me a new life then. I had become a truly freed person.[2]

What do you think about this testimony? I was deeply moved by this testimony because salvation—that is, the secret to victory over sin—was shown very clearly. The way to salvation, the secret to victory, is not in something else. It is in calling on the name of the Lord. This is the only way!

John Ryle said, "Habitual lively faith in Christ's presence and readiness to help is the secret of the Christian soldier fighting successfully."[3] Robert Murray M'Cheyne who lived a saintly life wrote in his book, *The Deeper Life*, which records his series of sermons:

> There are many peripheral ways to escape from sin, and we must never take them lightly. The examples of peripheral ways are marriage (1 Corinthians 7:2), running away (1 Timothy 6:11, 1 Corinthians 6:18), staying awake and praying (Matthew 26:41), etc. And Jesus defended himself with words, "It is written." But the important way to fight against sin is the act of throwing ourselves into the arms of Jesus like a little child, and the act of requesting the Lord that the Holy Spirit would fill us. "For everyone born of God overcomes the world. This is the victory that has overcome the world, even our faith" (1 John 5:4). What wonderful words![4]

Do you think this is foolish talk? Do you think it is not possible? No, it is possible! Even now, Jesus is saying to you:

> Come to me, all you who are weary and burdened, and
> I will give you rest.
>
> —MATTHEW 11:28

Therefore, call on the name of the Lord aloud now! Rely upon the powerful hand of Christ, and give all your burden of sin to the Lord. Then God's help and power will fall upon you, and you will be free from all your habitual sins.

I will give you concluding remarks.

> Everyone who calls on the name of the Lord will be
> saved.
>
> —ROMANS 10:13

One scriptural passage comes to my mind whenever I think about this verse. It is the record about two blind men.

> As Jesus and his disciples were leaving Jericho, a large
> crowd followed him. Two blind men were sitting by the
> roadside, and when they heard that Jesus was going by,
> they shouted, "Lord, Son of David, have mercy on us!"
>
> The crowd rebuked them and told them to be quiet,
> but they shouted all the louder, "Lord, Son of David,
> have mercy on us!"
>
> Jesus stopped and called them. "What do you want
> me to do for you?" he asked.
>
> "Lord," they answered, "we want our sight."
>
> Jesus had compassion on them and touched their
> eyes. Immediately they received their sight and
> followed him.
>
> —MATTHEW 20:29–34

I believe that we must act like these blind men in order to be saved. Like the blind men, we must put our hope in the Lord even in an absolutely hopeless situation and desperately call on the name of the Lord. We must call on the Lord's name before He passes us by. That is, before the opportunity called life passes us by, we must call on the name of the Lord. Like numerous souls in hell, we must not be the foolish one who calls again and again to the Lord despite the fact that there is no more promise of hope in the fiery pit of hell after the opportunity has passed. The Bible records that Jesus had compassion when He heard the cry of the blind men. Jesus is the Lord of love. Jesus cannot refuse the cries and weeping of those who call to Him, because His heart is filled with deep pity toward the sinners. Paul expresses this truth in the following passage.

> As the Scripture says, "Anyone who trusts in him will never be put to shame." For there is no difference between Jew and Gentile—the same Lord is Lord of all and richly blesses all who call on him, for "Everyone who calls on the name of the Lord will be saved."
> —ROMANS 10:11–13

When we look at this passage carefully, the words *anyone* and *everyone* appear. Between these words, the verse appears which explains the meaning of these words.

> The same Lord is Lord of all and richly blesses all who call on him.
> —ROMANS 10:12

That is right. The Lord richly blesses all those who call on Him. The Lord is never stingy. He never helps certain people, while rejecting certain other people. He will bestow His gift of salvation to all who call on His name.

We must also remember that He not only richly blesses all who call on Him, but He showers rich blessings on each individual person. What I mean is that someone might have received salvation by calling on the name of the Lord, and then he fell away. Even still, if that person calls on the name of the Lord again, he will not be destroyed, because the Lord will once again free him from sin.

How many times will the Lord do that? I believe He will do that without end, because the one who said to forgive "seventy times seven," (Matt. 18:22, NAS) is Jesus Himself. Therefore, do not waste time on useless feelings of condemnation and despair. The Lord loves everyone. The Lord is ready to help those who would call on Him. So I urge you to cry out the name of the Lord with the loudest voice! The Lord will free you from sin by His mighty power. Some people might say this after hearing my words, "Pastor, I did call on the name of the Lord. I cried out with the loudest voice, and I even fasted. But still, I am not free from sin. What went wrong?"

Actually, I had the same question before, but I discovered the answer through Mrs. Choo Thomas's book *Heaven Is So Real!* In this book, there is a record of the conversation between the Lord and Choo Thomas.

> "Lord, I know some Christians are very faithful, but they still have their old habits. Why can't You change them?"
>
> "Whoever wants to be changed will receive My help. If they ask Me for whatever they want I will give it to them if I know they are sincere and if they persevere. I will answer their prayers. Many of My children,

however, do not pray sincerely or long enough. If they do not have patience, they cannot receive a blessing.

"My daughter, you are so persistent. You never give up. You keep on asking Me for what you want in prayer. I hear your every prayer."

"Yes, Lord, I do not give up until I receive because I know You have all my answers. One of my Bible teachers told me to never give up praying for something you want. That's why I am very persistent in my prayers, Lord.

"I know You have the answers I need, especially in my personal prayers. You have answered more of my prayers than I ever expected. Thank You, Lord."

"I love persistent children. People's persistence proves their faithfulness, and by this I know that they believe I hold the answers to all their prayers."[5]

What important words! These words are light to those who are in despair. Pray! Pray with faith in these words: "With man this is impossible, but with God all things are possible" (Matt. 19:26). Do not let go of this faith, but "always pray and not give up" as Jesus told us in Luke 18:1. Jesus said, "When the Son of Man comes, will he find faith on the earth?" (Luke 18:8). The Lord wants to see such faith in the last days. Therefore, do not give up, but hold firmly to faith and pray continually. Then you will see salvation.

Remember! Heaven belongs to those who violently take it by force. A nation that hopes to capture another nation cannot win the war with just one shot. We must continually shoot until we take the nation by force. It is the same way with heaven when we violently take it by force.

Chapter 10

Up to Seventy Times Seven

Then Peter came to Jesus and asked, "Lord, how many times shall I forgive my brother when he sins against me? Up to seven times?" Jesus answered, "I tell you, not seven times, but seventy-seven times. Therefore, the kingdom of heaven is like a king who wanted to settle accounts with his servants. As he began the settlement, a man who owed him ten thousand talents was brought to him. Since he was not able to pay, the master ordered that he and his wife and his children and all that he had be sold to repay the debt. The servant fell on his knees before him. 'Be patient with me,' he begged, 'and I will pay back everything.' The servant's master took pity on him, canceled the debt and let him go. But when that servant went out, he found one of his fellow servants who owed him a hundred denarii. He grabbed him and began to choke him. 'Pay back what you owe me!' he demanded. His fellow servant fell to his knees and begged him, 'Be patient with me, and I will pay you back.' But he refused. Instead, he went off and had the man thrown into prison until he could pay the debt. When the other servants saw what had happened, they were greatly distressed and went and told their master everything that had happened. Then the master called the servant in. 'You wicked servant,' he said, 'I canceled all that debt of yours because you begged me to. Shouldn't you have had mercy on your fellow servant just as I had on you?' In anger his master turned him over to the jailers to be tortured, until he should pay back all he owed. This is how my heavenly Father will treat each of you unless you forgive your brother from your heart."

–MATTHEW 18:21-35

IDO NOT LIKE to beat around the bush, and so I will ask you one question first: "Beloved, have you with all your heart forgiven every person who has sinned against you? Is there any person whom you have not forgiven? Have you truly forgiven every single person who has sinned against you?"

This question is very important, because your eternal home will be decided according to your answer. This passage begins with the following familiar question:

> Lord, how many times shall I forgive my brother when
> he sins against me? Up to seven times?
> —MATTHEW 18:21

This question must be understood in the context of the cultural background at the time. During that period, the Jews were in the habit of quantifying their religious duties. In the Apocrypha, a man named Ben Sira mentioned that a neighbor who has committed a sin must be given two opportunities (see Ecclesiasticus 19:13–17); the rabbis taught that the neighbor's crime must be forgiven three times and no more (Amos 1:3; 2:1; Talmud, Yoma 86b). Peter, however, suggested that they forgive seven times. He was expecting a compliment when he said that. However, his expectation turned into shock when Jesus replied:

> I tell you, not seven times, but seventy-seven times.
> —MATTHEW 18:22

Generally, this command of Jesus cannot be understood easily. To forgive someone else's sin seventy-seven times was too extreme. Jesus knew what their reaction would be, so He went on to explain to His disciples why they must forgive seventy-seven times by telling a parable. This parable is called "the parable of the unmerciful servant."

This parable contains the greatest teaching on forgiveness in the whole Bible. Very important truths about forgiveness are implied in this parable. Unfortunately, there are not many people who honestly face the truths shown in this parable. So many people are in grave danger, yet they do not realize it.

The Absolute Duty Given to All Christians—Forgiveness!

Today, too many people believe in the wrong doctrine that says, "Once saved, never rejected." This doctrine gives birth to negligence, encouraging corruption and polluting other words of God. This doctrine pollutes our passage regarding forgiveness as well. Jesus gave a very serious warning in verse 35:

> This is how my heavenly Father will treat each of you unless you forgive your brother from your heart.
> —MATTHEW 18:35

Do you know to whom Jesus was speaking when He said that? He was speaking to believers. Jesus was not referring to unbelievers in the parable. In the passage, the servant received a tremendous cancellation of debt (salvation), and was called the servant of the master.

I will ask you this question. Are the unbelievers God's servants? Did they receive cancellation (forgiveness of sin) of their debt (sin)? No, therefore, the fearful warning in verse 35 is given to Christians—not just Christians by name, but genuine Christians.

Why did Jesus give such a warning? He said this because Christians who are saved can be unforgiving, and if they remain unforgiving, their souls will be destroyed. If there was no such possibility, Jesus would never have told this parable.

This parable has its basis on the teaching that those who are saved can be destroyed. (For those who would like to learn more about this truth, I recommend David Pawson's book *Once Saved, Always Saved?*) Besides this parable, many biblical warnings and words speak this truth. If one believes that a person who is saved once can never be rejected, he must inevitably dilute or alter the meaning of the words every time he encounters similar passages in the Bible, so that his creed can fit in.

In other words, this parable is given to Christians. Jesus reveals that forgiveness is absolutely essential to Christians. To a certain extent, it is acceptable if nonbelievers do not forgive because they are already bound for hell because of their sins. But since Christians are different from nonbelievers, they must always forgive.

Then why must Christians forgive others? There are two reasons for that.

1. They were forgiven.

The servant in the passage signifies Christians who have been forgiven a tremendous debt of ten thousand talents. How much is ten thousand talents?

At the time of Jesus, talents were circulated by the Judean and Roman societies to be the highest unit of currency. One talent was six thousand times the average worker's daily wage of one denarius. Therefore, one talent equaled twenty years of wage by one laborer. However, it was not just one talent, but ten thousand talents. Ten thousand talents, therefore, meant two hundred thousand years of wage by one laborer, which was an astronomical amount.

According to the Jewish historian Josephus, annual taxes levied from the whole region of Judea amounted to only eight hundred talents. By now, you can imagine what a tremendous amount of money ten thousand talents was.

This parable can be seen as too extreme and unrealistic. The king was overly generous. Without a doubt, the sin of the servant cannot be overlooked without any punishment. However, this is in reality the way God deals with those who approach Him with faith. Therefore, it is written in the Bible, "He does not treat us as our sins deserve or repay us according to our iniquities" (Ps. 103:10).

However, the parable does not end here. The servant who was miraculously forgiven of ten thousand talents came out and met a fellow servant who owed him a hundred denarii. During the time of Jesus, one denarius equaled a day's wage for an average laborer or a soldier, and amounted to only one six thousandth of a talent. Compared to ten thousand talents, one hundred denarii would be only six hundred thousandth of a talent. Therefore, the servant in the passage should have naturally forgiven his fellow servant. But astonishingly, he refused to forgive his fellow servant and threw the begging man into prison.

Ten thousand talents and one hundred denarii! The exorbitant difference between these two amounts shows how great is the difference between our sin against God and other people's sin against us. No matter how much other people have wronged us, it is nothing compared to the sin we have committed against God. Therefore, we must willingly forgive other people with all our hearts.

On the other hand, we must not fail to notice that although one denarius is nothing compared to ten thousand talents, it is still not a small amount of money. One hundred denarii is still a large sum—one third of a year's wages. If you were to lose one third of your year's salary, how would you feel? That is why many people have a difficult time forgiving other people.

We can learn an important lesson from this fact. Please listen carefully. If you want to forgive others, you must not linger on one hundred denarii. You must not think about one hundred denarii but one thousand talents. That is, you must not dwell on the sins that you need to forgive, but the sins of which you were forgiven. And you must consider the magnitude of your sins that were forgiven rather than the measure of sins committed against you. That is how you will be able to forgive others who have wronged you, no matter how grave their sins.

I will give you a real-life example regarding this truth. It occurred in Germany right after World War II. People were panic-stricken and torn by the war. One night a group of gangsters looted an isolated farm and ruthlessly murdered the entire family on that farm.

At the time, the police force on duty ran toward the scene after hearing a gunshot, and they arrested a few of the gangsters. They found that the oldest son was still breathing and took him to the emergency room at the hospital. As a result, the boy was able to make a narrow escape from the jaws of death.

Twenty years later, the oldest son, rising out of his painful memory, became a successful businessman and established a happy home. One day, he heard that one of the gangsters who had murdered his family had finished his prison term, but was not released by the authorities because he did not have any place to go. When he heard the news, he made an important decision after much agony. He decided to request the authorities to release the murderer, with himself as the guardian.

In the petition that he submitted to the authorities, he stated that we are all sinners and since Jesus Christ died for his sins and forgave him, he must forgive other people, too. (See Romans 3:23; 1 Corinthians 15:3; and Matthew 6:14.)

This is the reason we must forgive other people. At the same time, this is the secret to be able to forgive others sincerely.

Pastor John Flavel wrote this:

> The mercy of God to us should melt our hearts into mercy toward others. It is impossible that we should be cruel to others, except we forget how kind and compassionate God hath been to us. [1]

2. They need to be forgiven.

There are three daily necessities in life—our daily bread, God's forgiveness, and God's protection. We need these three every day. That is why Jesus taught us to pray the following prayer:

> Give us today our daily bread. Forgive us our debts, as we also have forgiven our debtors. And lead us not into temptation, but deliver us from the evil one.
> —MATTHEW 6:11–13

We must pray this prayer daily because these are essential to us. Jesus said in Matthew 18:35: "This is how my heavenly Father will treat each of you unless you forgive your brother from your heart." Likewise, those who do not forgive others cannot receive forgiveness themselves.

The following account happened a few years ago in America.

A woman in Denver, Colorado, had a daughter in her thirties in a seminary, but one day the daughter was ruthlessly stabbed to death by a murderer. That murderer had killed many other women before, and he was finally caught and arrested by a policeman. After the death of her daughter, the mother, a believer, fell into great sadness and despair. She blamed God and was filled with hatred toward the murderer.

One Saturday night, God spoke to her. "If you do not forgive the murder, I cannot forgive you as well. Since you cannot forgive the sin of another, I cannot forgive your sin."

After hearing God's voice, she came to her senses at last. She decided to forgive the criminal who had murdered her daughter and gave him a Bible through a member of the Gideon Society. When, by God's miraculous work, the murderer accepted Jesus Christ, she helped him to study in a seminary through correspondence courses. Afterward, the murderer became a prison missionary. The forgiven criminal became the servant of God instead of her daughter.

Beloved, as God spoke to the lady who lost her daughter, we cannot be forgiven if we do not forgive others.

Of course the Bible records, "If we confess our sins, he is faithful and just and will forgive us our sins and purify us from all unrighteousness" (1 John 1:9). As a result, we can easily assume that we will be forgiven only by confessing our sins. However, Jesus taught that we must pray, "Forgive us our debts, as we also have forgiven our debtors" (Matt. 6:12). Also, Jesus clearly said, "For if you forgive men when they sin against you, your heavenly Father will also forgive you. But if you do not forgive men their sins, your Father will not forgive your sins" (Matt. 6:14–15). Therefore, even if we confess our sins, we will never be forgiven if we have not forgiven other people's sins.

There is one very regrettable fact, however. Even though the Bible clearly records that those who do not forgive cannot receive forgiveness, many Christians do not accept this truth literally.

Pastor John Bevere wrote in his book *The Bait of Satan*:

> Today, I wonder how many Christians wish to receive God's forgiveness in the same way that they forgive others' sins against them? However, this is the only way to receive forgiveness. These days, too many hearts in the churches are unforgiving, and that is why we do not listen to God's word with seriousness. Whether or not unforgiving hearts are prevalent, the truth never changes. We will receive forgiveness in the same way that we forgive, pacify, and restore others.[2]

In reality, many people like to say this: "If only the ones who do the will of God can to go heaven, do you mean that many people will go to hell? (See Matthew 7:21.) How can that be?" People respond the same way to the issue of forgiveness. "Are you saying that the unforgiving cannot be forgiven? Then Christians who are unforgiving will all fall into hell? How can that be?" To those people, I say, "It is true!"

Those who will not forgive can never receive forgiveness themselves, no matter how much they believe in Jesus and confess their sins. Forgiveness of sins belongs to those who forgive others. Jesus said, "Do not judge, and you will not be judged. Do not condemn, and you will not be condemned. Forgive, and you will be forgiven" (Luke 6:37). Everyone reaps what he sows. Those who sow forgiveness will reap forgiveness; those who sow condemnation will reap condemnation.

Please repeat after me: "Forgiving others means forgiving myself, condemning others means condemning myself."

Therefore, I wish that we would all forgive other people who sin against us.

The Mark of Forgiveness That God Requires of Us

As I was saying before, forgiveness is a command of God that we must not disobey. We do not have the right to choose whether to forgive. We are God's forgiven ones. In other words, we are indebted to God's love.

Not only that, we need God's forgiveness every single day. Jesus said, "A person who has had a bath needs only to wash his feet" (John 13:10), and "Unless I wash you, you have no part with me" (John 13:8). Therefore, we do not have any right to choose. We must forgive others. In many cases, we thought we had forgiven others, but in God's eyes, the forgiveness did not occur. We must forgive the way God wants us to forgive, according to His standard.

> Get rid of all bitterness, rage and anger, brawling and slander, along with every form of malice. Be kind and compassionate to one another, forgiving each other, just as in Christ God forgave you.
> —EPHESIANS 4:31–32

God wants us to forgive others the way God forgave us. Then how did God forgive us? God forgave us using two methods. Therefore, we must follow His example and forgive others using these two methods as well.

1. God forgives us daily and ceaselessly.

When Peter asked how many times he should forgive his brother, Jesus answered that he must forgive even up to seventy-seven times. (See Matthew 18:21–22.)

He did not say to forgive just seventy-seven times. Therefore, this verse does not mean to forgive only four hundred ninety times. Jesus meant that we should forgive ceaselessly and unconditionally until He returns at His Second Coming.

Then why must we forgive someone unconditionally? It is because God forgives us unconditionally. I want to ask, how many times were you forgiven by God when you confessed your sins? Only seven? No, we must have been forgiven far more than four hundred ninety times.

How many times do you believe God will forgive you in the future? No matter how many times we will sin in the future, God will forgive us unconditionally when we realize our sin and sincerely repent. That is the reason why we must forgive others unconditionally.

About a month ago during our dawn prayer meeting, the Holy Spirit spoke to me regarding Peter's question and Jesus' answer: "What is important about forgiveness is not how many times we forgive, but our firm determination to forgive unconditionally. What Jesus is requiring in this passage is not how many times to forgive, but to live a life of forgiveness in this world as a person who forgives."

That is right. It is not the number that matters; the Lord wants us to live a life of forgiveness with firm determination. This is what the Lord wants of us.

2. God forgives us with all His heart.

When God forgives us, He forgives us with all His heart. That is why the Bible records the following:

> As far as the east is from the west, so far has he removed our transgressions from us.
>
> —PSALM 103:12

For I will forgive their wickedness and will remember their sins no more.

—JEREMIAH 31:34

But if a wicked man turns away from all the sins he has committed and keeps all my decrees and does what is just and right, he will surely live; he will not die. None of the offenses he has committed will be remembered against him. Because of the righteous things he has done, he will live.

—EZEKIEL 18:21–22

Who is a God like you, who pardons sin and forgives the transgression of the remnant of his inheritance? You do not stay angry forever but delight to show mercy. You will again have compassion on us; you will tread our sins underfoot and hurl all our iniquities into the depths of the sea.

—MICAH 7:18–19

Likewise, when God forgives us, He truly forgives us. Therefore, we must forgive others the way God forgives us. We must forgive sincerely from our heart. Sometimes we say that we forgive, but in reality, we have not really forgiven. In that case, we will recall the person's evil deed against us and be filled with anger or anguish. We feel this way because we have not truly forgiven the other person from our heart. In Matthew 18:35, Jesus says, "This is how my heavenly Father will treat each of you unless you forgive your brother from your heart." Therefore, we must not only forgive with our mouths, but must do so sincerely from our hearts.

Then what is forgiving from our heart? Forgiving from our heart means forgiveness in which our word and deed and heart coincide. In other words, it has no future recollection or revenge, or even a glimpse of hurt feelings. This is forgiving from our heart. In the passage, Jesus requires that first we forgive, and second, we forgive from our heart. The quantity of forgiveness must be endless, and the quality of forgiveness must be sincere. The point of the parable of the unmerciful servant is not simply endless number of forgiveness, but endless number of forgiveness from the heart. Therefore, we must always forgive others sincerely and endlessly.

The Great Price That Unforgiving Christians Must Pay

The Lord spoke of the frightening price that an unforgiving person must pay in this life and in the life to come.

> Then the master called the servant in. "You wicked servant," he said, "I canceled all that debt of yours because you begged me to. Shouldn't you have had mercy on your fellow servant just as I had on you?" In anger his master turned him over to the jailers to be tortured, until he should pay back all he owed. This is how my heavenly Father will treat each of you unless you forgive your brother from your heart.
>
> —MATTHEW 18:32–35

This passage contains the price that must be paid. Let us find out the price that the unforgiving must pay.

1. The unforgiving person loses his freedom.

In the passage, the master turned the evil, unforgiving servant over to the jailers. In other words, he had to be imprisoned in jail. Now, I would like to ask you. Can the person who lost his freedom be happy? To our eyes, those confined in prison and those who live in a communist country do not seem happy; that is because they do not have freedom.

Patrick Henry once said, "Give me liberty or give me death." Freedom is an essential element for human happiness. When a person does not forgive, he has lost his freedom. Because of that, he is miserable.

2. The unforgiving person will be tortured.

In the passage, the words "turned over to the jailers" appear (v. 34). In Greek, the "jailers" are called *basanistais.* Basanistais are not simply jail-keepers, but ones who torture. That is, they are troubleshooters who exert pressure upon the guilty and his family to take back the money that is owed.

To help your understanding, I will explain the situation during that period. At the time, people would often bury their money or treasure under the ground for safekeeping. Even when they needed to pay back their debt, they would pretend that they did not have any money. In that case, the creditor would hire a troubleshooter to exert pressure upon the debtors to find the buried money or treasure.

These troubleshooters would use torture as a means to find the buried treasure. In *Webster's Dictionary*, torture is defined as "a physical or mental pain" or "to inflict great pain in order to punish, force, or to receive sadistic pleasure." Then who exactly are the jailers—the troubleshooters—that Jesus mentions? They are evil spirits. God allows evil spirits to inflict physical or mental pain to those who are unforgiving, even if they are Christians.

Today, doctors and scientists relate disorders such as arthritis and cancer with unforgiving or grievous hearts. Also, many mental disorders are related to unforgiving hearts.

In reality, a great number of illnesses, and even demonization, is traced to unforgiving, hate-filled hearts. In many cases where prayers do not cure illnesses and drive out demons, the cause lies in the unforgiving heart. That is why Jesus said in Mark 11:22–26:

> "Have faith in God," Jesus answered. "I tell you the truth, if anyone says to this mountain, 'Go, throw yourself into the sea,' and does not doubt in his heart but believes that what he says will happen, it will be done for him. Therefore I tell you, what ever you ask for in prayer, believe that you have received it, and it will be yours. And when you stand praying, if you hold anything against anyone, forgive him, so that your Father in heaven may forgive you your sins."

3. The unforgiving person will not be forgiven himself.

> This is how my heavenly Father will treat each of you unless you forgive your brother from your heart.
> —MATTHEW 18:35

Such a message appears not only in this verse, but in many other verses in the Bible.

> For if you forgive men when they sin against you, your heavenly Father will also forgive you. But if you do not forgive men their sins, your Father will not forgive your sins.
> —MATTHEW 6:14–15

And when you stand praying, if you hold anything against anyone, forgive him, so that your Father in heaven may forgive you your sins.

—MARK 11:25

Do not judge, and you will not be judged. Do not condemn, and you will not be condemned. Forgive, and you will be forgiven.

—LUKE 6:37

Those who do not forgive others cannot be forgiven. Therefore, we must forgive others who sin against us.

4. The unforgiving person will spend eternity in hell.

Matthew 18:34 records that "in anger his master turned him over to the jailers to be tortured, until he should pay back all he owed." Here, "until he should pay back all he owed" suggests the possibility of attaining the limited end. That is why Catholics use this passage to assert the existence of purgatory. However, as Chrysostom well pointed out, this phrase excludes a fixed limited end. That is, the phrase "until he should pay back all he owed" is a strong expression of permanence and impossibility because it is impossible for an individual person to pay back ten thousand talents. Therefore, this phrase is pronouncing a life sentence, and symbolizes eternal punishment in the lake of fire in hell. Therefore, one who does not forgive others will go to hell even though he may be a Christian.

The famous evangelist D. L. Moody said, "Notice that when you go into the door of God's kingdom, you go in through the door of forgiveness."[3]

Also, John Ryle wrote:

Forgiven souls *are forgiving.* They do as they have been done by. They look over the offences of their brethren. They endeavour to "walk in love, as Christ loved them, and gave Himself for them" (Eph 5:2). They remember how God for Christ's sake forgave them, and endeavour to do the same towards their fellow-creatures....All ideas of heaven in which forgiveness has not a place, are castles in the air and vain fancies. Forgiveness is the way by which every saved soul enters heaven. Forgiveness is the only title by which he remains in heaven. Forgiveness is the eternal subject of song with all the redeemed who inhabit heaven. Surely an unforgiving soul in heaven would find his heart completely out of tune. Surely we know nothing of Christ's love to us but the name of it, if we do not love our brethren.[4]

John Ryle said that unforgiving people are unfit for heaven, and his words are true. This is illustrated clearly by the experience of Dick Mills, a famous evangelist. While Dick Mills was leading a meeting in a certain city, he was taken to the hospital emergency room because of his fever of 40° Celsius (104° Fahrenheit) due to pneumonia. He lay unconscious in the emergency room, and this is what he wrote about that time:

The moment I fainted, I heard a shout, "The pastor is dead!" Then I died and was moving toward heaven...It is not easy for me to share this because it does not show my good side, but I must be honest...While the emergency crew was endeavoring to administer oxygen inhalations to me, I was meeting Jesus and we shared a conversation. At that time, Jesus pointed to a city and asked, "Do you know that city exists eternally?" So I acknowledged, "Yes, I know that one of the names of heaven is the eternal city"... "Do you know that everything in that place is based on the rule of harmony?" Jesus asked again. So I answered, "Yes, I know." Then Jesus asked, "Do you know that you are losing the harmony?" Then I acknowledged, "Yes, I know."[5]

Mills had hostility toward a certain person who had become his competitor. During the subsequent conversation, Jesus reminded him of the tremendous debt of sin that Jesus had forgiven him and the fact that Jesus never mentioned that sin again. Despite that, he had nursed a dreadful poison in his heart to harm another person. Mills continued to confess his experience.

Jesus asked, "Don't you think that you need to go and love the person you had hostility toward?" So I answered, "Yes, I will do that. When I return and love the person, I will be victorious." Jesus said, "I will send you back." When I woke up, I was on the fourth floor of the hospital, and my wife and a nurse were cooling my fever and praying to God to bring me back.[6]

As he recollected his apparent death experience, Mills made an important confession.

As I trafficked between this world and afterlife, I realized how meaningless it was to harbor such hostility in my heart. Actually, I could not enter heaven because of that feeling. And as I traveled both worlds, I realized that my priority has suddenly changed. Now what I value the most is to stand pure and blameless before the Lord.[7]

As Dick Mills testified, unforgiving people are not fit to go to heaven. They cannot be in harmony with heaven, because heaven is the country of love. Therefore, those who do not forgive, no matter who they are, cannot go to heaven. This truth is also revealed through the testimony of a pastor in the Philippines.

That pastor became wealthy and successful in business, but he rebelled against the call of God. His disobedience brought misfortune in his life, as he ended up being carried to the hospital with a heart attack. During the operation, he died and saw himself standing outside heaven's door. There he saw Jesus about to judge his disobedience. He pleaded with the Lord, saying that if He would lengthen his life on earth, he would serve Him. The Lord answered his earnest prayer.

Before his soul returned to his body, the Lord showed him hell. He saw his mother-in-law burning in hell. He was shocked to see that view because his mother-in-law was a Christian who went to church diligently and always recited the "prayer of repentance."

Curious, he asked the Lord, "Why is she in hell?"

The Lord answered, "Because she did not forgive her friends, she cannot be forgiven."

Likewise, those who do not forgive others will not be forgiven themselves, and for their payment of sin, they will be thrown into hell.

The following account occurred a few days ago at dawn. I had a conversation with a deacon at our church. She said that her mother-in-law died, but without forgiving her husband, who caused so much heartache and pain throughout their marriage. She wanted to know if her mother-in-law had gone to heaven. This is what I told her: "If she died without having forgiven her husband, I believe she went to hell."

As I said that, once again I felt an acute sense of how important it is that preachers know the truth and teach it correctly. Not only for preachers, but for all who have elderly parents, I must ask you to listen carefully. Instead of assuming that "since they believe in Jesus, they will go to heaven," make sure that your parents repent thoroughly from all their sins and forgive all those whom they have not forgiven before they die. This is very important, because those who have not forgiven others can never go to heaven. That is the reason I included this message in this book even though it is not a direct message on the doctrine of salvation.

This is my conclusion. Today, we live in a culture where our intention and our words do not always have the same meaning. For example, when someone tells us something, his words and what he means by them do not always coincide. That is why, without our realizing, we are not seriously listening to what the other person is saying.

Such a phenomenon begins in childhood. A parent says to his child, "You will be spanked if you do that again!" Nevertheless, the child keeps doing the same thing repeatedly. Every time he repeats that action he receives the same warning from his parent, but no follow-up measures are taken to correct the child's behavior. Even when the punishment is given, it is either too light or too severe than the original warning.

Through these events, the child believes that his parents are not sincere about what they say; he may even believe their words to be lies. The child takes up a habit of thinking that the words of his parents and other authority figures are not all truthful. As a result, he becomes confused as to when he should listen seriously to the words of his elders, and whether to even listen to them at all. Such an attitude is projected unto all areas of life, so the child then sees his teachers, friends, leaders, employers from the same perspective. As he grows into adulthood, his frame of thought becomes normalized, and now his own words form insincere promises.

Let us take an example of a fictitious conversation. Let us pretend that a person met his acquaintance for the first time in a long while. At the time, he was in the middle of a busy schedule so he thought, *I do not want to talk with him now. I have no time!* He was not happy to see his acquaintance, but he greeted him, "I am so happy to see you!" After a short conversation, he ended the conversation, "Let's get together sometime for lunch."

In reality, the man was not glad to see his friend. He had no intention of having lunch with him. However, he said those empty words in order to escape the situation quickly and to feel less guilty about it. His words contained absolutely no sincerity.

Such a situation occurs frequently in real life. Today, most people speak the truth less than one quarter of the time. Therefore, it is very difficult to figure out when to take seriously the words of another.

Do you know why I am saying these words? I want to point out that people responded to the words of Jesus the same way. The Bible says, "Let God be true, and every man a liar" (Rom. 3:4). Though people may lie, God is the only being who cannot lie. Therefore, we must not take in the words of God the way we take in the words of our peers and superiors.

The words of Jesus contain His real intentions. The Lord is always sincere. The Lord always speaks honest words, transcending our cultures. Therefore, the words, "This is how my heavenly Father will treat each of you unless you forgive your brother from your heart" (Matt. 18:35), are literal truth. This word is not a bluff and will happen literally.

The words, "Not everyone who says to me, 'Lord, Lord,' will enter the kingdom of heaven, but only he who does the will of my Father who is in heaven" (Matt. 7:21), are not a bluff. These words are true, and this will surely happen. Therefore, when we receive God's Word, we must receive it as the word of truth. We must be fearful and tremble before the Word of God.

> This is the one I esteem: he who is humble and contrite in spirit, and trembles at my word.
>
> —Isaiah 66:2

— Chapter 11 —

SAINT CHUNHYANG

I am jealous for you with a godly jealously. I promised you to one husband, to Christ, so that I might present you as a pure virgin to him. But I am afraid that just as Eve was deceived by the serpent's cunning, your minds may somehow be led astray from your sincere and pure devotion to Christ.

—2 CORINTHIANS 11:2-3

MY LAST NAME is Byun. In my school days, my friends would jokingly give me the nickname, Governor Byun, who in Korean folklore tried to take Chunhyang by force when she was secretly married to a young lord named Yi. It is humorous that I am commenting on Chunhyang, but I believe that all of us must be like Saint Chunhyang, who represents "Ye-doryung" (Lord Jesus), rather than "Yi-doryung" (Lord Yi). We must be like Saint Francis, or Saint Anthony, or Saint Damien. That is why I chose the title of this message to be "Saint Chunhyang."

> But I am afraid that just as Eve was deceived by the serpent's cunning, your minds may somehow be led astray from your sincere and pure devotion to Christ.
> —2 CORINTHIANS 11:3

The most important part of this verse are the words, "to Christ." Our hearts must always be toward Christ. In the passage, Paul points out that our heart toward Christ must be "sincere and pure." Here, "sincere and pure" means not mixed and duplicated. That is, it means pure and not blended with other things. Sincerity and purity mean the singleness of devotion toward Christ. In other words, it means single-heartedness toward Christ.

During the thirty years of my Christian living, the emphasis in my faith life has changed several times. Only recently however, I have found the proper emphasis. Currently, my emphasis is to concentrate and fix my gaze only upon Jesus with a sincere and pure heart. That is, my emphasis is to seek Jesus as my purpose and to love Jesus. This is the emphasis of my faith.

Spiritual renewal, victory over sin, true freedom, internal peace, and standing firm without falling all depend upon this. Therefore, there is nothing more important than setting our hearts toward Jesus. That is why I want to take this time to speak to you about the importance of having a heart toward Jesus.

God's Concept of Corruption Is Different From Our Concept of Corruption

People consider almost everyone who goes to church as people belonging to God. However, before the coming of Jesus the rebellion will take place, and many people in the church will betray Jesus.

> Concerning the coming of our Lord Jesus Christ and our being gathered to him, we ask you, brothers, not to become easily unsettled or alarmed by some prophecy, report or letter supposed to have come from us, saying that the day of the Lord has already come. Don't let

anyone deceive you in any way, for that day will not come until the rebellion occurs and the man of lawlessness is revealed, the man doomed to destruction.

—2 THESSALONIANS 2:1–3

This does not only pertain to the future. Already there are too many people who are corrupted within the church. This statement sounds extreme, and so people may have a hard time accepting this fact. The reason people have difficulty accepting it is because they hold a shallow view of corruption.

Then what is corruption? Corruption does not merely signify denying Jesus as Peter did, or committing a moral sin as Samson and David did. The problem of corruption is far more essential and comprehensive.

The first person to become corrupt was Eve. Eve became corrupt after eating the forbidden fruit. However, her corruption does not simply lie in her act of eating. That is, corruption is not merely an action. It has an essential side to it. That is why Paul wrote in the passage:

But I am afraid that just as Eve was deceived by the serpent's cunning, your minds may somehow be led astray from your sincere and pure devotion to Christ.

—2 CORINTHIANS 11:3

Here, notice carefully the words "just as." Paul feared that the same thing that happened to Eve would happen to the Corinthian believers, that the believers' hearts would drift away from their sincere and pure devotion to Christ. This is what first happened to Eve, and this is what was about to happen to the Corinthian believers. That is why Paul warned them.

Therefore, corruption is nothing special. When our hearts wander away from sincere and pure devotion to Christ, we are corrupt even though we may not betray Him or commit a moral sin. Jesus does not consider corrupt only those who deny Him or fall into ethical decay. He regards everyone whose hearts are away from Christ as corrupt. Therefore, we must seriously examine where our hearts are pointed.

When rain falls from the sky, it flows down to the valley. The stream from the valley flows to the lake, the lake flows to the river, and the river flows to the ocean. Originally, the rain forms as the ocean water evaporates. Likewise, as the rainwater flows toward the ocean, our heart must continuously flow toward Jesus Christ. We must become a lake whose water is constantly flowing toward Jesus Christ.

However, do our hearts truly flow toward Christ? If our hearts do not flow toward Christ, but toward money, fame, authority, pleasure, even the Word of God, spiritual gifts, miracles, or prosperity, we are corrupt. Therefore, we must not think lightly but seriously about this. We must examine our current spiritual state. Then how can we know the direction of our hearts' flow? That is, how can we know whether we are in a corrupt state? We can know by the following three things.

1. We can know by examining our thoughts.

Our heart flows through our mind. Therefore, when we look at our thoughts, we will know where our heart is flowing.

> For he is the kind of man who is always thinking about the cost.
>
> —Proverbs 23:7

Dr. A. W. Tozer said that the true god a person serves is in the unconscious place where he spreads out his wings to fly and folds his wings to rest. When you go to that place, you will find that person's god.

This statement touches the core of the problem. Therefore, for those who daily think about how to make money, their god is money. For those who daily think about what other people think of them, their god is honor. For those who fall into dirty, sexual fantasy, their god is pleasure. Even though such people come to church and confess their faith, they are idolaters. Therefore, we must take every thought captive to Christ and "fix our eyes on Jesus" (Heb. 12:2), as the author of Hebrews exhorts. We must become the people who fix our gaze steadily upon Jesus.

2. We can know by examining what we value.

> No one can serve two masters. Either he will hate the one and love the other, or he will be devoted to the one and despise the other. You cannot serve both God and Money.
>
> —MATTHEW 6:24

Jesus declared that we cannot serve both God and money. He revealed that the reason is, "either he will hate the one and love the other, or he will be devoted to the one and despise the other." Jesus' words are so true, because they portray what true service is all about. True service is not simply confessing our faith and participating in worship and church services. It is not about giving tithes. True service is the expression of our hearts that love and cherish Him.

If we love and value someone, our heart will flow toward that person. Therefore, if we know what we truly love and value, then we will know the direction of our heart.

3. We can know by examining our heart's desire.

> As the deer pants for streams of water, so my soul pants
> for you, O God.
>
> —PSALM 42:1

> Whom have I in heaven but you? And earth has nothing
> I desire besides you.
>
> —PSALM 73:25

If these scriptural verses describe your spirit, then your heart is flowing toward Christ. In Psalm 105:4, it is recorded: "Look to the LORD and his strength; seek his face always."

Of course Jesus said, "Stay in the city until you have been clothed with power from on high" (Luke 24:49), and Paul said, "Eagerly desire spiritual gifts, especially the gift of prophecy" (1 Cor. 14:1). Therefore, to desire and seek power itself is not wrong. The problem is when we love and seek power more than God Himself. Before we seek God's power, we must first seek God Himself. This is not only true time-wise, but the first priority of our heart must be for God. When our priorities are mixed up, power changes from being a tool of serving God to becoming idolatry that replaces the position of God. We will have hearts that left the Lord. Therefore, carefully examine what your first priority is. Then you will see the direction of where your heart flows.

I have introduced these three ways of knowing the direction of your heart. Now use them to examine your heart. What does your heart flow toward? Like a lake, our heart also continuously flows toward some place, something, or someone. The final place of that flow must be Jesus. If our hearts are not flowing toward Jesus, we must repent and turn all of our heart toward Jesus.

The Serpent That Deceived Eve
Is Deceiving the Church Today

When we think of deception, we think of anti-Christ, false prophets, cult leaders, and false teachers, but deception does not merely creep in through these people. Deception can work through the mainline denomination's pastors and leaders. What do you think deception is? In the following passage, this is what Paul says:

> But I am afraid that just as Eve was deceived by the serpent's cunning, your minds may somehow be led astray from your sincere and pure devotion to Christ.
> —2 CORINTHIANS 11:3

We can come up with a simple definition concerning deception based on this word. Deception is Satan's strategy for turning our heart away from Christ to something else.

That is right. Deception is everything that causes our hearts to be turned away from Christ to something else. Therefore, those whose hearts are away from Christ are all deceived.

In the passage, Paul used the word *cunning* to express the strategy that Satan uses to deceive us. When we look at Satan's trick, we will realize how cunning it is. Just as the serpent used his cunning to deceive Eve, Satan deceives God's children through his cunning today. There are largely two of Satan's cunnings that he uses today.

1. Satan uses the Word to deceive God's children.

In the past when Satan deceived Eve, he used God's Word. When he was tempting Jesus, he also used the Bible. When he was deceiving the Jews, he used the Word as well.

> You diligently study the Scriptures because you think
> that by them you possess eternal life. These are the
> Scriptures that testify about me.
>
> —John 5:39

As such, the Jews worshiped the Scriptures but rejected Jesus, the topic of the Bible. The same thing is happening in today's churches. We think that because the Jews rejected Jesus and we believe in Jesus, our case is different from theirs. But the Holy Spirit spoke to me, "What happened to the Jews is happening to the churches today."

The preachers who do not realize the difference between preaching about Jesus Christ and testifying Jesus are largely responsible for this phenomenon. Many preachers preach concerning Jesus Christ, but they do not preach Christ. That is why today's circumstance is that many people love the things concerning Jesus—that is, the Bible and the doctrine—but their hearts are not toward Christ, and they do not have the love of Christ. In other words, the Bible, creeds, and doctrines have replaced Christ; they have become the church's idols. Rick Joyner wrote about this phenomenon is his book *The Harvest:*

> The Bible is a gift of infinite value, but our purpose
> is not to know the book about the Lord, but to know
> the Lord of the book…The church, ministry, spiritual
> truths, even the Bible can become our idols when they
> become the focal point of our interests.[1]

In the same book, Rick Joyner offers the following penetrating insight:

Whenever restoration movements took place, new truths were restored to the church despite many problems, lack of depth, and even deceptions and false doctrines. Out of these restored truths, many were driven toward extremes and error because the church focused on these rather than on the Only One who ought to be the focus of their interest. This caused the church to lose a sense of direction and will continue to do so if we allow this to happen.

The Way is not a principle or formula, but a person. To act by the truth means not simply consenting to the spiritual facts but following the Lord who is a person. Deception is not merely misunderstanding the doctrines and principles, but deception means not being in the will of God. We may know all the truths accurately and yet remain in disobedience. Our goal is not simply to know the Word of the Lord, but to know the Lord of the Word. We may recite the whole Bible and yet do not know the Lord Himself. Jesus is the Truth and the sum of all truths that were already restored and will be restored through the coming movements. We must never leave the pure devotion to Christ again.[2]

Please listen carefully. If our heart is not toward Christ, there is no consequential difference whether our hearts are toward anti-Christ or the Bible. Therefore, we must be careful not to fall into Satan's trap that causes us to lift the Word over Christ and follow the Bible rather than Christ.

2. Satan uses power to deceive God's children.

> But you will receive power when the Holy Spirit comes on you; and you will be my witnesses in Jerusalem, and in all Judea and Samaria, and to the ends of the earth.
> —ACTS 1:8

This word shows the purpose of why God poured His Spirit and His power into us. It is to make us into His witnesses, that is, the witnesses for Jesus Christ. The Holy Spirit came to witness Jesus Christ. Therefore, those who have received the Holy Spirit and His gifts must use them to lift the name of Jesus and to spread His name.

But what is the reality? God gives someone the gift of teaching. He uses that gift to interpret the Bible well and to prepare and deliver a tasty sermon. However, if he just ends there, he is not a witness for Jesus Christ; he is a witness of his own giftedness in preaching.

God gives some people the gift of prophecy. They know the secret to all mysteries and give amazing prophetic utterances that are very accurate. God pours the powerful gift of healing to some people, and they are able to heal patients and perform miracles. However, if they end here, they are merely witnesses of themselves, because people will not think about Jesus and will only marvel at the preachers, prophets, and miracle workers.

Some people may question, "That is too extreme a statement! How can the preachers or the gifted leaders only preach, prophesy, and perform miracles without spreading the name of Jesus?"

Of course they talk about Jesus, but preaching about Jesus is not the same as preaching Him. When the ministers preach about Jesus, people's hearts will not flow toward

Jesus but toward them. But when the ministers sincerely lift up Jesus and testify Jesus, people's hearts will flow toward Jesus no matter how wonderful the sermons, how accurate the prophecies, and how great the miracles. Hallelujah!

Let us pretend that there is a meeting being held at one place. As a speaker, an expository preacher was invited to lead the meeting. After the meeting, people only recalled how great his sermon was; their hearts are not moved to thirst and desire more of Jesus. This meeting was a failure, since all the gifts and power were given to testify Jesus, and such a meeting has failed to testify Him.

It is the same with prophetic conferences and healing conferences. If, when the meetings are over, people only recall how amazing the prophecies were and how awesome the miracles were, yet fail to have a stronger longing toward the Lord, such meetings are a failure.

However, many meetings today do not go beyond simply good sermons, prophecies, and miracles. In reality, there are not many meetings that lift the name of Jesus and testify Him so that people are drawn toward Him rather than just owning more knowledge about Him. This is the great proof that in today's churches, deception is strongly at work.

Beloved, Satan not only deceives people through heresy, but also through the Bible itself. Moreover, Satan does not only deceive people through fortunetellers, witches, and false signs and wonders of anti-Christians, but through genuine prophecies and miracles. Through these things, he can cause our hearts to leave Christ by focusing our attention on the Word, prophecies, and miracles. How cunning are Satan's deceptions! He is truly crafty! Therefore, we must be fully alert. We must rely humbly on the Lord's wisdom and discernment rather than make hasty conclusions and trust our own knowledge. That is the only way we will be victorious and not fall to Satan's tricks.

Those Who Do Not Pursue Jesus As Their Purpose Will Face God's Judgment

Corruption does not merely mean religious betrayal and moral failure, but it means turning our hearts away from sincere and pure devotion to Christ. As Satan deceived Eve, we will be swept away if we do not discern his craftiness, and we will face corruption even in the midst of sermons, prophecies, and miracles. Because this is real corruption, we will face God's judgment if we do not realize and repent from the sin.

These days, I recommend the book written by Choo Thomas, *Heaven Is So Real!* As I was reading the book, one person kept coming to my mind. It was Youngmi Jeong, the wife of Pastor Chang-Ryul Park at the Sang-Buk First Church.

There are many spiritually mature pastors and their wives in my vicinity. I have the privilege of meeting and having fellowship with them, for which I am grateful to God. Among the people I know, the spirituality of Youngmi Jeong is most similar to that of Mrs. Choo Thomas.

First, just as Mrs. Choo Thomas visited Christ in the spirit for the seventeenth time in the last seventeen years, Mrs. Youngmi Jeong also has that gift. She went in the spirit four consecutive times during our meeting, and since then, she often visits the Lord in the spirit.

In addition, just as Mrs. Thomas glorifies God through her spiritual dances, Mrs. Jeong cannot contain herself whenever there is the sound of praise. Like David, she becomes oblivious to people around her and becomes drunk with the Holy Spirit, glorifying God through her concentrated dance, which lasts for two to three hours. It is amazing how passionately she dances to the Lord as she praises Him.

Moreover, just as Mrs. Thomas is completely focused unto the Lord, Mrs. Jeong longs for Jesus and desires solely after Him. Even when she goes in the spirit, she does not pay attention to that fact. She does not think much of it. She only thinks Jesus is important and thirsts after Him. She goes before the Lord, wanting and praising Him.

> Whoever has my commands and obeys them, he is the one who loves me. He who loves me will be loved by my Father, and I too will love him and show myself to him.
>
> —JOHN 14:21

Whenever I read this verse I think about Mrs. Youngmi Jeong, because, as the Word shows, Jesus often appears to her because she only wants the Lord and loves Him passionately.

One time during a district pastoral meeting, I had the opportunity to meet and share with her husband, Pastor Chang-Ryul Park, and I heard the following testimony: one day, his wife went into the spirit while praising the Lord, and He told her twice, "Many people will fall and break away. Many churches will fall."

Afterwards, He showed her the burning lake of fire and said, "Many of my servants will fall away and will be thrown into this lake of fire because they did not seek Me."

As Pastor Park shared this testimony, he uttered a question, "But how can the Lord's servants and saints be thrown into the fire of hell just because they did not seek the Lord?"

At the time, his question was not his own question, but a constructive question inquired for the sake of other people's understanding. When I heard the testimony, I immediately knew in my spirit that this testimony was a true revelation. To convince you sufficiently, I can prove through Scripture that this revelation is true.

1. "Anyone who loves his father or mother more than me is not worthy of me; anyone who loves his son or daughter more than me is not worthy of me" (Matt. 10:37).

If there is anyone whom a person should properly love, it is his parents and children, but the Lord says that when a person loves his parents and children more than the Lord, he is not worthy of Him. In other words, he cannot be saved.

How much more should we despise money, glory, and pleasure, or Word, spiritual gifts, and ministry! The reason the Lord said this is not that loving other people is bad, but because of the seriousness of loving other people more than the Lord and not having the utmost love for the Lord. Therefore, our objects of love besides the Lord are not important, whether they are money, glory, pleasure, or the Word, gifts, or ministry. Any of these objects are a serious problem in the eyes of God. Therefore, whatever our object of love, if we end up loving it more than the Lord, we cannot go to heaven.

2. "Jesus replied: 'Love the Lord your God with all your heart and with all your soul and with all your mind. This is the first and greatest commandment" (Matt. 22: 37–38).

Jesus warned, "Not everyone who says to me, 'Lord, Lord,' will enter the kingdom of heaven, but only he who does the will of my Father who is in heaven" (Matt. 7:21).

The kingdom of God can be entered only by those who obey the commandments of God. The first commandment is to "love the Lord your God with all your heart and with all your soul and with all your mind" (Matt. 22:37). Therefore, even if we keep all other commandments but fail to love God passionately, we are not obeying Him. Those who do not love God passionately are disobedient people, because they have not followed His greatest commandment.

And, loving God is the secret to obeying all of His other commandments.

"This is love for God: to obey his commands. And his commands are not burdensome" (1 John 5:3).

Therefore, all those who do not love God are disobedient and cannot enter heaven.

> At that time the kingdom of heaven will be like ten virgins who took their lamps and went out to meet the bridegroom. Five of them were foolish and five were wise. The foolish ones took their lamps, but did not take any oil with them. The wise, however, took oil in jars along with their lamps. The bridegroom was a long time in coming, and they all became drowsy and fell asleep. At midnight the cry rang out: "Here's the bridegroom! Come out to meet him!" Then all the virgins woke up and trimmed their lamps. The foolish ones said to the wise, "Give us some of your oil; our lamps are going out." "No," they replied, "there may not be enough for both us and you. Instead, go to those who sell oil and buy some for yourselves." But while they were on their way to buy the oil, the bridegroom arrived. The virgins who were ready went in with him to the wedding banquet. And the door was shut.
>
> —MATTHEW 25:1–10

When Jesus returns, He will come as a bridegroom. Jesus will come to take His bride. Therefore, we must be ready as His bride. Then what is the most important preparation for the bride? That is having the true love for her bridegroom.

This occurred to me during one dawn prayer meeting. I was reading Luke 17:32–35 with the saints:

> Remember Lot's wife! Whoever tries to keep his life will lose it, and whoever loses his life will preserve it. I tell you, on that night two people will be in one bed; one will be taken and the other left. Two women will be grinding grain together, one will be taken and the other left.

Suddenly, the Holy Spirit came powerfully upon me. He spoke clearly to my spirit: "Do you know why when the Lord returns, two people will be in one bed but one will be taken and the other left, and why two women will be grinding together, and one will be taken and the other left? It is because one loved the Lord while living his Christian life, while the other did not love the Lord even while living his Christian life. As the Scripture is written, 'Look, the bridegroom!' Jesus will come as a bridegroom and will take away His bride. Therefore, only those who love the Lord sincerely will be lifted up."

That day, the word came so powerfully that the deacon Misoo Jeong, who was listening in the front pew, shook her whole body. She would often scream, fall, or run away whenever I would lay hands on her to pray, because the fire of the Holy Spirit was too hot for her to bear. That day, I was not even laying on hands, but she let out a scream after trying hard not to cry out while just listening. That day, I could clearly feel that the Lord was using my mouth directly to speak, and it was a very special time.

Beloved, do not forget this message. Jesus will come back

as a bridegroom. Therefore, only those who love the Lord will be lifted up. That day, people who fell in love with things other than the Lord, that is, those who fell into spiritual adultery, will be judged. That is why Paul gravely warned in 1 Corinthians 16:22:

> If anyone does not love the Lord—a curse be on him. Come, O Lord!
> I am jealous for you with a godly jealousy. I promised you to one husband, to Christ, so that I might present you as a pure virgin to him. But I am afraid that just as Eve was deceived by the serpent's cunning, your minds may somehow be led astray from your sincere and pure devotion to Christ.
> —2 CORINTHIANS 11:2–3

I will not explain long since I have already shared about this verse before. We have been betrothed to Jesus as His bride through evangelists, the matchmakers. We are not yet His wife since the wedding feast of the Lamb has not taken place. In other words, we are still being courted by Jesus. How should the dating couple behave? Shouldn't they think about each other continually, calling each other up every chance they get, dating and loving each other passionately?

> Strengthen me with raisins, refresh me with apples, for I am faint with love.
> —SONG OF SONGS 2:5

Like the Shulammite woman, we need to love the Lord with passion to the point of sickness. That is right. While we are engaged to the Lord, it is most important for us to date Him and love Him.

> To the angel of the church in Ephesus write: These
> are the words of him who holds the seven stars in his
> right hand and walks among the seven golden lamp-
> stands: I know your deeds, your hard work and your
> perseverance. I know that you cannot tolerate wicked
> men, that you have tested those who claim to be apos-
> tles but are not, and have found them false. You have
> persevered and have endured hardships for my name,
> and have not grown weary. Yet I hold this against you:
> You have forsaken your first love. Remember the height
> from which you have fallen! Repent and do the things
> you did at first. If you do not repent, I will come to you
> and remove your lampstand from its place.
>
> —REVELATION 2:1–5

The Ephesian church was sound in doctrine because they were able to discern false apostles. That is, they stood firm on the correct doctrines. Also, they not only possessed knowledge in their head, but were diligent in serving the Lord. They worked hard and persevered and were not lazy.

What do you think? Do you not think that they were faithful? Do you not think that this church should be considered a model church? But the Lord's perspective was different.

The church is not simply a religious organization. The church is the bride of Jesus Christ. Jesus will come as a bridegroom. How could the bride, the church, lose her first love toward the bridegroom, Jesus? That cannot be! Is that a small thing? That is why Jesus showed His disapproval and warned them severely, "Yet I hold this against you: You have forsaken your first love. Remember the height from which you have fallen! Repent and do the things you did at first. If you do not repent, I will come to you and remove your lampstand from its place."

The Lord will not see the church as a true church if it does not possess passionate love toward Him. There is nothing that can replace or make up this love. Therefore, having love for the Lord is a life-and-death matter. Besides this passage, take the following scriptural verses to consider their meaning and context and to compare with other Bible scriptures, and meditate upon them.

> But I know you. I know that you do not have the love of God in your hearts.
>
> —JOHN 5:42

> And we know that in all things God works for the good of those who love him, who have been called according to his purpose.
>
> —ROMANS 8:28

> But the man who loves God is known by God.
>
> —1 CORINTHIANS 8:3

> Listen, my dear brothers: Has not God chosen those who are poor in the eyes of the world to be rich in faith and to inherit the kingdom he promised to those who love him?
>
> —JAMES 2:5

> Though you have not seen him, you love him; and even though you do not see him now, you believe in him and are filled with an inexpressible and glorious joy, for you are receiving the goal of your faith, the salvation of your souls.
>
> —1 PETER 1:8–9

When we consider these verses, there is nothing more important in our faith walk than to love the Lord passionately. We must love the Lord and seek Him as our goal. Without this love, we cannot be lifted up as His bride. Therefore, fix your gaze upon Jesus and love Him deeply. In this urgent time before Christ's soon return, I wish that you would be thoroughly prepared as the Bride of Jesus Christ.

This is my conclusion now. Those around us know Great Faith Church as the church that moves in the "Holy Spirit movement," or the "spirituality movement." As I often say, among the people in the Holy Spirit movement, there are those with whom I feel rapport and those with whom I feel disparity. Both of these groups are part of those who make up the Holy Spirit or spirituality movement. Among them, there are people who are pure, humble, and truly love the Lord. But among them, there are also people who are most shameless, decayed, and corrupt, who try to fulfill their selfish ambition through God's power, like Simon the sorcerer.

While I became involved in the Holy Spirit movement, I realized that among the ones in this movement, there are many who are seeking the same thing we do, but still there are many who have a different focus than we do. Increasingly, I seriously felt how different they were to us. I felt the need to properly examine and disclose our church identity so that people would not misunderstand us. The term we came up with was "Bridal Movement." Though the filling and anointing of the Holy Spirit, spiritual gifts, and miracles are included, our pursuit is to seek Jesus as our goal and to become Jesus' lover by desiring to fall ardently in love with Him and to run toward Him.

Beloved, we must restore our first love and share a deep love with Jesus. That is the only way we will be lifted up when

Jesus the Bridegroom comes back. Furthermore, that is the only way the Lord will truly use us as strong warriors.

> Who is this that appears like the dawn, fair as the moon, bright as the sun, majestic as the stars in procession?
> —SONG OF SONGS 6:10

As the verse shows, we can become a strong warrior only when we have become the Lord's ardent lover and pure bride. Only when we become the beautiful bride of Jesus will we be threatening warriors to our enemy Satan. These two images are one and the same. Strong warriors are not made simply through spiritual gifts and power. Strong warriors are formed when we become united through our love to Jehovah's army general, Jesus. In other words, when the strong warrior Jesus roars like a lion and rises within us, we will become the strong warriors that will make hell tremble. That is why I think Rick Joyner wrote in his book *The Harvest:*

> In the coming days, there will be many emphases on the Lord Jesus Himself. As the moonlight becomes overshadowed when the sun rises, many past emphases will become overshadowed as the revelations of the Lord increase. When the church sees Him "in whom are hidden all the treasures of wisdom and knowledge" (Colossians 2:3), other truths that had been central in our eyes will not be considered important...When the apostolic position is restored, all the different visions of the churches will combine to focus on the Lord Jesus Himself. Since the Lord is God's final purpose, everything is summed up in the Lord. When God's deep knowledge and wisdom found in the Lord is revealed, every eye will fix on the glory of the Lord. Like the

concentrated light that becomes the immense strength of a laser beam, the focus of our interest that has been gathered on the Lord Himself will release a huge power in the church, enabling the church to finally fulfill the great commission.[3]

Therefore, fix your heart toward the Lord and love Him completely. That is the secret to receiving great power and effectively evangelizing the whole world. This can be proved from the scripture in 2 Chronicles 16:9:

> For the eyes of the LORD range throughout the earth to strengthen those whose hearts are fully committed to him.

To whom does the power belong? It belongs to those whose hearts are fully committed to the Lord. Through this scripture, we can understand why we lack power so much. That is because our heart is not fully committed to Him, but rather to money, glory, authority, and pleasure. Even if our hearts are toward Him, they are divided and not singly focused on the Lord. That is why God's power remains so weak among us.

Now that we know the cause of our lack of power, shouldn't we fix the problem? We have no time to hesitate; we only have time to make a determination. Now is not too late, so become fully committed to the Lord. Give your heart solely to the Lord. Then we will become a lovely bride to Jesus and the object of terror to demons. That is, we will become strong warriors, whose names will be known to hell like Paul's is, and we will be used mightily to conquer cities and nations for God.

AFTERWORD

"I Saw Your Books in Heaven's Library"

This is the vision by one of my church's prophetic ministry team leaders.

> When I was praying for my pastor's book, the Lord showed me his many books on his second-floor study, and told me that heaven's library is going to be filled with many of Pastor Byun's books.
>
> I felt as if I were on an observation tower when I saw houses coming into view. All of those houses were dark, desolate, and bleak. A short time later, I saw a light being turned on one at a time, and they grew brighter. "This means," the Lord explained to me, "that Pastor Byun's books are going to be used as a light to cast out the darkness."
>
> Then I saw a train station in the distance where many people were waiting for their trains. It had northbound and southbound railroad tracks, indicating that these people were soon to be divided into two groups. One group was bound for heaven, while the other group was bound for hell. Jesus said *Christians Going to Hell* will play a pivotal role in splitting up the people into two groups, and it will help many Christians to turn from their evil and back to the Lord.
>
> A moment later, I saw Pastor Byun's study again, and the edges of his bookshelf had turned to a golden hue. That golden hue reminded me of a remark I had heard: "In heaven, the covers of valuable books are covered with precious stones like gold or silver." Jesus

said that Pastor Byun's books will be memorable books in heaven because they will save many souls.[1]

A few days later, another deaconess was caught up to heaven and gave me her testimony. She saw my brain being filled with many books that will be written by me in the future. The Lord said that although the books in my brain were dimly visible now, they would soon be clearly revealed. They would become beautiful instruments for God's glory in Korea as well as among the nations.[2]

I have a solid confidence that the two visions came from God. The Lord verified them through Shawn Boltz, who is a very close friend of Heidi Baker, Bob Jones, Rick Joyner, Che Ahn and Mike Bickle. Shawn led a conference at Great Faith Church in May 2005. During the previous week, he had charge of a conference at a Presbyterian church in Pusan, Korea. More than one thousand congregation members came to hear Shawn Boltz. On the last day, he gave his personal testimony of having been to heaven. He recounted how he was caught up to heaven while driving. He spent eight hours in heaven; however, the time that lapsed on the earth was only three minutes. When he came back to the earth, he arrived exactly at the very destination that he had intended, a distance of four hours travel. Like Philip in the Bible, he was carried by God's hand in an instant. He has been caught up to heaven more than ten times. He shared his experience of heaven and told us about heaven's library. The following is part of his testimony.

> When I was in heaven, I saw one place marked, "The Library of Heaven." It was equipped with books from the past, the present, and the future. In the middle of them was the Book of Life. There were a tremendous

number of books on the walls, and all of them were "the books of heaven."

I was looking for a certain book, but I could not find it. I asked an angel why the book was not there, because I had read it previously. The angel showed me the original copy, saying, "That book was plagiarized from this book." Using his intellectual ability, he employed heavenly property as his own book however he pleased.

In heaven's library, you cannot find a myriad of books that exist now. Nevertheless, the authors are enjoying prosperity from the fruit they are bearing. However, their books have no eternal value in heaven.

In the section marked, "The Past," there were a large number of books written by highly respected people. In spite of their fame, their books were torn from the section because their books did not give glory to God. New pages were added to those books.

If you could not find something of eternal value on earth, you would find them in heaven. Almost all of the books today record historic and cultural things; they do not record about eternal life.

The angel continued, "People clothed the church with wisdom in order to make money or to enlighten people with human wisdom."

However, there were stacks of books in heaven's library whose titles you have never heard before. The Lord calls them the finest books.

I also approached a section labeled "The Future." Two of the largest angels were guarding the future books. Although the angels prevented me from entering, some authors' names were visible even from ten meters away. I thought to myself, *I have no idea who that is, or this one, and I've never heard of that one either.* So many books of heaven's library are going to be published by God's unknown people.

Many books that I saw in heaven will be published in the future. Those authors are not yet known to us, but God knows who they are. I believe God is blessing Korea, who will pour out heavenly books within the next ten years. Right now, God is blessing those who are faithful and devoted to heaven's books. Some of these books will change the present secular culture, some of them will reflect heavenly kingdom, and some of them will give a blueprint of how to build up the churches. All the resources for God's glory are already there. The present books are not worth comparing with the future books that will come out.[3]

After the sermon, many of the congregation members were caught up to heaven when Shawn laid hands on them. At that time, Shawn called me forward and continued, "Pastor Byun! I saw a lot of your books in heaven, and I saw a section prepared for your books. There were many books of yours, not just one or two. *Christians Going to Hell* was one of them. Your books are going to be translated into various languages in many countries, and they will proclaim God's glory wherever they go."

Hallelujah! To God's name be the glory. So far, I have introduced my book with bold confidence, and I may have appeared proud to some people. Nonetheless, I dared to urge people to read my book, because—more than anyone else—I know my book is not a product of mere human wisdom. It is a gift from God, who chooses the foolish things of the world to shame the wise.

Hallelujah! May God be glorified solely! Amen! Amen!

NOTES

Preface

1. Choo Thomas, *Heaven Is So Real!* (Lake Mary, FL: Creation House Press, 2003), 193.

2. Ibid., 177.

3. Ibid., 46–47.

4. Ibid., 193.

Chapter 1
Do Not Go to Hell!

1. John Wesley, "Sermon 112," text from 1872 edition, http://gbgm-umc.org/umhistory/wesley/sermons/serm-112.stm (accessed July 15, 2005).

2. Theophylactus, *The Explanation by Blessed Theophylact of the Holy Gospel According to St. Mark by Theophylactus* (House Springs, MO; Chrysostom Press, 1993).

3. Maurice Rawlings, MD, *Beyond Death's Door* (Nashville, TN; Thomas Nelson, 1978), 3.

4. Quoted in John Wesley's "Sermon 112," text from 1872 edition, http://gbgm-umc.org/umhistory/wesley/sermons/serm-112.stm, (accessed July 15, 2005).

5. Tryon Edwards, *A Dictionary of Thoughts* (Lincoln, NE; F.B. Dickerson, 1905), 225.

6. John Wesley, taken from a letter "To John Smith, ST. IVES, July 10, 1747" (Wesley Center Online, Wesley Center for Applied Theology at Northern Nazarene University, http://wesley.nnu.edu/john_wesley/letters/1747.htm (accessed July 14, 2005).

7. Jonathan Edwards, quoted by Martyn Lloyd-Jones in *The Puritans: Their Origens and Successors* (Edinburgh, Scotland: Banner of Truth, 1987).

8. Thomas á Kempis, *The Imitation of Christ* (Trans. by William Griffin), (San Francisco, CA: HarperSanFrancisco, 2000), 48.

9. Maurice Rawlings, MD, *Beyond Death's Door* (Nashville, TN; Thomas Nelson, 1978).

10. Richard Baxter, *The Saints' Everlasting Rest* (John T. Wilkinson,

ed.), (Vancouver, BC, Canada: Regent College Publishing, 2004).

11. Samuel Davies, "Things Unseen to be Preferred to Things Seen, www.scripturestudies.com/Vol7/G3/top.html (accessed July 15, 2005).

12. Thomas Watson, *The Doctrine of Repentance* (Carlisle, PA: Banner of Truth, 1987).

13. Quote available on the Internet at http://www.gospeltruth.net/1847OE/470721_prvl_prayr_3.htm (accessed December 22, 2005).

14. Quote available on the Internet at http://www.worthynews.com/Sermons/spurturnorburn.htm (accessed December 22, 2005).

15. T.L. Osborn, *How to Be Born Again* (Tulsa, OK: Osborn International, 1977).

16. Mary K. Baxter, *A Divine Revelation of Hell* (New Kensington, PA: Whitaker House, 1993), 42.

17. Jung Pyeo Lee, *The Sound of Thunder From Heaven* (Seoul, Korea: Qumran Publishers, 1997).

18. Quote available from the Internet at http://www.gospeltruth.net/1853OE/531109_richman_lazarus.htm (accessed December 22, 2005).

19. Joan Wester Anderson, *Where Angels Walk* (New York, NY: Ballantine Books, 1993), 17.

20. Rev. David Nelson, "Cause and Cure of Infidelity", 1846, http://angelfire.com/nh/politicalscience/1841davidnelsoninfidelitynde.htm (accessed July 20, 2005).

Chapter 2
The Repentance That Leads to Salvation

1. Thomas Watson, *The Doctrine of Repentance* (Carlisle, PA: Banner of Truth, 1987).

2. Joseph Alleine, *An Alarm to the Unconverted* (Lafayette, IN: Sovereign Grace Publishers, 2000).

3. Charles Finney, *Lectures to Professing Christians* (New York, NY: Garland Publishing, 1985).

4. Watson, *The Doctrine of Repentance* (Carlisle, PA: Banner of Truth, 1987).

5. D. L. Moody, *Your Victory in Jesus* (New Kensington, PA: Whitaker House, 1997), 48.

6. Charles H. Spurgeon, *My Conversion* (New Kensington, PA: Whitaker House, 1996), 51.

7. Adoniram Judson Gordon, *The Ministry of the Spirit* (Minneapolis, MN: Bethany House Publishers, 1986).

8. Young Moon Park, *I Will Keep My Eyes on It* (Seoul, Korea: Inshin Publishing, 1997).

9. Charles Hodge, *Systematic Theology* (Peabody, MA: Hendrickson Publishers, 1999).

10. D. L. Moody, *Secret Power* (New Kensington, PA: Whitaker House), 131.

11. Quote available from the Internet at http://www.wicketgate .co.uk/issue48/e48_5.html (accessed December 29, 2005).

12. Charles Finney, *Lectures to Professing Christians* (New York, NY: Garland Publishing, 1985).

13. Thomas Watson, *The Doctrine of Repentance* (Carlisle, PA: Banner of Truth, 1987).

14. Charles Finney, *Experiencing the Presence of God* (New Kensington, PA: Whitaker House), 208.

15. Saint Augustine, *Confessions* (Trans. by Henry Chadwick), (New York, NY: Oxford University Press).

16. Charles Finney, *Experiencing the Presence of God* (New Kensington, PA: Whitaker House), 218.

17. John Bunyan, *Acceptable Sacrifice* (London, UK: Fresh Bread, 2001), 90.

18. Charles Spurgeon, *Evening by Evening* (New Kensington, PA: Whitaker House, 2001), 96.

19. Joseph Alleine, *An Alarm to the Unconverted* (Lafayette, IN: Sovereign Grace Publishers, 2000).

20. Quote available on the Internet at www.gospeltruth.net/ 1836LTPC/ltpc09_tandf_repentance.htm (accessed December 29, 2005).

21 Thomas Watson, *The Doctrine of Repentance* (Carlisle, PA: Banner of Truth, 1987).

22. Quote available on the Internet at http://searchwarp.com/ swa6134.htm (accessed December 29, 2005).

23. Joseph Alleine, *An Alarm to the Unconverted* (Lafayette, IN: Sovereign Grace Publishers, 2000).

24. Quote available on the Internet at www.whatsaiththescripture

.com/Fellowship/Spurgeon/Faith.Checkbook/December.text.html
(accessed December 29, 2005).

25. Quote available on the Internet at http://www.reference
.com/browse/wiki/Charles_Grandison_Finney (accessed January 23,
2006).

26. Quote available on the Internet at http://wesley.nnu.edu/john_
wesley/christian_library/vol29/CL29Part6.htm (accessed January
30, 2006).

27. Yong-Kyu Park, evangelism booklet for free distribution. To
obtain free booklets, call Seoul, Korea, at 82-2-593-8165.

28. St. Thomas Aquinas, *Summa Theologica* (Wheaton, IL:
Christian Classics, 1981).

29. D. L. Moody, *Secret Power* (New Kensington, PA: Whitaker
House), 142.

30. Thomas Watson, *The Doctrine of Repentance* (Carlisle, PA:
Banner of Truth, 1987).

Chapter 3
Faith More Precious Than Gold

1. Charles Price, *Real Christians* (Colorado Springs, CO: NavPress,
1940).

2. Charles Finney, *Revival Lectures* (Grand Rapids, MI: Fleming
H. Revell, 1993).

3. Charles Hodge, *Systematic Theology* (Peabody, MA: Hendrickson
Publishers, 1999).

4. Charles Finney, *Power From On High* (Fort Washington, PA:
Christian Literature Crusade, 1962).

5. Gary Collins, *The Biblical Basis of Christian Counseling for
People Helpers* (Colorado Springs, CO: NavPress, 1993).

6. Richard Baxter, *A Call to the Unconverted* (Lafayette, IN:
Sovereign Grace Publishers, 2000).

7. Charles Spurgeon, *Grace and Power* (New Kensington, PA:
Whitaker House, 2000), 58.

8. A.W. Tozer, *The Root of the Righteous* (Edmonton, Alberta:
Christian Publications, 1955), 128.

9. John Stott, *Romans: Encountering the Gospel's Power* (Downers
Grove, IL: InterVarsity Press, 1998), 73.

10. Oswald J. Smith, "What Does It Mean to Believe?," cassette series (distributed by World Literature Crusade).

11. Charles Price, *Real Christians*, (Colorado Springs, CO: NavPress, 1940).

12. Rick Joyner, *The Final Quest*, (New Kensington, PA: Whitaker House, 1997), 12.

13. Flora Slosson Wuellner, *Feed My Shepherds* (Nashville, TN: Upper Room Books, 1998).

14. Choo Thomas, *Heaven Is So Real!* (Lake Mary, FL: Creation House, 2003).

15. Thomas Manton, *The Life of Faith* (Fearn, Scotland: Christian Focus Publications, 1994).

16. Jonathan Edwards, *Charity and its Fruit* (Carlisle, PA: Banner of Truth, 1978).

17. Charles Hodge, *Systematic Theology* (Peabody, MA: Hendrickson Publishers, 1999).

Chapter 4
Faith and Obedience

1. William Barclay, *The Letters of James and Peter*, The Daily Study Bible Series (Philadelphia, PA: The Westminster Press, 1960).

2. See also http://en.wikipedia.org/wiki/Epistle_of_James (accessed January 23, 2006).

3. Eusebius, *The History of the Church*, G.A. Williamson, translator (New York: Penguin, 1990).

4. Quote available on the Internet at http://www.theopedia.com/Martin_Luther (accessed December 30, 2005).

5. Charles Finney, *Power From on High* (Fort Washington, PA: Christian Literature Crusade, 1962).

6. Rick Joyner, *The Call* (New Kensington, PA: Whitaker House, 1999), 65.

7. Charles Finney, *The Autobiography of Charles G. Finney* (Minneapolis, MN: Bethany House Publishers, 1977).

8. Quote available on the Internet at http://www.gospeltruth.net/1837LTPC/lptc05_just_by_faith.htm (accessed January 23, 2006).

9. John Stott, *Life in Christ* (Grand Rapids, MI: Baker Books, 2003).

10. Quote available on the Internet at http://www.gospeltruth.net/ 1836LTPC/ltpc01_self_deceivers.htm (accessed January 30, 2006).

11. John Ryle, *Holiness*, (Moscow, ID: Charles Nolan Publishing, 2001).

12. Charles Hodge, *The Way of Life*, (Carlisle, PA: Banner of Truth, 1996).

13. Stephen Charnock, *New Birth*, (Carlisle, PA: Banner of Truth, 1987).

14. Quote available on the Internet at http://www.gospeltruth.net/ 1837LTPC/lptc05_just_by_faith.htm (accessed January 30, 2006).

15. Quote available on the Internet at http://www.biblebb.com/ files/edwards/justification.htm (accessed December 30, 2005).

16. Quote available on the Internet at http://www.gospeltruth.net/ 1837LTPC/lptc05_just_by_faith.htm (accessed December 30, 2005).

17. Jonathan Edwards, *Justification by Faith* (Orlando: Soli Deo Gloria Ministries, 2000).

18. Ibid.

19. Ibid.

20. Ibid.

21. Source unknown.

22. Ed Silvoso, *That None Should Perish* (Ventura, CA: Regal Books, 1994).

Chapter 5
Rebirth I

1. General William Booth, quotes by author, http://www.weeks -g.dircon.co.uk/authorsB.htm (accessed July 14, 2005).

2. Kenneth Hagin, *The New Birth*, (Tulsa, OK: Faith Library Publications, 1911).

3. Ibid.

4. Oswald Smith, *The Gospel We Preach* (London, UK: Marshall, Morgan & Scott; 1962).

5. T. L. Osborn, *How to Be Born Again* (Tulsa, OK: Osborn International, 1977).

6. Quote available on the Internet at http://www.csec.org/csec/ sermon/stott_2719.htm (accessed January 6, 2005).

7. In-Chan Jung, ed. *The Bible Encyclopedia* (Seoul, Korea:

Christian Wisdom Publishing, 1980).

8. Quote available from the Internet at http://www.monergism .com/thethreshold/articles/onsite/monergism_grid.html (accessed January 6, 2006).

9. Sadhu Sundar Singh, *Reality and Religion: Meditations on God, Man, and Nature* (Madras, India: Christian Literature Society, 1968).

10. Quote available on the Internet at http://www.the-highway .com/regcon_Hopkins.html (accessed January 6, 2006).

11. John Wesley, *Sermon 45*, http://gbgm-umc.org/umhistory/ wesley/sermons/serm-045.stm, taken from 1872 text edition (accessed July 14, 2005).

12. Sadhu Sundar Singh, *At the Feet of the Master* (Madras, India: Christian Literature Society, 1971).

13. Quote available on the Internet at http://gbgm-umc.org/umw/ wesley/serm-045.stm (accessed January 6, 2006).

14. Quote available on the Internet at http://www.crossroad.to/ Excerpts/books/faith/tozer-faith.htm (accessed January 6, 2006).

15. Quote available on the Internet at www.the-highway.com/ regcon_Hopkins.html (accessed January 12, 2006).

16. T. L. Osborn, *How to Be Born Again* (Tulsa, OK: Osborn International, 1977).

17. Further information available at http://wesley.nnu.edu/ holiness_tradition/manton/sermon2.htm (accessed January 12, 2006).

Chapter 6
Rebirth II

1. Quote available on the Internet at http://jmm.aaa.net.au/ articles/4612.htm (accessed January 12, 2006).

2. A. W. Tozer, *Born After Midnight,* (Edmonton, Alberta: Christian Publications, 1986).

3. Quote available on the Internet at http://www.abideinchrist .com/messages/1jn2v1.html (accessed January 13, 2006).

4. John Wimber and Kevin Springer, *The Dynamics of Spiritual Growth* (London, UK: Hodder & Stoughton, 1995).

5. Quote available on the Internet at http://www.gotothebible

.com/HTML/newnessoflife.html (accessed January 13, 2006).

6. Kenneth Hagin, *The New Birth* (Tulsa, OK: Faith Library Publications, 1911).

7. Quote available on the Internet at http://www.iclnet.org/pub/resources/text/ipb-e/epl-10/web/charnock-necessity-regeneration.html (accessed January 30, 2006).

8. Quote available on the Internet at http://www.seegod.org/sanctification_-_ryle.htm (accessed January 30, 2006).

9. Quote available on the Internet at http://www.twolisteners.org/At%20The%20Masters%20Feet.htm (accessed January 13, 2006).

10. Sadhu Sundar Singh, *At the Feet of the Master* (Madras, India: Christian Literature Society, 1971).

11. For further information see http://www.ondoctrine.com/2cha0102.htm (accessed January 13, 2006).

12. Sadhu Sundar Singh, *At the Feet of the Master* (Madras, India: Christian Literature Society, 1971).

13. Quote available on the Internet at http://www.eaglevision.com.my/ssvisions.htm (accessed January 13, 2006).

14. Sadhu Sundar Singh, *At the Feet of the Master* (Madras, India: Christian Literature Society, 1971), author's paraphrase.

15. Quote available on the Internet at http://www.lamblion.net/Quotations/ryle_jc.htm (accessed January 13, 2006).

16. Quote available on the Internet at http://www.gospeltruth.net/1852OE/520929_salv_impossible.htm (accessed January 13, 2006).

17. Quote available on the Internet at http://www.ccel.org/c/charnock/nec_regen/nec_regen.html (accessed January 13, 2006).

18. Charles Finney, *True Revival* (Grand Rapids, MI: Fleming H. Revell, 1993).

19. Charles Finney, *God's Love for a Sinning World* (Grand Rapids, MI: Kregel Publications, 1975).

20. Quote available on the Internet at http://www.iclnet.org/pub/resources/text/ipb-e/epl-10/web/charnock-necessity-regeneration.html (accessed January 18, 2006).

21. Kenneth Hagin, *The New Birth* (Tulsa, OK: Faith Library Publications, 1911).

22. Quote available on the Internet at http://www.ccel.org/c/charnock/nec_regen/nec_regen.html (accessed January 17, 2006).

23. Quote available on the Internet at http://www.iclnet.org/pub/

resources/text/ipb-e/epl-10/web/charnock-necessity-regeneration
.html (accessed January 18, 2006).

24. John Stott, *Christ the Controversialist* (Carol Stream, IL: Tyndale House Publishers, 1970).

Chapter 7
There Is No Such Thing As Shameful Salvation!

1. Saint Augustine, *Confessions* (Trans. by Henry Chadwick), (New York, NY: Oxford University Press).

2. Charles Hodge, *1 Corinthians* (Wheaton, IL: Crossway Books, 1995).

3. *Hokma Comprehensive Commentary: New Testament, vol. 7* (Seoul, Korea: Christian Wisdom Publishing, 2001).

4. *The Grand Synthetic Commentary, vol. 17* (Seoul, Korea: Discipleship Publishing, 2004).

5. David Lowley, *The Bible Knowledge Commentary 1 & 2 Corinthians* (Seoul, Korea: Tyrannus Publishing, 1994).

6. Quote available on the Internet at http://homepage.mac.com/shanerosenthal/reformationink/chfeelings.htm (accessed January 18, 2006).

7. Quote available on the Internet at http://www.cfan.org/_includes/printerfriendly.asp?id=0000509&page=01&printversion=true&server=www.cfan.org&lang=english-intl&site=uk_site (accessed January 18, 2006).

8. Quote available on the Internet at http://www.christiantruth.com/savingfaithandtheologians.html (accessed January 18, 2006).

9. Kenneth Hagin, *Art of Prayer* (Tulsa, OK: Faith Library Publications, 1992).

Chapter 8
The Kingdom That Only the Victorious Can Enter

1. Quote available on the Internet at http://www.openheaven.com/library/pastoral/victory.htm (accessed January 18, 2006).

2. Quote available on the Internet at http://www.thechristian.org/resources/testimonies/wesley.pdf (accessed January 19, 2006).

3. Quote available on the Internet at http://www.biblebb.com/files/ryle/great_battle.htm (accessed January 19, 2006).

4. D. L. Moody, "The Christian's Warfare," a sermon, http://www .hissheep.org/past/the_christians_warfare.html (accessed July 15, 2005).

5. Quote available on the Internet at http://www.gospeltruth.net/ 1845OE/451105_victory_faith.htm (accessed January 19, 2006).

Chapter 9
Je-e-sus!

1. Larry Lea, *Wisdom—Don't Live Life Without It,* (Surrey, England: Highland Books, 1991).

2. Stephen Hill, *The Pursuit of Revival,* (Lake Mary, FL: Creation House, 1997).

3. Quote available on the Internet at http://www.biblebb.com/ files/ryle/are_you_fighting.htm (accessed January 19, 2006).

4. Robert Murray M'Cheyne, *The Deeper Life* (Charlotte, NC: World Wide Publications, 1994).

5. Choo Thomas, *Heaven Is So Real!* (Lake Mary, FL: Creation House, 2003).

Chapter 10
Up to Seventy Times Seven

1. Quote available on the Internet at http://www.housechurch.org/ spirituality/john_flavel/flavel_on_keeping.html (accessed January 19, 2006).

2. John Bevere, *The Bait of Satan* (Lake Mary, FL: Charisma House, 2004).

3. Quote available on the Internet at http://underground.orcon .net.nz/articles/moody_prayer.html (accessed January 19, 2006).

4. Quote available on the Internet at http://www.mountzion.org/ fgb/Summer03/FgbS2-03.html (accessed January 20, 2006).

5. Dick Mills, source unknown.

6. Ibid.

7. Ibid.

Chapter 11
Saint Chunhyang

1. Rick Joyner, *The Harvest* (New Kensington, PA: Whitaker House,1997), 111.

2. Ibid.

3. Ibid., 218.